Mathematical Structure in Human Affairs

Mathematical Structure in Human Affairs

R.H. Atkin
University of Essex

Crane, Russak & Company, Inc.
New York

© R. H. Atkin 1974
First published 1974

Library of Congress Catalog Card No. 73-93383

ISBN 0-8448-0319-7

Published in the United States by:
Crane, Russak and Company, Inc.
347 Madison Avenue
New York, N.Y. 10017

Typeset by Tecprint Ltd., Loughborough.

Printed in Great Britain by The Pitman Press, Bath.

Preface

I have written this book in an attempt to show the relevance of a mathematical approach to the study of various fields of human endeavour. It is also intended to provide a background for the extensive research into a structural language which has occupied me during recent years and which has been illustrated by numerous applications in the fields of urban and community structures.

In one sense the mathematics is as old as the hills, being essentially combinatorial, but in another sense it is modern as it develops structural ideas on a basis of set theory. In this latter sense it needs to be described in both an algebraic and a geometric manner, either of which requires the language of a multi-dimensional space. Such a concept, as that of an n-dimensional space, seems to me to be no more abstract (in the worst sense of that word) than is that of the traditional 3-dimensions wherein the physicist finds his electrons and protons.

I believe that the old-fashioned idea of 3-dimensional real-space, like the poor, will always be with us, but that it is an idea which is necessary rather than one which is sufficient. The real-space (what I have referred to as actual-space), the space wherein we can describe how we live (not just how we exist), where we have sufficient elbow-room to distinguish between the living and the dead, is multi-dimensional. It is the space in which we can be creative, where we paint our pictures, play-act our politics, and where we must not only describe the action but equally well the metaphor which gives it depth. By comparison we can only live in the scientist's 3-space if we can make ourselves small enough to do so. Time in that space seems to be fast running out; now we must surely seek for our Time in a space which is sufficiently rich to match the aspirations of the young as well as the metaphysics of the old.

This book is therefore a plea for the thesis that we can find a mathematical language capable of expressing not only a traditional scientific view of the universe (whatever that is) but also that more flexible and creative view normally associated with the artist and man-of-affairs. Hopefully this thesis is the beginning of a constructive reaction to the shallow philosophy of the two cultures.

I would like to thank many friends and colleagues for encouragement of all kinds, the University of Essex for the time and space in which to write the book, Mrs Cromarty for permission to reproduce her construction of the map of Saffron Walden (1600), and particularly the publishers for their encouragement and help.

Colchester, 1974 R. H. Atkin

to my wife

who Phylls our garden
with flowers

Contents

PREFACE   *page* v

Chapter 1   Ideas Associated with Set Theory
1.1   Introduction   1
1.2   Set membership   2
1.3   Aristotle's *Politics*   3
1.4   Galileo's sets and relations   6
1.5   Logical paradoxes   8
1.6   Probability and sets of events   10
1.7   Chess and relations Γ_W, Γ_B 14
1.8   The university bar   17

Chapter 2   People and Complexes
2.1   Does the barber shave himself?   22
2.2   Everyman is a polyhedron   26
2.3   Top-q and bottom-q 33
2.4   Weighted relations and slicing parameters   35
2.5   The idea of a pattern on a complex   44

Chapter 3   The Game of Chess
3.1   Lasker on chess   46
3.2   Q-analysis for mode [0, 0]   47
3.3   Positional motifs and structure   50
3.4   Checkmate   54
3.5   Time in chess   55
3.6   The Immortal Game (1851)   56
3.7   Computers and chess   63

Chapter 4   Multi-dimensional Art
4.1   A search for structure   65
4.2   Checkerboard, Bright Colours 1919 – Piet Mondrian   65
4.3   Mondrian picture with card $X = 1$ 67
4.4   Mondrian picture with card $X = 4$ 68
4.5   Mondrian picture with card $X = 16$ 73
4.6   Mondrian picture with card $X = 64$ 77
4.7   Forces inherent in a change of view   79

Chapter 5	Space is full of Holes	
5.1	Real-space and actual-space	82
5.2	The idea of the cocycle law	88
5.3	The cocycle law in macrophysics	90
5.4	The cocycle law in classical mechanics	93
5.5	The cocycle law in Maxwell field theory	96
5.6	The transition to quantum theory	99
5.7	Quantum theory and special relativity	101
5.8	The direct use of the cocycle law by Bohr	103
Chapter 6	Urban Structure	
6.1	Multi-dimensional town	107
6.2	A Tudor village in Q-space	108
6.3	A general analysis for a town	117
6.4	Patterns and t-forces on an anciente towne	127
6.5	Algebraic patterns for town planning	138
Chapter 7	Politics and the University Bar	
7.1	Shall we move the bar?	142
7.2	The political backcloth	148
7.3	Round-1	151
7.4	Round-2	153
7.5	The referee stops the fight	162
APPENDIX A	Sets and Relations	164
APPENDIX B	The Structure of a Relation	174
APPENDIX C	Homology and Relations	189
APPENDIX D	An Algebra for Patterns	200
REFERENCES AND BIBLIOGRAPHY		208
INDEX		211

1 Ideas Associated with Set Theory

1.1 Introduction

The introduction of what is commonly called 'modern mathematics' into our educational system has at least had the beneficial result of focussing attention on the mathematical notion of a *set*. This idea is central to the theme of this book, and therefore it will not be amiss if we examine various illustrations of it — chiefly as a preliminary to finding our way to a fruitful concept of mathematical structure. More formal details of set-theory, and of other mathematical ideas, will be found in the relevant appendices to this book. This latter treatment possesses the virtue of providing a formal algebra, or calculus — in the language of pure mathematics — for the logical manipulation of set-theory ideas. But when, as applied mathematicians, we come to use any such calculus to describe what we believe to be real-world situations, then the crucial matters are the relevance of the fundamentals of the calculus to our intuitive recognition of those situations. When the layman plaintively asks 'what is set-theory all about?', he is speaking as a would-be applied mathematician. We cannot be surprised when he remains unmoved by the pure mathematician's reply, *viz.*, 'it is about definitions, axioms, and logically-deduced theorems'.

In asking for the semantics of a piece of pure mathematics the layman is asking for a translation from one language to another, and when he is an earnest student trying to (say) become a mathematician, then he is trying to achieve a mental condition in which translation is unnecessary. But probably the chief difficulty in this translation process lies in the fact that the mathematical language is dedicated to the elimination of ambiguity whereas, for example, English is not. This elimination of ambiguity, or the introduction of the mathematician's 'well-defined', is the starting point of Science and of the scientific method. It is much more important, and more profound, than the introduction of numbers in that old-fashioned sense of 'measuring things'. Failure to appreciate just such a point could well account, at least in part, for the modern growth of disillusionment with the methods of science.

In this respect it is important for us to discuss various fields of human endeavour, spanning both the (traditional) scientific and the non-scientific, if we are to see a unifying theme in the intellectual achievements in human affairs. But, firstly, we must begin at the beginning; we must begin with the idea of a mathematical set.

1.2 Set membership

By a mathematical set, S, we mean a collection or class of well-defined objects, and of any object whatsoever it must be possible for us all to agree on the answer to the question, 'is this object a member of the set S?'. Furthermore, the answer to this question must either be yes or no; the question (answer) falls within the orbit of the binary (2-valued) logic of the propositional calculus. Answering yes or no to the set-membership question is equivalent to saying that the proposition, 'this object x is a member of this set S', has one of two truth values, *viz.*, true or false. This is the significance of the words 'well-defined'.

Since the word 'object' might be unduly restrictive on the use of our imaginations it is usual to replace it by the word *element;* we speak of the elements of a set S. Often, when we are trying to make abstract mathematical points, we can abide by a convention to denote sets by upper-case letters S, A, X, etc., and the elements by lower-case letters, s, a, p, q, etc. But in real-life situations this can be ignored and the elements of a set might have humorous names like Tom, Dick, Harry.

If we wish to specify all or some of the members of a set S we shall try to consistently use curly brackets and write, for example,

$$S = \{a, b, c, d\}$$

or

$$F = \{Tom, Dick, Harry\}$$

The fact that some element x is a member of a set A is usually denoted by the Greek letter ϵ, and the statement

$$x \in A$$

is read as 'x is a member of the set A'

or as 'x belongs to (the set) A'.

The negation of ϵ is simply $\notin$, so that

although $\qquad 2 \in \{1, 2, 3\}$

we notice that $\qquad 4 \notin \{1, 2, 3\}$.

Listing all the members of a set, as in F above, is obviously only possible when the set contains only a finite number of elements. An example of a set which is not finite is J, the set of all integers. If it is not misleading we might denote this set by

$$J = \{0, \pm 1, \pm 2, \ldots\}$$

On the whole we shall be concerned with finite sets, but this should not be interpreted as meaning that we try to avoid considering infinite sets. Indeed set-theory, as first developed by Cantor, was designed to clarify the possible meanings of the word infinite.

Whether finite or infinite a set is therefore characterized by two basic ideas,

(1) the idea of element (the things which are members) and
(2) the idea of set-membership (a proposition with two truth values).

This property of membership of a set, which the members share, is a crucial and profound concept, for it distinguishes between two *qualities, viz.,* the one quality of being (only) an object with some specified properties, and the other quality of being a collection of such objects which is held together by this peculiar property. Thus the 'membership' acts like a kind of *cement* which creates out of the individual objects some new thing which is different in quality, in kind (what Russell described as of different types [36]). This idea constitutes our interpretation of the ancient Aristotelian view that

the set is more than (different from) the sum of its parts.

We are not here using 'more than' as a numerical measure. The Aristotelian notion was largely discredited in the early days of set-theory when 'more than' was obstinately interpreted as 'numerically greater than': clearly, with infinite sets, a 'part' can be numerically equal to the 'whole' — thus, the set J of integers is properly contained in the set Q of rational numbers, yet Cantor showed that J and Q are equally numerous.

On the contrary, we are expressing the essential and characteristic nature of set-membership — what led Russell to postulate the theory of types — when we accept the phrase 'the set is more than the sum of its parts'. We notice too that the meaning we wish to ascribe to this statement requires an interpretation also of the words 'sum of its parts'. (So much qualification of a short statement in English illustrates forcibly our meaning about ambiguities in the language — perhaps only politicians and lawyers fully value that ambiguity.) The final, if tedious, description of the statement, and that which contains the substance of our interpretation, is the following:

'the collection of elements together with the
cement of set-membership'   *(the set)*

'is qualitatively different from'   *(is more than)*

'the collection of elements without the cement'   *(the sum of its parts).*

We shall return to this point many times as we discuss the crucial points of applying set-theory notions to real-world situations, whether in the physical or the social sciences. But first we can gain insight into the problems of application by considering some historical precedents.

1.3 Aristotle's *Politics*

In his *Politics* [51] Aristotle went to great pains to define the 'State' in terms which we can now recognize as those of set-theory. His ideal State was to contain 2000–3000 individuals, then (1) a household was a set of individuals, (2) a village was a set of households, and (3) a State was a set of villages. The crucial feature of this particular sequence is perhaps contained in the following extract:

'... in the order of Nature the State is prior to the household or the individual. For the *whole must needs be prior to its parts.* For instance, if you take away the body which is the whole, there will not remain any such thing as a foot or a hand..... For a hand separated from the body will be a disabled hand; whereas it is the function or faculty of a thing which makes it what it is....'

This 'function' or 'faculty' of the set-member is precisely what is to make it a member of the set. In the same way the Aristotelian State was more than a collection of arbitrary villages. A village, as a member of the State, possessed functions or faculties which it could not otherwise possess. These functions, or this membership, performed the role of cementing the villages into a new (qualitative) thing, *viz.,* the State. Thus the idea of a set (the State) as a whole-thing serves as a *connectivity* (cementing) between its members (the villages) – this word 'connectivity' can be given a well-defined mathematical significance, as we shall see in the sequel, although 'cementing' might be more concrete.

The other idea which springs from the above extract is that the whole (the set) must be prior to its parts. This characteristically Aristotelian view is most certainly deeply opposed by the modern (post-medieval) scientific method. If it is accepted then it leads to a physics which, in its theories, explains the significance of the set-members in terms of the significance of the set (the whole). Modern physical theories do exactly the reverse of this; the whole is 'explained' in terms of the (ultimate) parts. Thus Eddington [21] was able to discuss the two tables (scientific and intuitive), the one being a set of electrons and protons, the other being familiar and macroscopic.

We distinguish the two views of science – the Aristotelian and the post-medieval – as the *holistic* and the *atomistic.* Although through the work of Epicurus and Democritus, the atomistic view was not unknown to the ancient Greeks, nevertheless it was the Aristotelian view which dominated effective scientific thinking until the modern experimentalist era began. Now, in the twentieth century, we see many signs of a revival of holistic theories, sending us all back to that other Aristotelian notion of 'moderation in all things'.

The Aristotelian discussion of *Politics* contains ample illustrations of the concept of *subset* (*v.* Appendix A) of a given set. In particular Aristotle, in reviewing the State as a set of individuals (in which he was not consistent) divided the latter into two categories (not counting the women), *viz.,* freemen and slaves. Thus all the freemen formed a subset of the State – which was the set of all men. If F is the set of all the freemen in the State S then $F \subset S$, F is a subset of S, meaning that:

'if $x \in F$ then $x \in S$, for all possible $x \in F$.'

Studying the *Politics* from the point of view of set theory leads to questions of definition which Aristotle never answers. For example, are we to understand that the State is defined as a set whose members are villages, households, or individuals? If the State is a set of individuals then 'households' is a subset of 'State', as is also 'village'. This is illustrated diagrammatically opposite.

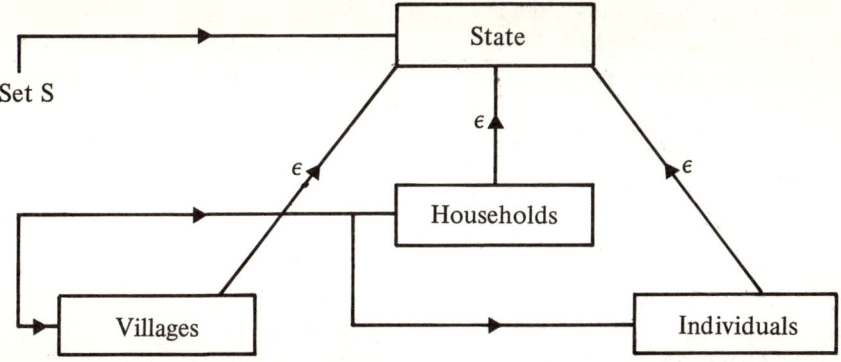

the relation between subsets being

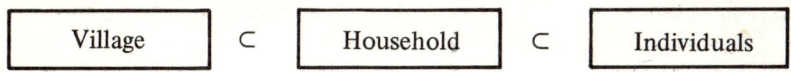

The question of which entities are the set-elements and which are the subsets is an important one because the discussion later on considers various attributes (such as virtue, morality, justice) which are applicable exclusively to elements or to subsets of State, but not to both. Thus Aristotle claimed that 'justice' is applicable to (is a quality of) the set State, not to individuals. Similarly the polity of the State could only exist if it possessed subsets distinct from the single-member subsets (the individuals as elements of S). It was not possible to be a senator (a member of the subset 'senate') if the State did not exist.

In toto, if we insist that Aristotle's State is defined as a set of individuals (as set elements) then we must also allow that certain subsets (e.g. village) are more significant than others. When he is discussing the characteristics of Oligarchy, Democracy, and Tyranny then the significant subsets are the Households and the Villages. When he is discussing the most suitable recipients of political power then he takes as the significant subsets the Rich, the Freemen, the Nobles, the Virtuous, and the Majority. When he is discussing the questions of property and the so-called natural finance then the most significant subsets are the Households.

Thus, although, in any purely abstract theory of sets, the mathematician must allow every possible sub-collection of set-members to form a subset, when we are concerned with the theory as an *application* of mathematics we must make distinctions between possible subsets.

But although it appears reasonable, in the case of the *Politics,* to accept the definition of the State in terms of set-membership applied to individuals we find that this interpretation is only consistently possible for the first five Books (there are eight Books in all). In Book Six Aristotle rocks the boat by asserting that the State consists of two kinds of elements *viz.,* (1) a qualitative kind (freedom, wealth, culture, and nobility) and (2) a quantitative kind (numbers of individuals). He is now enlarging the set of elements beyond the individuals, including for example the element 'wealth'. Unfortunately he has previously insisted that wealth, whilst being indispensable is nevertheless not to be a part of the State. Perhaps the most remarkable feature of the *Politics* is the extent of the consistency, vis-à-vis set-theory, rather than the reverse.

1.4 Galileo's sets and relations

If we move on some two thousand years from Aristotle we come to the time of Galileo [16, 46] and the birth of modern scientific enquiry. At that time the Aristotelian philosophers were still absorbed in the concepts of his scientific analysis, the *Physics*. In laying the foundations of the science of mechanics Galileo had to do battle with the ancient ideas about motion [38]. Tied up closely with the idea of a natural 'place' for every object, motion could be classified as 'natural' or otherwise. The Aristotelian view was that circular motion (such as that apparently of the planets) was natural, rectilinear motion was not. Hence, in order to understand the motion of a body a *set of concepts* was required which consisted, in the main, of the elements {place, nature, potential}. Strange to our minds is the thought that 'time' is not a prerequisite of motion but comes after it, that is to say, time is a consequence of motion, the latter being a 'natural property' of objects. Essentially, we are to believe that motion is the fulfilling of what exists (in the 'nature' of the body) potentially.

But it all had its lighter side. The Aristotelian principles led to a theory of the projectile (due essentially to Albert of Saxony [16]) which viewed its motion as compounded of three successive parts; during the first two the impressed 'impetus' declined to zero, and during the last part the body fell vertically to the ground.

As far as the application of set-theory is concerned we can see that the set of concepts which were available for the discussion of motion was quite unacceptable to Galileo and his contemporaries. The Aristotelian set was not suitable for a (modern) *description* of the motion of an object, however suitable it might have appeared to be for an *explanation* of the phenomenon. Galileo set his mind against the pursuit of the 'why' of the motion and concentrated on describing the 'how'. This required hypotheses about possible basic sets of elements and experiments to test their validity. The interested reader will find many fascinating details of that work in the modern edition of Mach's book [38].

Accepting the Cartesian postulate that Euclidean geometry is an actual description of our 3-dimensional space, Galileo set about the problem by studying the rolling of a ball down an inclined plane. The *set* which he required for the description was therefore a collection of *geometrical points* (which could be numbered by their distances from the origin) together with a collection of *time intervals* (which were numbers attached to various amounts of water which flowed from a suitable container). Thus the Galileian set, as opposed to the Aristotelian, was what we would now call the *cartesian product* $S \times T$, S being a set of geometrical points, and T being a set of times,

$$S = \{s_1, s_2, \ldots s_n, \ldots\}$$

$$T = \{t_1, t_2, \ldots\} \qquad [v.\ \text{Appendix A}].$$

But this Galileian set, $G = S \times T$, now contained the possibility of a description of all possible motions (accelerated, uniform, zero) of bodies on the inclined plane. The particular motion of the rolling of a ball down the plane (from the rest position) was then to be found by identifying a particular subset of G; that is to say, of a collection of the s_i and the t_j which correspond as near as possible to the points-cum-times at which the ball was to be actually observed. If this particular subset is denoted by B then $B \subset G$ and the description of this particular motion is equivalent to a specification of set-membership for elements of B. Each element of G is a pair of numbers, say, (s_i, t_j) and each element of B is a pair of numbers, say, (s_i, t_i) — where the labels attached to each pair of corresponding s and t are made to coincide.

We can now describe this Galileian picture of the motion of the ball as follows:

> *the motion is described by a subset B of the set $G = S \times T$ where $(s, t) \in B$ if, and only if, $s = k t^2$, k being a constant number characteristic of B and independent of the particular pair (s, t).*

Nowadays we would say that $k \propto g$, g being the symbol for the acceleration due to gravity at the surface of the earth.

This formula $s = kt^2$, which is expressed in elementary algebra, tells us of a functional dependence between the allowed values of s and the corresponding values of t. It can be understood as a *formula* which describes the motion of a ball rolling down an inclined plane. But equally well it is an expression of a *mathematical relation* between the sets S and T, or of the set G. If we denote this relation by λ_G then all the possible elements of S being denoted by $s_1, s_2, \ldots$ and all the elements of T by $t_1, t_2, \ldots$ we can denote λ_G by the scheme in the following array.

λ_G	t_1	t_2	t_3	t_4	t_5	t_6	t_7	t_8	t_9	t_{10}	t_{11} →
s_1	1	0	0	0	0	0	0	0	0	0	0
s_2	0	1	0	0	0	0	0	0	0	0	0
s_3	0	0	1	0	0	0	0	0	0	0	0
s_4	0	0	0	1	0	0	0	0	0	0	0
s_5	0	0	0	0	1	0	0	0	0	0	0
s_6	0	0	0	0	0	1	0	0	0	0	0
s_7	0	0	0	0	0	0	1	0	0	0	0
s_8	0	0	0	0	0	0	0	1	0	0	0
↓											

The set $G = S \times T$ is represented by all the pairs (s_i, t_j) but B is the set corresponding only to the positions of the 1's, along the main diagonal. Thus λ_G puts a 1 in that time t_i which is related to the position s_i by the formula $s_i = kt_i^2$, and it puts a 0 where the relation does not apply. If the t's were renumbered so that, for example, s_i were related to t_{i+2} then the 1's would no longer appear on the leading diagonal, but there would still be only one 1 in each row or column.

This relation describing the motion exists between the sets S and T of position (or distance) and time (time interval of travel) which Galileo actually measured. It is significant to point out therefore that the description does not depend for its validity on being able to measure *all* the Euclidean points of a line (whatever 'all' means in this context). Thus the set-theory description allows the use of finite sets in the actual observations of mechanics.

This formulation of the description of a common kind of motion led Galileo to the notion of *acceleration* (as we use it today) as a change of velocity per unit of time, and to what is referred to as the *law of inertia* — which asserts that rectilinear motion is the 'natural' motion. The mathematical method introduced by Galileo consisted in using the language of elementary algebra together with Euclidean geometry to name the basic set-members (of S and of T), then to specify the relevant set-membership by obedience to some specific relation. A knowledge of the set B is equivalent to a knowledge of λ_G, to a knowledge of 'the formula'.

We are still reeling from the effects of this revolutionary way of thinking.

1.5 Logical paradoxes

The idea that a scientific (unambiguous) study can be expressed in terms of set-theory is closely tied up with the role we wish to give to our 2-valued (binary) logic. We have seen that set-membership is a special illustration of this idea and it is not surprising if attempts to apply set-theory to actual-world situations fall down on this point. If we wish to theorize about concepts with English names and yet are unable to identify these concepts in an unambiguous way — that is to say, if the concepts are not well-defined — then the assumption of a set-theoretical setting for the theory will take us from bad to worse. There are valuable lessons for us in the work of mathematicians and logicians themselves. [36]

In the early days of the set-theory initiated by G. Cantor many paradoxes were unearthed, and these were the consequences of trying to apply set-theory definitions in inappropriate situations — often to (imagined) sets themselves.

Cantor originally defined a *set* S as *any collection of definite, distinguishable objects of our intuition or of our intellect to be conceived as a whole*. This certainly allows us to entertain the idea of *the set of all sets*, denoted (say) by U. This set (if so it be) U will possess the property of belonging to itself, $U \in U$, since U is a set. Contrariwise it is easy to think of sets which do not belong to themselves: the set of all dogs is not a dog. Let us denote by T the set of all sets which are not members of themselves. This gives rise to a famous paradox (Russell's paradox) discovered independently by Zermelo and Russell. It arises when one tries to answer the question: is $T \in T$ (is T a member of itself)?

Since membership of a set is decided in a 2-valued logic we expect the answer to be either Yes or No. Assuming that the answer is Yes, $T \in T$, then T is a set to be found in a set (*viz.,* T) of sets which are not members of themselves; hence $T \notin T$. Hence we must have been wrong in our original assumption; the answer must be No. Hence $T \notin T$; and so T is a set which does not belong to the set (T) of sets which are not members of themselves; hence $T \in T$. Now we have the genuinely paradoxical situation that to the question:

is T a member of T?

we can answer Yes and No. Then the set-membership requirement has fallen down.

Bertrand Russell gave a homely popularization of this paradox in the following form.

'A certain village contains a man who is the village barber. The barber shaves all and only those men in the village who do not shave themselves. Does the barber shave himself?'

If we assume that the barber shaves himself then he must be one of the men who is not shaved by the barber; hence he does not shave himself; the opposite case can also be deduced. Clearly the paradoxical situation is concerned with the fact that the set is confused with the set-elements. Thus the set of men who do not shave themselves is a definition of the barber *per se,* and the question assumes that the barber (i.e. the set) is only a member of the set. Such a view of the problem led Russell to his theory of types – in which he sought to demand a strict hierachy of elements, sets of elements, sets of sets of elements, etc.

The same paradox is involved in the problem of the librarian who sets out to compile a reference book, for his library, of all the reference books in his library which do not refer to themselves. Does his new reference book refer to itself?

Or the very ancient liar-paradox (or the Cretan paradox) in which Epimenides, the Cretan, says 'all Cretans are liars'. Is he speaking the truth?

Finally in the same vein, and perhaps the most attractive – expressing a saga of the triumph of wit over adversity, is the ancient *dilemma of the crocodile.* The crocodile has stolen a child and promises the father to return the child provided the father can guess whether the crocodile will return the child or not. What is the crocodile to do if the father guesses that the crocodile will not return the child? [There can be no prize for remarks about crocodile tears.]

Such problems, and there are many more [36], are introduced to demonstrate to the unwary that the requirements we place upon set-identification and set-membership are non-trivial. If we seek to apply set-theory notions to actual-world situations then we must expect to examine our fundamental assumptions with great care. To say, for example, that the science of mechanics, or the science of economics, is erected on a basis of set-theory is to say something profound about the observational basis of that discipline. And this occurs long before we need wrestle with formalistic problems of algebra, arithmetic, calculus, or structure in general.

1.6 Probability and sets of events

Another important example of the application of set-theory arises in the modern theory of probability (and therefore of statistics). This arose from a consideration of *games of chance,* such as dice, roulette, and other human vices. When a single die is thrown it is apparent that we have so little knowledge about the 'how' of its motion that we cannot resist speaking of an 'equal chance' of a six or a three turning up. Of the set-members (*viz.*, 1, 2, 3, 4, 5, 6) which constitute the set of 'all possible results of a throw' we must express our complete ignorance vis-à-vis the outcome. We speak of this by saying that any one of the six values of the die is 'equally likely' or has an 'equal probability' with any of the others. Continued throwing of the die seems to give a reasonable justification for this attitude since, if there is a large number N of throws, the actual number of occurrences of any one number is near-enough equal to $N/6$; at least under normal conditions — when the die is not deliberately loaded.

The set of all possible results of a throw is generally referred to as the *set of (possible) events,* E. If we are interested in a successful throw of a six then that event would be called a *success;* all possible successes constitute a subset S of E. In this simple case of a single die, if S refers to the throw of a six, then card E = 6 and card S = 1.

Probability theory says that,

the probability of a success S *is* card S/card E,

that is to say, in this case, the probability of throwing a six is 1/6. Its relevance becomes more convincing if we consider the result of throwing a pair of dice simultaneously. Then a result (or event) is the number pair (x, y), with x and y taking any one of the numbers $1, \ldots, 6$. Hence E contains 36 possible events. If we ask the question, in how many ways can we obtain a result in which $x + y = 8$, we see that the answer must be 5 — being given by the events

$$(2, 6), (3, 5), (4, 4), (5, 3), (6, 2).$$

Let this set be the successes we are looking for in a particular throw. Then card S = 5 and theory gives the probability of a success as

$$p\{x + y = 8\} = \text{card S}/\text{card E} = 5/36.$$

Such an approach to a formulation and quantification of a theory of probability can clearly make a lot of sense when both E and S are finite sets and when the subsets of E are, in some well-defined observational sense, accessible without bias. But when card E = ∞ and card S $<$ ∞ then p{S} = 0, for any finite subset S; and when card S = ∞ = card E what happens to the value of p{S}?

This latter predicament is usually avoided (?) by a definition of p{S} which is the *limiting value* of card S_n/card E_n, as $n \to \infty$, and where both S_n, E_n are finite subsets of S and E respectively. This requires the identification of a sequence of sets $\{E_n\}$, with $E_n \subset E_{n+1}$, and *experimental conditions which ensure* that

$$\lim_{n \to \infty} \{\text{card } S_n/\text{card } E_n\}$$

actually exists.

What is more awkward for this limiting view of probability is the fact that *ordinality concepts* have been introduced into the whole notion, and if this ordinality is to be avoided it is necessary for the experimental conditions to ensure that, for *all* observable monotone sequences $\{E_n\}$, the value of lim $\{\text{card } S_n/\text{card } E_n\}$ must not only exist but be invariant. These are very demanding conditions to be placed on the experimental observations of the sets S and E. Furthermore, the limiting-view can hardly be regarded as a satisfactory generalization of the ratio-view since the results are not necessarily consistent. This arises from the fact that an infinite sequence of numbers, tending to a limit l as $n \to \infty$, does so independently of the values of any finite set of those numbers contained in the portion $n < k$ (k arbitrary but finite).

An attempted way out of this limiting view of probability, due to R. A. Fisher [24], and followed by the majority of contemporary statisticians, is to regard the actual data (the set S_n) as constituting a *random sample* of a hypothetical infinite population. But it takes us out of our theme to discuss the idea of a random sample in this chapter. Suffice it to point out that, generally, the 'problem' of defining probability values centres around the 'problem' of infinite sets E and S. [33]

But although it seems to correspond with observation that the ratio-view of probability (p{S} = card S/card E; S and E both finite) represents certain actual-world situations (dice, roulette, lotteries, gambling generally) it is by no means obvious that such a situation is commonplace. If this is so, it is not that we are criticising the set-element/set-membership decisions which are involved but rather warning against the relevance of the associated ratio of cardinalities which is involved when speaking of probability or chance. The point we are trying to make concerns the *status of the subsets* of E, and this question is distinct from the above problem of finding some definition of probability which works for an ever-widening class of sets.

When we wish to apply the notion and calculus of probability to an actual-world situation we must be sure that the *subsets of E are observationally accessible without bias*. This is the condition of play for the gambler, and only when this applies can gambling odds be offered *before the event*. If a die is thrown then E has cardinality 6 and the observational events are any one of the six faces; hence the observationally accessible subsets of $\{1, 2, 3, 4, 5, 6\}$ are the following, and no others,

$$\{1\}, \{2\}, \{3\}, \{4\}, \{5\}, \{6\}$$

Assigning a probability of p{S} = 1/6 to an observational subset can now be of great interest and relevance to the gambler only if it can be so assigned *prior* to the event. It can be so assigned, as a piece of applied mathematics, if it turns out (*after* the event) to model the actual experimental situation. It is unavoidable that this should have all the ingredients for a *circulus in definiendo* or a chicken-or-the-egg state of affairs, as illustrated for a set E with observable subsets S_i.

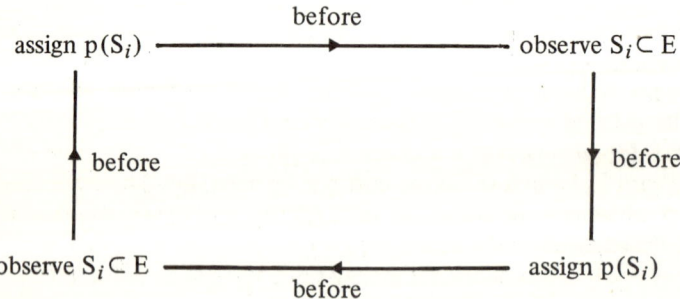

We shall refer to the situation represented by this diagram as the *probability loop*. The assignor in this probability loop is inevitably looking both backwards and forwards. In the Backward-Look condition the assignor has the observed knowledge of the frequency counts whereby he may identify card S and card E in the actual-world. In the Forward-Look condition the assignor possesses the probability model (the set of values he calls $p(S_i)$) and hopefully he expects the results of observation to give values of card S and card E which fit p(S).

When the assignor adopts the Backward-Look condition in the probability loop he naturally describes the numbers $p(S_i)$ as relative frequency counts of the observed events. When he adopts the Forward-Look condition he changes his mode of speaking and says 'the probability of the event S_i occurring in an actual-world observation is $p(S_i)$'.

The assignor's ever-present predicament lies in the fact that his probability numbers $p(S_i)$ are ultimately derived from cardinalities, from counting heads (only). Hence he cannot appeal to another set of well-defined observations, as a criterion for deciding whether or not the Forward-Look is likely to be justifiable. If, for example, there were some connection between S_1 and S_2 — such as S_2 must follow S_1 — then the system possesses certainties and conditional dependencies which affect the probability values. The calculus of probabilities makes provision for certainty by allowing the value p = 1, and *via* the concept of conditional probability it can also contain other types of dependence. But in the end, the justification for the Forward-Look lies in the Backward-Look. There is no escape from the probability loop.

But is this situation at all alarming? Is there not a 'loop-problem' in any piece of applied mathematics, from which we cannot escape?

The answer to the first question must be No, and to the second it must be Yes. There is however a difference between the sorts of system studied by

Galileo and those studied by the probabilists, or rather in the attitudes adopted by the investigators in the two cases.

In broad terms we can say that one method is based on asking the question *how?*, the other is based on asking the question *how often?*. When Galileo examined the system of a ball rolling down an inclined plane he was trying to find suitable sets of observations in terms of which he could describe the *how* of the motion. In the results of this study we see that he thereby produced a description of a specific type of event, or phenomenon. The *event was identified as a certain relation* λ_G between certain sets S and T; it was implicitly assumed that the sets S and T could themselves be identified without ambiguity by the (well-defined) techniques of the experimental set-up.

When we ask *how often* we can obtain a total of 8 in throwing a pair of dice we are assuming that the event is already well-defined in the observational technique. We are not looking deeper than the set E of all events to some other set (or sets) Y in terms of which the *how* of throwing an 8 can be described. To this extent we can say that we are ignorant of *how* the 8 occurs: we either do not know how or we believe that it is irrelevant to know. What matters to us, what is the *content* of our knowledge, is the frequency count of the event S = {throw a total of 8} in the totality E. If the observational set E consists of events $E_1, E_2, \ldots E_n$ and the successes are $S_1, S_2, \ldots S_k$ then each S_i is a subset of E, being defined as a set of the E_j. Thus the recognition of an S_i — a necessary preliminary before we can count them — implies a relation λ_p between the S_i and the E_j. For example, let E be the set of events obtained by throwing a pair of dice simultaneously, and let S_1 = {throw a total of 5}, S_2 = {throw a total of 6}, and S_3 = {throw a total of 10}. If we label the events of E by E_{rs}, meaning that die-1 shows the number r and die-2 shows s, we get

$$S_1 = \{E_{14}, E_{23}, E_{32}, E_{41}\}$$
$$S_2 = \{E_{15}, E_{24}, E_{33}, E_{42}, E_{51}\}$$
and
$$S_3 = \{E_{46}, E_{55}, E_{64}\}$$

The relevant portion of the incidence matrix for λ_p looks like the following.

λ_p	E_{11}	...	E_{14}	E_{15}	...	E_{23}	E_{24}	...	E_{32}	E_{33}	...	E_{41}	E_{42}	...	E_{46}	...	E_{51}	...	E_{55}	...	E_{64}	...
S_1	0	...	1	0	...	1	0	...	1	0	...	1	0	...	0	...	0	...	0	...	0	...
S_2	0	...	0	1	...	0	1	...	0	1	...	0	1	...	0	...	1	...	0	...	0	...
S_3	0	...	0	0	...	0	0	...	0	0	...	0	0	...	1	...	0	...	1	...	1	...

This relation is the counterpart to Gaileo's λ_G above and it comes prior to any question of counting S_i. It identifies the set-membership for the experimental successes in terms of a basic set of (unquestioned) events E_j. When a single die is thrown then $S_i = E_i$ and λ_p contains a line of 1's down the leading diagonal — as does λ_G.

But λ_G relates two distinct sets S (space-points) and T (time-points), whilst λ_p relates {subsets of E} to {elements of E}. Hence whilst λ_G is a relation on the Cartesian product S × T, λ_p is a relation on the Cartesian product P(E) × E, P(E) being the *power set* of E. Starting from this initial position of λ_p (which identifies the experimentally accessible subsets S_i) the probabilist goes round and round the probability loop until he stabilizes a set of numbers $p(S_i)$. These are rational numbers and may be seen as given by a *mapping* π from the subsets of E (that is to say, from P(E) to the rationals $\mathscr{Q}$. We therefore represent the probability model by identifying this map

$$\pi : P(E) \to \mathscr{Q}$$

with the obvious understanding that if $S_i \neq S_1, S_2,$ or S_3 then

$$\pi(S_i) = 0$$

We now obtain a new set of numbers, *viz.*, the values of $\pi(S)$ for every $S \in P(E)$, and this is the simple relation of the mapping π; it looks like the following.

π	.... $\pi(S_1)$	$\pi(S_2)$	$\pi(S_3)$ ....
S_1	1	0	0
S_2	0	1	0
S_3	0	0	1

We shall return to this procedure in Appendices C and D, when we discuss the ideas of a *pattern* on a simplicial complex, but the point which is relevant in the present discussion is the recognition of a *specially favoured* collection of subsets (the S_i) of a set E; and what is more, we cannot assume that *all* subsets of E are so favoured — the relation between the S_i themselves (what we shall call q-connections) play a significant role in identifying *structure*.

1.7 Chess and relations Γ_W, Γ_B

From what we have said so far it is clear that much of human thinking is concerned with firstly, identifying specific sets, and secondly, with mathematical relations between selected sets. It is in the study of such relations that we shall find a great deal of basic structure; most of the technicalities required will emerge in subsequent chapters, the formal discussion will be found in the Appendices.

An uncomplicated kind of relation between well-defined finite sets can be seen in the game of chess, an activity invented by and for the human mind and which must contain features peculiar to the latter. It is therefore no accident that research workers in the field of machine-intelligence have long been fascinated with the problem of constructing a chess-playing computer. A basic method of attacking this problem was provided by C. Shannon and, as a matter of interest, the progress which had been made by 1966 was tested in a computer-match between those at ITEP in Moscow and at Stanford University in the U.S.A. The result of a four-game match at the time was a 3–1 win for the Soviet 'player'.

We can appreciate some of the chess-player's difficulties by noticing that the game is played between two opponents, White and Black, on a board of 64 squares. Each player commences with 8 pieces (2 Rooks, 2 Knights, 2 Bishops, 1 Queen, 1 King) and 8 pawns. They are placed in position, at the commencement of the game, as shown in Figure 1.1, which also shows the method of labelling the squares a1 ... h8.

Figure 1.1 Mode [0, 0] in the game of chess

The sets are well-defined, being WM (the White Men), BM (the Black Men), and S (the squares). The position in Figure 1.1 can be said to be in *mode* [0, 0], with White to move; after White's move we shall say that the game is in mode [1, 0], etc. The rules of the game are sufficiently well-known not to need repetition here — no one should go through life without obtaining at least a smattering of them.

There is a standard international algebraic notation for describing a move; this is illustrated by the following pitiful sequence.

(1) e2–e4   : e7–e5
(2) B–c4   : N–f6
(3) B × f7 + : K × f7
(4) Q–h5 +   : N × h5
(5) Resigns

A pawn is not denoted by the letter P but by the square on which it sits; 'moves to' is denoted by — captures by ×; + means 'check' N stands for Knight (the American influence on the English language!); 'resigns' means that White has had enough.

There is one obvious relation for White between WM and S, *viz.*, that relation which tells us where the pieces are positioned on the board; similarly for Black. This relation is a *mapping* WM → S and so its incidence matrix cannot contain more than one 1 in any row or column; denote it by Π_W (or Π_B).

The relation Π_W is not very helpful when the game is played because it does not embody the rules of the game. These are involved however in the definition of a much more interesting relation which we shall denote by Γ_W (or Γ_B).

If WM = $\{X_1, \ldots X_{16}\}$, where X_i is either a piece or a pawn, and S = $\{S_1, \ldots S_{64}\}$, where S_j is a square of the board, then we define Γ_W in the following way:

given X_i and S_j, then $(X_i, S_j) \in \Gamma_W$ if and only if X_i attacks S_j.

By 'attacks' we mean that one of the following holds true:

(1) if it is White's move, and if X_i is not a pawn or the King, then 'X_i–S_j' is a legal move;
(2) if X_i is a pawn then S_j is a capturing square for X_i;
(3) if there is a White man Y on S_j then X_i is protecting Y, in ordinary chess-player's parlance;
(4) if X_i is the White King then S_j is an immediate neighbour to the square occupied by X_i; horizontally, vertically, or diagonally;
(5) if the square S_j contains a Black piece or pawn Z (other than the King) and if it were White's move, then 'X × Z' is a legal move;
(6) the Black King is on square S_j and is in check to White's X_i.

A similar definition clearly holds for Γ_B. In either case we notice that X_i cannot attack its own square, a fact of practical significance which is well-known to chess-players the world over.

We see too that Γ_W is a function of the mode $[I, J]$ which describes the state of play. Identifying Γ_W and Γ_B for each mode of a game takes us through the whole range of attack and defense experienced by either player. Each player must likewise be mentally aware of the relation Γ of his opponent.

In Γ_W (and Γ_B) lies the secret of the game – if we can only discover it. In a chess-player's ability to comprehend the subtleties of Γ_W and Γ_B, either in his conscious or subconscious mind, lies a profound clue to assessing that peculiar chess-intelligence which we admire. If Emmanuel Lasker was right, and intelligence-for-chess is the same as intelligence-for-life, then a deep understanding of Γ_W and Γ_B should tell us something about ourselves which is much coveted. [37]

An example of a simple Γ_W is illustrated by the position shown in Figure 1.2 opposite.

In Γ_W the Pawn (on e2) is related to {d3, f3}
the King (on c2) is related to {b1, c1, d1, b2, d2, b3, c3, d3}
the Rook (on c4) is related to {c3, a4, b4, c4, d4, c5, c6, c7, c8}
the Queen (on d3) is related to {c2, d1, d2, e2, c3, e3, f3, g3, h3, c4, d4, e4}

Since the Black King is on square e4, which is related to the White Queen, it is in check in this mode.

In the inverse relation Γ_W^{-1} we notice, for example, that the square c3 (containing the Black pawn) is related to {R, Q, K}; in other words, it is attacked three times by the White pieces.

Figure 1.2 Black King is in check

1.8 The university bar

Every organization, institution, business, political party, or what-have-you, demonstrates the occurrence of relations between finite sets. Let us illustrate what this might be by taking a university as an example — the more so since university dons are well-known for their subtle sense of humour and tolerance about being exposed to public gaze — but let us undertake not to uncover any features which a hot-blooded undergraduate might interpret as sinister.

In England (1974) a university is organized through a committee structure which is designed to deal with both academic and non-academic matters. At the top is the Council, which contains distinguished lay-members, and immediately below this is found the Senate where the academic dons and professors engage in friendly chaffing about the facts and fantasies of the scholastic life. There is then a collection of school-(or faculty-) boards and departmental committees (but sometimes there is only one member to each one of these). Besides these academically-oriented committees there will be sub-committees of both Council and Senate which will be required to deal with various non-academic matters, such as minor finance, major finance, maintenance of building and plant, catering, sporting and recreational facilities, discipline (for the students), residence and lodgings, spiritual and bodily welfare matters in general. Most of these committees have the right, which they frequently exercise, of setting up sub-committees and/or working parties to hive off the onus of studying specific problems and recommending decisions. The total hierachy of committees is not linear (totally ordered) although it is sometimes a puzzle to know whether or not it is so intended. The result of this is that the committee activities — the policy matters they are designed to discuss and the decisions they are expected to take — can overlap, and the same substantial matter can be injected into, say, the Senate by more than one route.

If we create a list of all university activities which are relevant to, say, the month of January 1974. then hopefully this list is well-defined and forms a finite set — both questions can give rise to hours of good-humoured debate among the community of scholars.

There is now a natural relation between this set of activities and the set of committees which make up the whole hierachy. An understanding of this relation can be important for the practical matter of reaching decisions which are implemented as well as for the theoretical understanding of the whole structure.

Of course, the committees possess members and these are people (*sic*). They are drawn from the academic staff, by and large, but can also include students (undergraduate and graduate) and lay-members from 'outside'.

There is now a relation between the set of people who serve on any committee and the set of university activities mentioned above. This relation contains that information relevant to the much-vaunted and fashionable *decision-making process*. Some members of the set of people will be related to many activities, by being on many important committees; some activities will be related to many people, by being legitimately discussed by many committees or by many people on a few committees. Often some one person (a chairman or probably the vice-chancellor) will be technically on all committees of a certain pedigree. That could mean that he possesses great influence, or it could not.

But in any event we can see that the running of an organization through a committee structure amounts to discussion and decision against a background of specific mathematical relations. These must be relations between people and policy matters (activities) and between committees (which are subsets of the set of people) and these same matters. Whether or not these relations contain all the intangible qualities which make the differences between individual people is not immediately significant. It is not essential that these relations should be *sufficient* to encompass the whole decision process but only that it be seen to be *necessary*. Without these relations this style of government could not exist; the secrets of the style must therefore be in the mathematical relations.

Let us illustrate the relations involved by considering a fictitious example which might arise when it is proposed that the university bar should be moved from Position-A to a new Position-B.

In Position-A the features include the following:

(A1)   the floor area is $50\,m^2$;
(A2)   the bar is on ground level (floor-0);
(A3)   the entrance to the bar is from an open quadrangle;
(A4)   the bar is adjacent to a retail shop and to two administrative offices;
(A5)   the bar is beneath a common-room (known as a quiet room);
(A6)   bar deliveries are by way of a lift from a loading bay beneath floor-0;
(A7)   the distance from the bar to on-campus student residences is 300 m;
(A8)   the distance to the open car park is 500 m;
(A9)   the distance to the lecture theatres is 200 m;
(A10)   the bar is opposite a coffee-and-snacks bar (30 m) in the quadrangle.

In Position-B the features would include the following:

(B1) the floor area is to be extended to 75 m^2;
(B2) the bar is to be on the first floor (floor-1) level;
(B3) the entrance is not visible from the outside;
(B4) two large seminar rooms are to be converted to form the bar;
(B5) the bar is to be adjacent to increased toilet facilities;
(B6) the distance to student residences is to be 100 m;
(B7) the distance to the car park is to be 600 m;
(B8) the distance to the lecture theatres is to be 250 m;
(B9) the bar is to be more luxuriously furnished than before;
(B10) deliveries will be by a different lift from level floor-(-1);
(B11) the bar is to be adjacent to administrative offices;
(B12) the bar will be above the students' launderette;
(B13) the bar will be beneath a small lecture room.

If we assume that these features are the main ones which influence people in coming to a decision about the wisdom of the proposal then we must see what set of university activities (practical and theoretical) is likely to be involved.

Since physical alterations are involved (B4) some *capital expenditure*, albeit of a minor nature, will be required. When Position-A is vacated something must be done with the inside and the outside of the old bar; the *external decor* will need to be settled therefore and also the question of *room/space allocation* will arise — the more so since Position-B requires a loss of two large seminar rooms to the academically-used pool of rooms. Hence *departmental space requirements* need to be discussed, and also *faculty space requirements* might need to be reshuffled. Since the bar is to be moved to an inside position (A3 → B3) there will be an effect on the *cleaning arrangements* and also *security requirements* will alter — because of what will now be adjacent to the bar. Since the bar provision generally is the concern of the *catering section*, this must be discussed; for example, the financial effect on both the bar itself and the coffee-and-snacks bar. Naturally, the bar provision is part of the general *facilities for student recreation* as well as being part of the university's *overall amenities*. Since these latter are also open to the public at large (by general invitation) the affair is also a problem in *public relations (cf.* A8, A2, A1 with B1, B2, B3, B7). Because many students live on the campus the questions A7 and B6 are relevant in the context of *student residences,* and matters like B9, B13 are likely to be the concern of *staff amenities.*

Let us rest content with this set of 13, for the moment, and label them as follows:

Y1	capital expenditure	Y6	cleaning detail	Y11	public relations
Y2	external decor	Y7	security	Y12	student residences
Y3	room allocation	Y8	catering provision	Y13	staff amenities
Y4	departmental rooms	Y9	student recreation		
Y5	faculty rooms	Y10	general amenities		

Now let us suppose that it so happens that all these university activities can be dealt with by the following set of 12 committees (cttee):

X1 minor-works finance cttee
X2 student welfare cttee
X3 landscape cttee
X4 catering cttee
X5 academic department cttee
X6 faculty board
X7 social amenities cttee
X8 housing cttee
X9 student affairs cttee
X10 senate
X11 finance cttee
X12 council

Some of these committees are subcommittees of others but this feature is temporarily irrelevant for us. The relation which we first find, denoted by Γ_1, is set out in the following incidence matrix, which shows the positions of the 1's only, in the relation; all the other entries are zeros.

Γ_1	X1	X2	X3	X4	X5	X6	X7	X8	X9	X10	X11	X12
Y1	1	0	0	0	0	0	0	0	0	0	1	0
Y2	0	0	1	0	0	0	0	0	0	0	0	0
Y3	0	0	0	0	1	1	0	0	0	1	0	0
Y4	0	0	0	0	1	1	0	0	0	0	0	0
Y5	0	0	0	0	0	1	0	0	0	1	0	0
Y6	0	0	0	0	0	0	1	0	1	1	0	0
Y7	0	1	0	0	0	0	0	0	1	1	0	0
Y8	0	0	0	1	0	0	1	0	0	1	1	1
Y9	0	1	0	0	0	0	0	0	1	1	0	0
Y10	0	1	0	0	0	0	1	0	0	1	0	1
Y11	0	0	1	0	0	0	1	0	0	1	0	1
Y12	0	1	0	0	0	0	0	1	1	1	0	1
Y13	0	0	0	0	1	1	0	0	0	1	0	1

This relation Γ_1 must contain the background to the formal business of discussing the proposal and of making decisions.

Another relation, say Γ_2, will exist between the people who sit on the various committees and the committees. In practice this set of people will number, perhaps, 200; for our purposes we will demonstrate Γ_2 by assuming that the number is much smaller. This amounts to saying something ludicrous like 'there are only 10 people on senate, 5 on the council', etc., but the point will be sufficiently clear when we return to this example for more analysis later. The only identifications which might be helpful will be the people P1, P2, P3, P4 – which we propose to label vice-chancellor, chairman of an academic department, dean of a faculty, dean of students, respectively. We then assume a Γ_2 between the people set and the committee set, with the following incidence matrix.

Γ_2	X1	X2	X3	X4	X5	X6	X7	X8	X9	X10	X11	X12
P1	1	1	0	0	0	1	0	0	0	1	1	1
P2	0	0	0	0	1	1	0	0	0	1	0	1
P3	1	0	0	1	0	1	0	0	0	1	0	1
P4	0	1	0	0	0	0	1	0	1	1	1	1
P5	1	0	1	0	1	0	0	0	0	0	0	0
P6	0	1	0	0	0	1	0	1	0	0	1	0
P7	0	0	0	0	0	0	1	0	0	0	0	1
P8	0	0	0	1	0	0	0	0	0	0	0	1
P9	0	0	0	0	0	0	0	1	0	0	1	1
P10	1	0	0	1	0	0	0	0	1	0	0	0
P11	0	0	1	0	0	1	0	0	0	1	0	0
P12	0	1	1	0	1	0	0	0	0	1	0	0
P13	0	0	0	0	0	0	0	0	0	0	0	0
P14	0	0	0	0	0	0	0	0	0	1	0	0
P15	0	0	0	1	0	0	0	0	0	0	0	0
P16	0	0	0	0	0	1	0	0	0	1	0	0
P17	0	1	0	0	0	0	0	0	0	0	0	0
P18	0	0	0	0	0	0	0	0	0	1	0	0
P19	0	0	0	0	0	1	0	0	0	0	0	0
P20	1	0	0	0	0	0	0	0	0	0	0	0
P21	0	0	1	0	0	0	1	0	1	0	0	0
P22	0	0	0	0	0	0	0	0	0	0	0	0
P23	0	1	0	0	1	0	1	0	0	1	0	0
P24	1	0	0	0	1	0	0	0	0	0	0	1
P25	0	0	0	0	0	0	0	0	0	0	1	1

In the face of these (simplified) relations Γ_1 and Γ_2, who would dare propose that 'we move the bar'?

2 People and Complexes

2.1 Does the barber shave himself?

It is our intention to explore further the consequences of basing a study of people and their communities on the ideas of set-theory and the related structures. The problem of finding the most significant sets (most significant from the point of view of ultimate pay-off) of elements is likely therefore to be crucial. The confrontation between the followers of Aristotle and those of Galileo is an illustration of this problem in one particular field, and our discussion in section 1.4 demonstrated the importance played by the notion of a mathematical relation, in the final Galileian solution.

There are warning signs too in the matter of knowing when we have a set, in the sense of it being well-defined, and when not. In section 1.5 we have drawn attention to the Russell paradox and its popular illustration of the barber who shaves all and only those men who do not shave themselves. It is not possible to answer Yes or No to the question 'does the barber shave himself?' — but the *paradox* is not just a *dilemma,* it is not the same as the dilemma found in the question 'have you stopped beating your wife?'. The barber question is a logical paradox because if we answer Yes then we can logically deduce the answer No, and *vice versa.*

The barber-question is a set-identification/set-membership question; how to identify, to make well-defined, the set of 'men who shave themselves' — or the complementary set of 'men who are shaved by the barber'. Leaving aside the Russell theory of types, which amounted to an algorithm for categorizing well-defined sets, we can also throw some light on the situation by referring to the notion of a relation between sets (*v.* also Appendix A).

In the barber's town the set of men — other than the barber — may be denoted by M. This is a well-defined set, a Yes-or-No answer can be given to the question 'is $X \in M$?', for if X is a man and if X is not the barber then $X \in M$, otherwise $X \notin M$. Now denote the set which contains the barber by B; card B = 1. The business about being-shaved-by-the-barber is now a well-defined mathematical relation, say σ, between the well-defined finite sets B and M. Precisely, we regard σ as a subset of $M \times B$, $\sigma \subset M \times B$, so that if

$$M = \{M_1, M_2, \ldots M_n\}$$

and $$B = \{B_1\}$$

the pair $(M_i, B_1) \in \sigma$ if and only if 'M_i is shaved by B_1'. This is illustrated, in the case of $n = 6$, by the following incidence matrix.

σ	M_1	M_2	M_3	M_4	M_5	M_6
B_1	1	0	0	1	1	0

The logical paradox of the Russell barber-question can now be seen as a consequence of the *confusion between sets and a relation* on the sets. If we try to extend the set M so as to include the set B and to do this by defining the whole 'set' M ∪ B by the relation σ we are deeply involved in a *circulus in definiendo* (to say the least).

The lesson we must therefore learn, and which profoundly dominates any attempt to apply set-theory notions in any field of human affairs, *is to clearly distinguish in our minds between well-defined sets of elements and well-defined relations between these sets.*

The *structure* which we are seeking lies in the *relation between two sets* (like this σ); it does not lie in the sets *qua* sets. This structure is what mathematicians have called a *simplicial complex* (or complex of simplices, commonly denoted by the letter K). Perhaps the simplest way to introduce the idea is to describe the associated geometry which formally represents such a structure of simplices (the reader is advised to compare this with details elaborated in Appendix B).

The characteristic of a relation between two sets Y and X, seen most easily in the incidence matrix of 0's and 1's (compare sections 1.7 and 1.8) is that any one $Y_i \in Y$ is usually related to more than one of the X_j. If a particular Y_i (say, Y_1) is related to just one member of X we call it a zero-order simplex (written 0-simplex). If Y_1 is related to two members of X, say X_1 and X_2, we call it a first-order simplex and write $Y_1 = \langle X_1, X_2 \rangle$, a 1-simplex, and so on. If Y_1 is a p-simplex then it must be related to $(p + 1)$ members of the set X.

In a geometrical interpretation of these words we think of a 0-simplex as a point (or vertex), each 1-simplex as a line joining two vertices, each 2-simplex as a triangle formed by the collection of three specified vertices, etc. Thus a p-simplex can be thought of as a convex polyhedron with $(p + 1)$ vertices, and these vertices are labelled by the members of the set X. Thus if we are thinking of a particular relation λ between sets Y and X we can encompass the whole thing by going through each of the Y_i in turn and identifying it as a p-simplex (or its polyhedron); the collection of all simplices thus obtained will be the simplicial complex K we are interested in. To be precise we denote this collection of simplices by $K_Y(X; \lambda)$, meaning that the set X provides us with the vertices of our polyhedra (simplices) and the set Y provides us with names or labels for the simplices which λ has somehow created out of the two sets. It then follows quite clearly that we can use the associated inverse relation λ^{-1} to give ourselves the so-called conjugate simplicial complex $K_X(Y; \lambda^{-1})$, in which the set Y provides the vertices and the set X provides the labels for the simplices built out of them by the relation λ^{-1}. (λ^{-1} is easily obtained from a typical incidence matrix by reading down the columns instead of along the rows.) Thus we usually need to acquire the mental habit of associating two simplicial complexes with each relation λ, viz., $K_Y(X; \lambda)$ and $K_X(Y; \lambda^{-1})$.

In any event we obtain a structure which represents all the features of the mathematical relation λ, which somehow contains in it the essence of the 'cement' which λ has introduced into the set Y (and which λ^{-1} has introduced into the set X) in its relation with X (or Y). Using the geometrical way of thinking gives us a feeling, however vague at this stage, of the way in which the simplices (polyhedra) Y_i are all interconnected. It is this suggestion of abstract geometrical connections which justifies us in using the word 'structure' to describe the property of the relation λ. The pursuit of it in more or less greater detail is the task outlined in this book. In the illustration of the barber-question above ($n = 6$) the structure is perhaps particularly simple. The element B_1 is related *via* σ to elements M_1, M_4, M_5. Hence in $K_B(M; \sigma)$ there is one 2-simplex $\langle M_1 M_4 M_5 \rangle$, together with all its faces. In $K_M(B; \sigma^{-1})$ there is one 0-simplex $\langle B_1 \rangle$, representing (equally well) the three men M_1, M_4, and M_5. The barber-question therefore has a well-defined structure once it is expressed as a relation between well-defined sets, and this structure has a geometric representation shown in Figure 2.1. The paradox is resolved in the sense that the original question cannot be put since it is in some sense improper (more of the problem of question-putting later) in the context of the sets M, B, and the relation σ.

Attempting to identify the set M ∪ B by the relation σ requires us to replace σ by another relation which naturally includes the original. This new relation is defined by the open statement '—— is shaved by ——' and denoted, say, by μ. This μ is a subset of (M ∪ B) × (M ∪ B) and, in the above case of $n = 6$, its incidence matrix looks like the following.

μ	M_1	M_2	M_3	M_4	M_5	M_6	B_1
M_1	0	0	0	0	0	0	1
M_2	0	1	0	0	0	0	0
M_3	0	0	1	0	0	0	0
M_4	0	0	0	0	0	0	1
M_5	0	0	0	0	0	0	1
M_6	0	0	0	0	0	1	0
B_1	0	0	0	0	0	0	?

The incidence matrix gives trouble when we come to the entry for the pair (B_1, B_1), because in all the other rows and columns the set-membership conditions require

$$(M_i, B_1) \in \mu \text{ whenever } (M_i, M_i) \notin \mu$$

and

$$(M_i, B_1) \notin \mu \text{ whenever } (M_i, M_i) \in \mu.$$

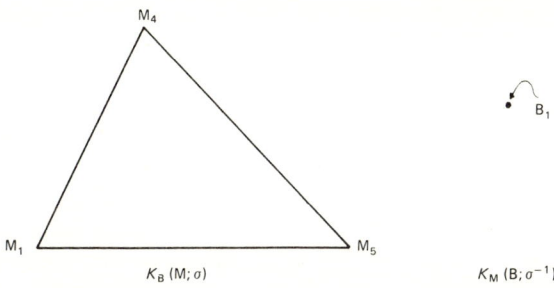

Figure 2.1 Structure of the barber-paradox relation

Thus B_1 (a proposed set-member of $M \cup B$) is part of the definition of the relation μ which defines the set. If we put a 1 in the matrix opposite (B_1, B_1) then we must put a 0 in the same place, and *vice versa*. Hence the *proposed set $M \cup B$ is not well-defined when μ must be one of its subsets.*

We can therefore keep to the set $M \cup B$ and reject μ as a (sub)set-defining relation $[\subset (M \cup B) \times (M \cup B)]$ or we can keep the relation μ and express it as a subset of a different set. In the latter case μ becomes a combination of our earlier σ (which defines a subset of $B \times M$) and a subset of $M \times M$. In either event, we avoid the logical paradox by refusing to allow the notions of set-membership and relation-between-sets to be improperly confused with each other.

Some of the difficulties which can arise are not so striking as this logical paradox but nevertheless they show up the binary Yes-No nature of set-membership, and some can involve the logical paradox if they are pushed too far.

Suppose there are two sets of people, one is called Montague and denoted by M, the other is called Capulet and denoted by C. The classical struggle between M and C might be manifest *via* a relation λ defined by '——— loves ———'. Then membership of M or C can be inextricably involved with λ by asserting (plausibly)

if $R \in M$ and $R \lambda X$ then $X \notin C$

and if $J \in C$ and $J \lambda X$ then $X \notin M$.

The Shakespearean problem now arises acutely by asking if λ is well-defined as a subset of $(M \cup C) \times (M \cup C)$, in the following manner.

If $R \in M$ and $J \in C$ is $(R, J) \in \lambda$?

assuming $R \lambda J$ then $J \notin C$ which is a contradiction, and

assuming $J \lambda R$ then $R \notin M$ which is also a contradiction.

Hence there is only one solution, which amounts to the Shakespearean plot, *viz.*, that R and J cannot exist.

Problems of *ranking* contain dangers if they are too involved; by 'ranking' we mean the assignment of (usually) a scale of integers to a given set of qualities or activities. In a particularly simple case one might assign the integer 0 or 1 to a set of qualities, these might represent 'bad' or 'good'. But of course people can rank people who rank qualities etc. Suppose Y is a person who ranks the opinion of his acquaintances 0 or 1 according as they rank a certain political opinion; precisely, if X ranks the certain political opinion 0 then Y ranks X at 1 and if X ranks the opinion at 1 then Y ranks X at 0. This is fine, it makes for unending chat at cocktail parties, Y is an interesting (if slightly obtuse) fellow with a strong character and a bold ability to judge everyone in sight. But what kind of opinion is Y able to form of himself if he sticks to his eccentric method?

If Y tries to rank that certain opinion as 0 then Y must rank his own opinion as 1 and *vice versa*. Consequently if Y selects a set S of people by defining membership *via* this ranking (X ϵ S if Y's ranking of X's opinion is 1) then he can neither include nor exclude himself. The set S is not well-defined if the selection is from a collection which includes Y.

2.2 Everyman is a polyhedron

The idea of relations, between various sets of people or between sets of people and other sets, constitutes the hard currency of social intercourse. *How to make friends and influence people* is an invitation to share the supposed secrets of a particular set of relations. Each individual person in a social *milieu* feels the pressures of the relations which exist between himself and other people — members of his family, his colleagues at work, the authorities, etc. [14, 48, 49] These pressures can produce various effects; they can act as a binding, adhesive social force, what we have called *social cement;* they can act as a decisive (even revolutionary) influence. But taken together they constitute a *backcloth,* setting a stage on which the individual plays his part — not necessarily the kind of dramatic part which has been entirely written by a strange author but a part which might well involve writing the plot as it is played. It is not therefore a static picture, frozen in an external time dimension, but a dynamic interplay of past and present with each man charting his own time, his own future. We can surely accept the poet's 'and one man in his time plays many parts' without insisting that these parts are consecutive, they make up a jumble of parts, interdependent and tripping over each other. Yet however appealing such a poetic analogy might be, we must notice that the metaphor is merely a device for replacing one set of relations by another set. If the image of actors-playing-their-stage-roles is helpful to us it is surely due to the encouragement it gives us to be somewhat more detached from our personal involvement in multiple relations, an encouragement to go outside ourselves and therefore to *see* relations as abstract entities rather than merely to *feel* the relations as pressures and enticements.

The sense we have of the quality of our lives, the richness or barrenness, the complexities of our mutual dependencies, the opportunities for thought or action, the rewards or punishments which might come our way, all these intangibles are our intuitively apprehended sense of mathematical relations which exist between us and others, between us and physical things — and surely these relations can well include relations between (well-defined) sets of relations. And it is the *structure of a relation* — of the *simplicial complexes* which represent that relation — which contains an expression of its *quality*.

Let us take a simple hypothetical example of a relation λ between a finite set of people P and a finite set of human activities A, $\lambda \subset P \times A$. Suppose there are twenty people in P with names P1, P2, ... P20 and suppose that the names of the activities in A are given by the following list,

- A1 the pastime of playing golf
- A2 an interest in local people and gossip
- A3 the activity of gardening
- A4 being a local-authority employee
- A5 active in a political organization
- A6 employment in the retail trade
- A7 enthusiasm for motoring
- A8 studying a foreign language
- A9 active interest in young people
- A10 an interest in conservation and environment

where it is obvious that we are using the words human activity in a very wide sense to include interests, actions, hobbies, professions of all kinds.

We can illustrate the significance of our structure by considering a hypothetical relation $\lambda \subset P \times A$, a relation which can be defined without any danger of logical paradox by a routine data collecting procedure. Suppose that, in our hypothetical community, the relation λ possesses the incidence matrix shown on page 28.

Using the definitions and theory of a Q-analysis (*v.* Appendix B) we can obtain the structures of the two complexes $K_P(A; \lambda)$ and $K_A(P; \lambda^{-1})$.

In λ, P1 is related to A1 because he plays golf in his leisure time, he is related to A3 because he indulges in gardening, he is related to A6 because he is a small shopkeeper, he is related to A8 because he is studying the French language, he is related to A9 because he is on the School Board of a local primary school, and he is related to A10 because he belongs to a national wild-life preservation society.

In the language of complexes P1 is a 5-simplex in $K_P(A; \lambda)$, possessing 6 vertices out of the vertex set A. In a geometric representation P1 is a *hexahedron* in a *5-dimensional space,* say, E^5. In the same way P17 is the 4-simplex ⟨A2, A3, A7, A8, A9⟩ in $K_P(A; \lambda)$; he is related to A2 because he is an avid student of the local newspaper, to A3 because his roses are the envy of his neighbours, to A7 because he just is, to A8 because he too is studying the French language at the local night school, and to A9 because he tries to help with a local youth club. In the geometric representation P17 is a *pentahedron* in some *4-dimensional space*.

What matters about the relation λ is the *connectivity pattern* of the complexes; *this is what the people are aware of in their community lives.*

λ	A1	A2	A3	A4	A5	A6	A7	A8	A9	A10
P1	1	0	1	0	0	1	0	1	1	1
P2	1	1	0	0	0	0	1	1	0	0
P3	0	1	1	1	1	0	0	1	0	1
P4	1	0	1	0	0	0	0	0	0	0
P5	0	1	0	0	0	1	0	0	1	1
P6	0	1	0	0	0	0	0	1	0	0
P7	0	0	1	0	0	1	0	0	0	0
P8	0	1	0	0	1	0	0	1	0	1
P9	1	0	1	0	0	1	0	0	0	0
P10	0	1	0	1	0	0	0	0	0	0
P11	1	0	0	0	1	0	1	0	1	0
P12	0	0	1	0	0	0	0	0	0	1
P13	0	0	0	1	0	0	0	1	0	0
P14	1	1	0	0	1	0	1	0	1	0
P15	1	0	1	0	0	1	0	1	0	1
P16	0	1	0	0	1	1	0	1	0	0
P17	0	1	1	0	0	0	1	1	1	0
P18	1	0	1	0	1	1	0	0	0	0
P19	0	1	0	1	0	0	1	0	0	1
P20	1	0	1	0	1	0	0	1	1	0

Thus we notice that, in this relation, Messrs. P1 and P17 share a 2-face, *viz.*, the 2-simplex ⟨A3, A8, A9⟩. This is simply the expression of the three activities out of the set A which they share. If we consider that our set A is exhaustive (or sufficiently so) then this shared face is what enables P1 and P17 to communicate, to develop some rapport, to have the opportunity of joint action to achieve some common end, or to find some common ground on which to do battle. The three simplices

$$P1 \qquad \langle A3, A8, A9 \rangle \qquad P17$$

are an example of a *chain of connection* of *order* 2 (*v*. Appendix B), it is a 2-*connectivity* in the *complex* $K_P(A; \lambda)$, with P1 as a typical σ_P, P17 as a typical σ_r and ⟨A3, A8, A9⟩ as a typical β_1 (or α_1 or α_h). A schematic representation of this chain of connection is shown in Figure 2.2.

People and Complexes 29

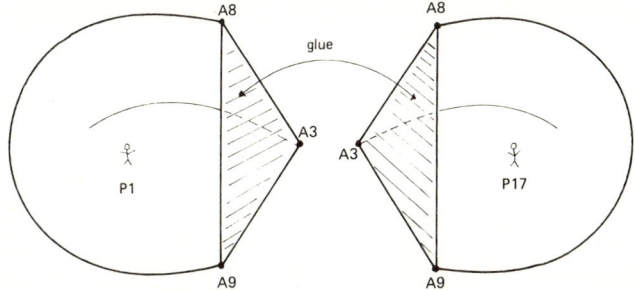

Figure 2.2 Messrs P1 and P17 2-connected

⟨A3, A8, A9⟩ is the *face* which P1 *shows to* P17, and *vice versa*, in the context of this relation λ; this is *the face* of *common speech*. It is not surprising therefore if (e.g.) P1 appears to be very different to different people. We see for example that P1 and P10 share no common face, they are disconnected ($q = -1$); P1 can therefore have (at the best) a second-hand view of P10. One such second-hand view might well arise *via* P19 because it is possible to see from the relation λ that

P1 is 0-connected to P19

and P19 is 1-connected to P10

There is therefore a (rather weak?) connection between P1 and P10, *viz.*, a 0-chain of connection:

$$\begin{array}{ccc} \langle A1, A3, A6, A8, A9, A10 \rangle & \langle A2, A4, A7, A10 \rangle & \langle A2, A4, \rangle \\ P1 & P19 & P10 \\ & \updownarrow & \updownarrow \\ & \langle A10 \rangle & \langle A2, A4 \rangle \end{array}$$

and a schematic diagram of this is shown in Figure 2.3.

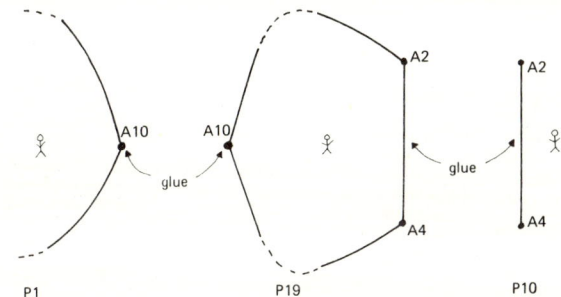

Figure 2.3 A chain of connection between P1, P19, P10

In this connection P19 and P10 offer faces to each other which coincide with the 1-simplex ⟨A2, A4⟩, each is a local-authority employee and each is a local-man. In fact P10 = ⟨A2, A4⟩ is a face of P19 in the complex $K_P(A; \lambda)$ - perhaps P19 appears to be 'deep' to P10, 'there is more to him' than P10 can

30 Mathematical Structure in Human Affairs

properly apprehend. If P19 and P10 can develop communication at this 1-level then P19 and P1 only communicate *at a vertex*, the 0-simplex ⟨A10⟩, *via* discussions of the environment (which might include entities like P10?)

In this way we can see how to obtain a complete picture of the structural connectivity pattern of $K_P(A; \lambda)$. As a practical algorithm for producing the connectivities in Table 2.1 we can proceed as follows.

P1	P2	P3	P4	P5	P6	P7	P8	P9	P10	P11	P12	P13	P14	P15	P16	P17	P18	P19	P20	
5	1	2	1	2	0	1	1	2	–	1	1	0	1	4	1	2	1	0	3	P1
	3	1	0	0	1	–	1	0	0	1	–	0	2	1	1	2	0	1	1	P2
		5	0	1	1	0	3	0	1	0	1	1	1	2	2	2	1	2	2	P3
			1	–	–	0	–	1	–	0	0	–	0	1	–	0	1	–	1	P4
				3	0	0	1	0	0	0	0	–	1	1	1	1	0	1	0	P5
					1	–	1	–	0	–	–	0	0	0	1	1	–	0	0	P6
						1	–	1	–	–	0	–	–	1	0	0	1	–	0	P7
							3	–	0	0	0	0	0	1	2	1	0	1	1	P8
								2	–	0	0	–	0	2	0	0	2	–	1	P9
									1	–	–	0	0	–	0	0	–	1	–	P10
										3	–	–	3	0	0	1	1	0	2	P11
											1	–	–	1	–	0	0	0	0	P12
												1	–	0	0	0	–	0	0	P13
													4	0	1	2	1	1	2	P14
														4	1	1	2	0	2	P15
															3	1	1	0	1	P16
																4	0	1	2	P17
																	3	–	2	P18
																		3	–	P19
																			4	P20

Table 2.1 q-connectivities in $K_P(A; \lambda)$, from $\Lambda\Lambda^T$

Denoting the incidence matrix by Λ and its transpose by Λ^T, with $\Lambda = (\lambda_{ij})$ and $\Lambda^T = (\sigma_{rs})$ and $\sigma_{rs} = \lambda_{sr}$, we notice that since each λ_{ij} is 0 or 1 a typical inner product

$$\sum_j \lambda_{ij} \sigma_{js}$$

has a value which equals the number of 1's which are common to the ith row in Λ and the sth column in Λ^T. This value is therefore equal to the number of 1's common to the simplices (people) P_i and P_s. Hence the q-value of the face common to P_i and P_s equals

$$\left\{ \sum_j \lambda_{ij} \sigma_{js} \right\} - 1$$

This means that the q-values of the faces common to every possible pair of people are given by first evaluating the matrix product $\Lambda\Lambda^T$ and then subtracting 1 from every element. This gives the connectivities of the simplices in $K_P(A; \lambda)$, and since they are symmetric it is only necessary to show half the matrix, so that Table 2.2 contains these in a triangular array.

	A1	A2	A3	A4	A5	A6	A7	A8	A9	A10	
	8	1	5	–	3	3	2	3	3	1	A1
		9	1	2	3	1	3	5	2	3	A2
			9	0	2	4	0	4	2	3	A3
				3	0	–	0	1	–	0	A4
					6	1	1	2	2	1	A5
						6	–	2	1	2	A6
							4	1	2	0	A7
								9	2	3	A8
									5	1	A9
										6	A10

Table 2.2 q-connectivities in $K_A(P; \lambda^{-1})$, from $\Lambda^T \Lambda$

By a similar reasoning we obtain Table 2.2 for the connectivities of the simplices in $K_A(P; \lambda^{-1})$ by forming the matrix product $\Lambda^T \Lambda$ and subtracting 1 from each element.

In the tables we represent $q = -1$ (disconnection) by the symbol –, for ease of reference. Since Λ is a 20 × 10 matrix it follows that $\Lambda \Lambda^T$ is 20 × 20 and $\Lambda^T \Lambda$ is 10 × 10.

Referring to Table 2.1 we can readily obtain the Q-analysis (v. Appendix B) for $K_P(A; \lambda)$ as the following set of equivalence classes:

$K_p(A; \lambda)$

q-value	Q_q-value	Components
5	$Q_5 = 2$	{P1}, {P3}
4	$Q_4 = 5$	{P1, P15}, {P3}, {P14}, {P17}, {P20}
3	$Q_3 = 9$	{P1, P15, P20}, {P19}, {P18}, {P17}, {P16}, {P14, P11}, {P8, P3}, {P5}, {P2}
2	$Q_2 = 1$	{P10, P19, P18, P17, P16, P15, P14, P11, P9, P8, P5, P3, P2, P1}
1	$Q_1 = 1$	{all}
0	$Q_0 = 1$	{all}

Figure 2.3 illustrates the fact (which follows from Table 2.1) that although all the simplices fall into one component at $q = 1$, this does not mean that every pair share a 1-face, only that a chain of 1-connection exists which includes any pair. Thus P1, P19, P10 can be found in the 1-chain of connection

$$P1 - P2 - P19 - P10$$

We notice too, from the Q-analysis of $K_P(A; \lambda)$, that the whole set of twenty people is not connected until we reach the level of $q = 1$. If it had happened that, even at $q = 0$, the value of $Q_0 = 2$, then this would mean that the people were naturally divided into two disconnected sets and that all communication between the two sets would be impossible. Naturally the inattentive reader objects at this point to declare that communication, in practice, among twenty people, would not break down because our proposed A-set is inadequate in representing the possible interests of the people. Precisely — but the lesson is there to see, the size of A is irrelevant to the validity of the analysis. If we find a situation in which $Q_0 > 1$, and all (sympathetic) communication has ceased, then it can only be repaired by extending the set A — finding or proposing suitable vertices A11, A12, etc., until we obtain $Q_0 = 1$, and possibly (as an insurance) $Q_1 = 1$, $Q_2 = 1$, etc. The stability of the 'social scene' is clearly measured by the *structure vector* Q, in this sense.

If we turn our attention to the conjugate complex $K_A(P; \lambda^{-1})$ we obtain the connectivities in Table 2.2. The values of Q_q and the identification of the components (equivalence classes) are as follows.

$K_A(P; \lambda^{-1})$

q-value	Q_q-value	Components
9	3	{A8}, {A3}, {A2}
8	4	{A8}, {A3}, {A2}, {A1}
7	4	{A8}, {A3}, {A2}, {A1}
6	7	{A8}, {A3}, {A2}, {A1}, {A10}, {A6}, {A5}
5	8	{A10}, {A9}, {A8, A2}, {A6}, {A5}, {A3}, {A2}, {A1}
4	5	{A10}, {A9}, {A8, A6, A3, A2, A1}, {A7}, {A5}
3	2	{A10, A9, A8, A7, A6, A5, A3, A2, A1}, {A4}
2	1	{all}
1	1	{all}
0	1	{all}

In this complex $K_A(P; \lambda^{-1})$ the highest dimensional simplices are A8, A3, A2, each being a 9-simplex; hence each possesses 10 vertices (10 people). Our hypothetical community is therefore noted for the outstanding activities, viz., A2 — local affairs and gossip, A3 — gardening, and A8 — studying a foreign language. The next striking feature is the interest shown in the golf course *via* A1. These four simplices, A1, A2, A3, A8 dominate the structure from $q = 9$ to $q = 6$; they are the outstanding features of life seen by a stranger visiting our community. These simplices only connect at $q = 5$ — and then only A8 and A2; a serious chain of 4-connection occurs in the set

$$\{A1, A2, A3, A6, A8\}$$

which characterizes one feature of the structure, *viz., the internationally-minded retail traders are meeting on the golf course to exchange local schemes and gossip and to exchange plants and cuttings from their well-attended gardens.* In comparison with $K_P(A; \lambda)$ we notice that all the vertices form a single connected component at the level of $q = 2$.

We notice that our language of connectivity naturally expresses the structure of the community life (via $K_A(P; \lambda^{-1})$) as well as the structure of the interaction of the people (via $K_P(A; \lambda)$). We can begin to see something of the conjugate natures of what might be called the *social community* and the *political community* in these complexes, which arise from the same relation λ. Matters which are primarily thought of as political are those which refer to the framework which allows interaction between people, to the channels of discussion, agreement, conflict, decision-making — all in a structure which is dominated by simplices with individual people at the vertices (or groups of people). Such a backcloth of structure is provided by the simplicial complex $K_A(P; \lambda^{-1})$, whatever the set A actually represents. By comparison the complex $K_P(A; \lambda)$ provides us with a structure which is person-oriented, with the chains of connection which provide a social *milieu* for the interaction of individuals. It is therefore possible to associate, in a broad sense, the complexes $K_A(P; \lambda^{-1})$ and $K_P(A; \lambda)$ with political and social views of the community — more strictly perhaps, to speak of the *political* and *social views of the relation* $\lambda \subset P \times A$, for presumably we might well wish to reserve the word 'community' for a situation involving a number of relations λ_i, for various values of i. In a later section (v. Chapter 6) we shall see how a holistic view of such a set of relations can be obtained.

2.3 Top-q and bottom-q

From Table 2.1 and the Q-analysis of the previous section we can obtain a pair of integers $(\check{q}, \hat{q})_i$ for each simplex (person) P_i in $K_P(A; \lambda)$. The value of $\hat{q}$ is to be taken as dim P_i, which also means the maximum connectivity of P_i, whilst the value of $\check{q}$ is to be the largest q-value at which this particular P_i is connected to a distinct P_j. Thus $\check{q}$ is the first q-value, descending from $\hat{q}$, for which P_i finds itself in a component containing some other P_j. Clearly we must always have

$$\hat{q} \geqslant \check{q}$$

We shall refer to the pair $(\check{q}, \hat{q})$ as the *pair of extremes* for the simplex to which it refers; separately we shall call $\hat{q}$ (or dim P_i) the *top-q* and $\check{q}$ the *bottom-q*, of that simplex.

The pairs of extremes for all twenty people in $K_P(A; \lambda)$ are as follows.

P1 = (4, 5)	P6 = (1, 1)	P11 = (3, 3)	P16 = (2, 3)
P2 = (2, 3)	P7 = (1, 1)	P12 = (1, 1)	P17 = (2, 4)
P3 = (3, 5)	P8 = (3, 3)	P13 = (0, 1)	P18 = (2, 3)
P4 = (1, 1)	P9 = (2, 2)	P14 = (3, 4)	P19 = (2, 3)
P5 = (2, 3)	P10 = (1, 1)	P15 = (3, 4)	P20 = (3, 4)

and Figure 2.4 shows these points represented as a lattice in the $(\check{q}, \hat{q})$-plane with bottom-q as abscissa and top-q as ordinate.

The point labelled P19 also represents the simplices P18, P16, P5, and P2, whilst the point labelled P4 also represents the simplices P6, P7, P10, and

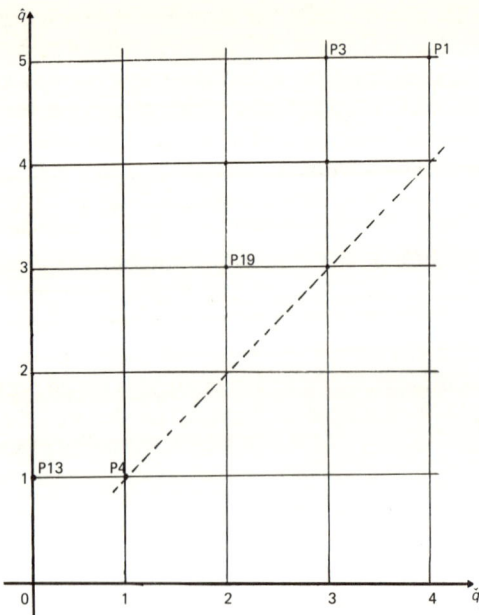

Figure 2.4 Points $(\hat{q}, \check{q})$ in $K_P(A; \lambda)$

P12. Since $\hat{q} \geqslant \check{q}$ it follows that there can be no points below the dotted line, which corresponds to $\check{q} = \hat{q}$. Now, for example, P3 corresponds to the pair of extremes (3, 5); the bottom-q is 3, and this is a measure of the greatest q-level at which P3 is connected to some other P_i; at this bottom-q value P3 ceases to be isolated (to be its own equivalence class), ceases to stand apart from all the others, ceases to be eccentric, begins to be admitted into some larger group, begins to be socially integrated, begins to conform habitwise. By comparison, the top-q value is a measure of the individual's personal maximum dimension (as far as this particular relation is concerned). The difference between the top-q and the bottom-q, $\hat{q} - \check{q}$, is therefore a *measure of the unusual, non-conforming, eccentric nature* of P3. Of course a value of $\hat{q} - \check{q} = 2$ is presumably more revealing if $\check{q} = 1$ than if $\check{q} = 10$, and to allow for this we shall prefer the ratio $(\hat{q} - \check{q})/(\check{q} + 1)$ as a measure of the eccentricity of the simplex. In the case of P3 this equals 2/4 whilst for P1 it equals 1/5. We therefore say that, *in any relation* $\lambda \subset P \times A$ *the eccentricity of a simplex P is the rational number* $(\hat{q} - \check{q})/(\check{q} + 1)$ *where $\check{q}$ is the bottom-q of P and $\hat{q}$ is the top-q of P.*

Denoting this eccentricity by Ecc(P) then, in the context of our relation λ, between people and activities, a large value of Ecc(P) indicates a person P with a large number of unusual attributes relative to the number of his 'usual' attributes. In the extreme case that $\check{q} = -1$ the simplex P (or σ) is totally disconnected from the rest and this gives an infinite value for the eccentricity; Ecc(P) = ∞ This seems reasonable since P cannot be more eccentric than when he is totally disconnected.

When Ecc$(\sigma) = 0$ the representative point of σ lies on the dotted line, since $\check{q} = \hat{q}$. If all the simplices of $K_P(A; \lambda)$ have representative points on the dotted line then there is a great uniformity about the structure.

If we turn our attention to the conjugate complex $K_A(P; \lambda^{-1})$ we obtain the following pairs of extremes and eccentricities for the activities.

A1 = (5, 8), 3/6   A6 = (4, 6), 2/5
A2 = (4, 9), 5/5   A7 = (3, 4), 1/4
A3 = (5, 9), 4/6   A8 = (5, 9), 4/6
A4 = (2, 3), 1/3   A9 = (3, 5), 2/4
A5 = (3, 6), 3/4   A10 = (3, 6), 3/4

The activity with the largest eccentricity is A2, with 1, top-q equal to 9 and bottom-q equal to 4. This activity is 'interest in local people and gossip'; the fact that the eccentricity is highest suggests that (1) a large number of people are λ-related to A2, and (2) interest in A2 dominates other (connecting) interests. The fact that $q = 4$ is illustrated by the only chain of 4-connection

$$A2 \text{ --- } A8$$

where A8 is the activity of 'studying a foreign language'.

By comparison with A2 we see that the smallest eccentricity is provided by A7, with bottom-q equal to 3 and top-q equal to 4. This means, as far as our community and relation λ are concerned, that

$$A7 = \text{enthusiasm for motoring}$$

is not an eccentric kind of interest in the sense that the people who share it also share other interests. A typical chain of 3-connection involving A7 is

$$A1 \text{ --- } A3 \text{ --- } A8 \text{ --- } A2 \text{ --- } A7$$

and between $q = 4$ and $q = 3$ we have noticed that A7 changes from being in a class by itself to being in an equivalence class which is large, *viz.*, {A10, A9, A8, A7, A6, A5, A3, A2, A1}

We can conclude that A7 is an activity which is 'well-integrated' into the social scene.

2.4 Weighted relations and slicing parameters

Let us now suppose that the names we have been using for individual people, P1, P2, etc., are replaced by the names of *types of people*, say, T1, T2, etc., and let us consider how to analyse a relation

$$\mu \subset T \times A$$

where A is another set of activities, A1, A2, etc.

The point of this discussion is to show how the structures of μ can refer to a large collection of people, provided they can be reasonably well-described in terms of types or groups (but the word group has a precise mathematical meaning, so we try to avoid using it in any other context). By 'type' we mean not only such things as 'possessing rosy cheeks' or 'of blood group O', but also such descriptions as 'in the income bracket £5000 – £10 000' or 'member of the Conservative party'. Thus our word 'type' is *to mean a set* T *whose members define finite sets of people;* naturally we exclude the set T itself as a member, so that T $\notin$ T.

Depending on our own inclinations we can therefore select a collection T1, T2, ... Tk as the members of T and then consider a relation μ between this T and a relevant set A of 'activities'. If we are students of *sociology* then we might choose for A various generalized interests associated with kinship, friendship, antagonisms, or habits associated with hobbies, religious observances, gang warfare, juvenile delinquency, or etc. If we are students of *political theory* and/or *practice* we might choose for A various activities concerned with voting habits (locally or nationally), attendances at party meetings, or at town council occasions, acceptance or rejection of party-political doctrines and party-political tactics. If we are students of *economics* then we might choose for A such activities as investment habits, petty-cash habits, things which housewives buy in various kinds of shops, capital and recurrent costs for a variety of enterprises, and so on. If we are students of *town planning* and the *environment* we might choose for A such activities as location of residences, types of residences, enjoyment of cultural amenities, enjoyment of public parks, use of sporting facilities, accessibility to shopping areas, ease of travel to places of employment, conservation of historic buildings, preservation of *flora* and *fauna,* use and abuse of motor cars, buses, trains, and aeroplanes – and so on.

But having finally selected a suitable set T and a suitable set A we are here concerned with the kind of data which is a generalization of the incidence matrix A, already considered. Now *we expect the relation* $\mu \subset$ T $\times$ A *to be described by a matrix array in which the entries are integers* (not merely 0 or 1) *over a wide range.* This will arise, for example, since the element T1 (say, rosy-cheeked people) might be related to A1 (living in the countryside) by the number 500 – because 500 people of type T1 live in the countryside. The resultant data for μ is therefore a matrix M = (μ_{ij}) where $\mu_{ij} \in$ J; we do not thereby exclude negative entries. Schematically we indicate this relation μ by

μ	A
T	M(J)

We shall illustrate the possibilities by setting up a relation between types of traffic (people driving types of vehicles) and a set of traffic routes in a hypothetical town. We therefore take a set T as follows:

T1	private car	T4	public transport bus
T2	small commercial van	T5	taxi
T3	large commercial van	T6	long distance coach

The set A will be a set of 11 roads, indicated in Figure 2.5.

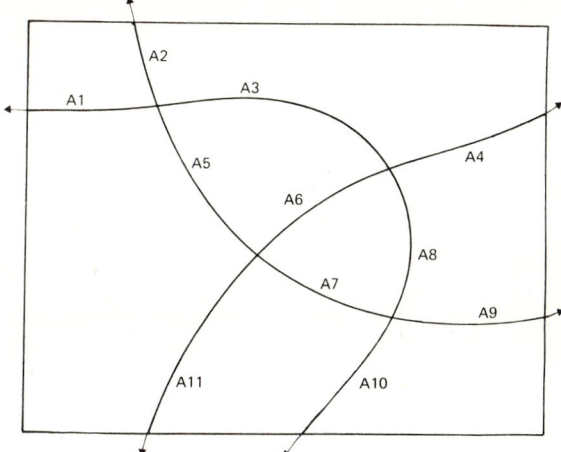

Figure 2.5 A set of traffic routes

We consider the relation $\mu \subset T \times A$ which is defined by the open statement 'n vehicles of type — travel on the road — between the hours 08.30 and 09.30 of a specific Saturday'. The number n is an entry in the matrix M; it does not distinguish between the directions of traffic flow. Suppose therefore that M has the following composition.

M	A1	A2	A3	A4	A5	A6	A7	A8	A9	A10	A11
T1	48	30	72	12	80	146	184	200	21	42	53
T2	11	4	28	5	22	24	38	32	9	8	16
T3	0	0	4	0	6	12	14	19	3	2	0
T4	4	6	8	2	10	14	9	13	4	2	4
T5	0	1	4	5	7	12	16	14	2	0	2
T6	4	2	6	3	2	0	0	0	4	1	5

Such an array will be called a *weighted relation* (weighted by the values of n). This matrix M(J) contains in it many binary relations μ_i, with their corresponding structures. If we imagine that in each position in M a column of bricks is erected containing the number n, then M looks like a mass of buildings — rather like a modern city. We can now produce a particular binary relation, say, μ_1, by taking a horizontal slice through this pile of columns, and if there is any part of the column above our slice we put a 1 in the incidence matrix of μ_1, otherwise we put a zero. For example, if we take a slice at the level of $\theta \geqslant 20$ (where θ represents any position in the matrix M) the corresponding incidence matrix for $\mu_1 \subset T \times A$ looks like the following.

$\theta \geqslant 20$

μ_1	A1	A2	A3	A4	A5	A6	A7	A8	A9	A10	A11
T1	1	1	1	0	1	1	1	1	1	1	1
T2	0	0	1	0	1	1	1	1	0	0	0
T3	0	0	0	0	0	0	0	0	0	0	0
T4	0	0	0	0	0	0	0	0	0	0	0
T5	0	0	0	0	0	0	0	0	0	0	0
T6	0	0	0	0	0	0	0	0	0	0	0

We naturally refer to θ as a *slicing parameter,* clearly we need not select the same slicing value for each row (or for each column). In fact if M is an $m \times n$ matrix then we must allow for the possibility of selecting mn values of θ to obtain one binary relation such as μ_1. The choice of any particular θ_{ij} (for the element in the ith row and jth column of M) may well be of significance for the elements Ti and Aj. Often, however, we can find that 'slicing by rows' (in which the same value of θ is used for all the elements in a particular row) or 'slicing by columns' gives us an adequate structural analysis.

For example, suppose we slice M by columns and take the following values for the slicing parameters, viz., $\theta_j = 1$ if $j \neq 8$ and $\theta_8 = 250$. Then in the resulting relation μ_1 there must be a column of zeros under A8, and this means that *effectively the road A8 is totally absent from the set* A. Thus we have, by this means, *sliced out* the road A8, and this might correspond to the physical reality of closing that particular road for some road-works purpose. By the same token, if we wish to contemplate the situation in which all long-distance coaches are banned from A6 then (among other things) we must slice out (T6, A6) by, say, taking $\theta_{66} = 1000$ (or some other sufficiently high integer). If, on the other hand, we can allow up to 5 coaches per hour in the road A3 we take slicing parameters so that $\theta_{63} = 6$. In the same way, if all the public transport drivers go on strike we can take it into consideration by slicing by rows and slicing out T5 by $\theta_5 = 100$.

As an exercise we now contemplate the results of a Q-analysis in different binary relations derived from M by specific slicing operations.

(1) How are the roads 'connected' with respect to a traffic distribution defined by the slicing-by-rows: $\theta_1 = 50, \theta_2 = 20, \theta_3 = \theta_4 = \theta_5 = \theta_6 = 1$? The incidence matrix for μ_1 follows from M and the connectivities are given (by evaluating $\Lambda\Lambda^T$ and $\Lambda^T\Lambda$ in the usual way) as follows.

$\underline{K_T}(A; \mu_1)$

	T1	T2	T3	T4	T5	T6	
	5	4	4	5	5	3	T1
		4	4	4	4	1	T2
			6	6	5	3	T3
				10	8	7	T4
					8	5	T5
						7	T6

The structure vector is

$$Q = \{\overset{10}{1} \ 1 \ 1 \ 1 \ 1 \ 1 \ 1 \ 1 \ 1 \ \overset{0}{1}\}$$

with components

    at $q = 10$ {T4}   at $q = 6$ {T4, T5, T6, T3}
    at $q = 9$ {T4}   at $q = 5$ {T1, T3, T4, T5, T6}
    at $q = 8$ {T4, T5}   at $q = 4, 3, 2, 1, 0$ {all}
    at $q = 7$ {T4, T5, T6}

$\underline{K_A}(T; \mu_1^{-1})$

A1	A2	A3	A4	A5	A6	A7	A8	A9	A10	A11	
1	1	1	1	1	0	0	0	1	1	1	A1
	2	2	2	2	1	1	1	2	1	2	A2
		5	2	5	4	4	4	3	2	3	A3
			2	2	1	1	1	2	1	2	A4
				5	4	4	4	3	2	3	A5
					4	4	4	2	1	2	A6
						4	4	2	1	2	A7
							4	2	1	2	A8
								3	2	2	A9
									2	1	A10
										2	A11

The structure vector is

$$Q = \{\overset{5}{1} \ 1 \ 1 \ 1 \ 1 \ \overset{0}{1}\}$$

40 *Mathematical Structure in Human Affairs*

with components

at $q = 5$ {A3, A5}
at $q = 4$ {A3, A5, A6, A7, A8}
at $q = 3$ {A3, A5, A6, A7, A8, A9, A11}
at $q = 2$ {A2, A3, A4, A6, A7, A8, A9, A10, A11}
at $q = 1$ {all}
at $q = 0$ {all}

Either of these complexes, $K_T(A)$ or $K_A(T)$, is a structure relative to a hypothetical *norm*, namely, that traffic level defined by the row slicing parameters $\{\theta_i, i = 1, \ldots 6\}$ given above. Precisely, the norm corresponds to the observation, in the specified period of time and on the specified data, of 50 private cars, 20 small commercial vans, 1 large commercial van, 1 public transport bus, 1 taxi, and 1 long-distance coach. Against this projected norm the complex $K_A(T; M_1^{-1})$ gives the connectivity pattern of the road system — not of course to be confused with the physical road-building connectivities displayed on the map of Figure 2.5. Thus we notice that road A3 and A5 are each 5-simplices (and $5 = \dim K_A(T)$) and identical since they are also 5-connected. This means that *every type of traffic is manifest on these roads at the level of the norm.* At $q = 4$ the roads A6, A7, and A8 enter as 4-simplices, being faces of A3 and A5. The norm is therefore reached, on A6, A7, A8, for all but the long distance coaches. At $q = 3$ the roads A9, A11 enter the complex; on A9 the norm for private cars and small commercial vans is not reached, whilst on A11 it is the small commercial vans and the large commercial vans which are missing. At $q = 2$ the road A10 enters, attaining the norm for larger commercial vans, public transport buses, and long distance coaches. At $q = 1$ all the roads lie in the single 1-connected component; and therefore they are all present at $q = 0$.

We notice now that the structure of $K_A(T; \mu_1^{-1})$ elevates the roads to the dimensional level of the simplices. It is no longer sufficient to think of a road, say, A5 as a line (or a lane) drawn on a map between points A and B. The map-view of a road is a 1-dimensional view, an arc which joins two 0-dimensional points. The map-view of A5 is the result of forcing the 5-simplex A5 into a representation in the Euclidean space E^2, whereas the structure of the actual complex $K_A(T; \mu_1^{-1})$ requires a representation in E^5, for A5, and in this instance the same E^5 will suffice to represent the whole of $K_A(T)$. In some way yet to be determined the physical road A5, on the surface of the earth, must be so constructed as to constitute a faithful representation of the simplex road A5.

We notice, for example, that A6 is 0-connected to A1, these roads sharing the simplex $\langle T4 \rangle$, *viz.*, the public transport bus norm; A8 is 1-connected to A2, these roads sharing the simplex $\langle T4, T5 \rangle$ — formed by the bus and taxi traffic.

We notice too that, for every road in the complex, the top-q equals the bottom-q — which is the same as saying that every eccentricity is zero. It is reasonable, therefore, to regard the roads in this complex, relative to this norm, as well-integrated into the traffic scene?

Turning our attention to the conjugate complex $K_T(A; \mu_1)$ we see again that the structure vector is unity in all dimensions. The traffic type T4 (town buses) are present on all roads, since dim T4 = 10 = dim K and card A = 11. Hence we must congratulate the corporation on its bus service during the Saturday early morning rush? The town buses are indeed noticeable above all other traffic because T4 has a pair of extremes in top-q equals 10 and bottom-q equals 8. Relative to the rest of the traffic T4 possesses a non-zero eccentricity; by comparison every other type of vehicle possesses zero eccentricity, with $\check{q} = \hat{q}$.

The smallest simplex is the 4-simplex of T2 = ⟨A3, A5, A6, A7, A8⟩, the small commercial vans. This suggests that (relative to the norm of $\theta = 2\bar{0}$) these vans are to be found in a restricted part of town. Surely we deduce that the roads A2, A5, A6, A7, A8 probably enclose the commercial shopping areas of town? By comparison the long-distance coaches T6 form a 7-simplex which is only 1-connected with T2. Hence the coaches are spread around the town in areas away from the shopping areas where T2 is to be found. No doubt the coach parking areas are to be sought in areas adjacent to A1, A2, A4, A9, A10, A11?

The private cars T1 form a 5-simplex ⟨A3, A5, A6, A7, A8, A11⟩, suggesting that people are travelling into town by A11 and that A3, A5, A8 probably border extensive residential areas convenient for employment and shopping in the centre of town. It is not therefore surprising that T1 and T4 (the town buses) should be highly connected at $q = 5$, indeed they share the common face ⟨A3, A5, A6, A7, A8, A11⟩.

We notice too that all the types of traffic (at this slicing level) are connected at the level of $q = 4$. This means that there is always a set of 5 roads (not always the same 5) which are shared by any two traffic types. This suggests that the roads are being well used, without obvious discrimination, at this time and on this day. A particular vehicle (a T1 or a T2, say), finding its way through the traffic routes will therefore have a wide choice of alternative in that it can be found in at least 5 ($q = 4$) roads — usually more. This property is indicated by the value of the *obstruction vector* $\hat{Q}$ (v. Appendix B) on $K_T(A; \mu_1)$. In this we have

$$\hat{Q} = Q - U$$

where U is the vector representing the unit point in Q-space. Hence we obtain

$$\hat{Q} = \{\overset{10}{0} \ 0 \ 0 \ 0 \ 0 \ 0 \ 0 \ 0 \ 0 \ 0\}$$

and so the 'obstruction' is in some sense zero. People, or things, who travel on the road system presumably distribute themselves throughout the types of vehicle T1 — T6 and this distribution is necessarily a function of the road system. Hence we have the situation that the mobility of this distribution — as it tries to move from one pattern to another — must depend on the q-connectivity values which link the T-simplices. The more highly are these simplices connected the more mobile is the potential distribution of travelling public (or goods). The obstruction vector $\hat{Q}$ is a measure of the lack of mobility (or amount of obstruction to free movement) for any such distribution on the T-set. Since a simplex possesses a structure vector of unity and is also an example of maximum connectivity it must be accorded an effective obstruction vector of zero. The definition of $\hat{Q}$ ensures this zero vector in the case of a single simplex.

In this example the structure vector is essentially that of a single simplex, viz., T4, and so it is not surpirsing that $\hat{Q} = 0$. There is therefore, in this complex $K_T(A; \mu_1)$, maximum mobility for any distribution of people or goods travelling *via* the (whole) T-set as a function of the A-set. There is therefore no in-built obstacle to any change in a particular parcel distribution over the vehicle types.

(2) Due to planned roadworks in the future we need to contemplate the following situation: A6 to be closed to all traffic except T1, T3; A3 to be closed to all buses, coaches, and large commercial vans T3, T4 and T6; A8 to be closed to all private cars and taxis, T1 and T5. Subject to this we impose a norm defined by slicing the rows as follows: for T1, $\theta = 50$; for T2, $\theta = 20$; for T3, $\theta = 10$; for T4, $\theta = 6$; for T5, $\theta = 10$; for T6, $\theta = 4$. We assume that the pattern in M is not sufficiently upset to alter the effects of slicing since the period of time to which it relates suggests the possibility of filtering traffic through by-roads not considered in the set A.

The induced binary relation $\mu_2 \subset T \times A$ now possesses an incidence matrix as follows.

μ_2	A1	A2	A3	A4	A5	A6	A7	A8	A9	A10	A11
T1	0	0	1	0	1	0	1	0	0	0	1
T2	0	0	1	0	1	1	1	1	0	0	0
T3	0	0	0	0	0	1	1	1	0	0	0
T4	0	1	0	0	1	0	1	1	0	0	0
T5	0	0	0	0	0	0	1	0	0	0	0
T6	1	0	0	0	0	0	0	0	1	0	1

This gives the following connectivity patterns.

$K_T(A; \mu_2)$

T1	T2	T3	T4	T5	T6	
3	2	0	1	0	0	T1
	4	2	2	0	–	T2
		2	1	0	–	T3
			3	0	–	T4
				0	–	T5
					2	T6

with structure vector

$$Q = \{\overset{4}{1} \ 3 \ 2 \ 2 \ \overset{0}{1}\}$$

with components

at $q = 4$ {T2}
at $q = 3$ {T1}, {T2}, {T4}
at $q = 2$ {T1, T2, T3, T4}, {T6}
at $q = 1$ {T1, T2, T3, T4}, {T6}
at $q = 0$ {T1, T2, T3, T4, T5, T6}

Notice that T5 is not connected until the level $q = 0$.

$K_A(T; \mu_2^{-1})$

A1	A2	A3	A4	A5	A6	A7	A8	A9	A10	A11	
0	–	–	–	–	–	–	–	0	–	0	A1
	0	–	–	0	–	0	0	–	–	–	A2
		1	–	1	0	1	0	–	–	0	A3
			–	–	–	–	–	–	–	–	A4
				2	0	2	1	–	–	0	A5
					1	1	1	–	–	–	A6
						4	2	–	–	0	A7
							2	–	–	–	A8
								0	–	0	A9
									–	–	A10
										1	A11

with structure vector

$$Q = \{\overset{4}{1} \ 1 \ 1 \ 2 \ \overset{0}{1}\}$$

with components

at $q = 4$ {A7}
at $q = 3$ {A7}
at $q = 2$ {A5, A7, A8}
at $q = 1$ {A3, A5, A6, A7, A8}, {A11}
at $q = 0$ {A1, A2, A3, A5, A6, A7, A8, A9, A11}

Here we notice that the roads A4 and A10 are not part of the complex $K_A(T)$ because, with this slicing, the traffic (of any kind) is so light as to be discounted.

44 Mathematical Structure in Human Affairs

The types of traffic in $K_T(A; \mu_2)$ is no longer uniform; T1, T2, T4, and T6 possessing non-zero eccentricities *via* the pairs of extremes,

T1 = (2, 3), T2 = (2, 4), T4 = (2, 3), and T6 = (0, 2).

Also the *obstruction vector* $\hat{Q}$ is

$$\hat{Q} = \{\overset{3}{2} \quad 1 \quad 1 \quad 0\}$$

as compared with the earlier 0.

The roads in $K_A(T; \mu_2^{-1})$ have also altered their roles considerably. The pairs of extremes are as follows:

A1 = (0, 0), A2 = (0, 0), A3 = (1, 1), A5 = (2, 2),
A6 = (1, 1), A7 = (2, 4), A8 = (2, 2), A9 = (0, 0),
A11 = (0, 1)

Thus the road A7 has the largest value of $\hat{q} - \check{q}$, being 2; A7 is therefore the most eccentric road in the town. Also the obstruction vector is now

$$\hat{Q} = \{\overset{1}{1} \quad 0\}$$

and is again not zero.

The increase in the obstruction vector on $K_T(A; \mu_2)$ reflects the obvious fact that the new restrictions on the town roads have *increased the rigidity of the traffic distribution*. This idea of rigidity can now be given mathematical expression *via* this obstruction vector concept. The vector $\hat{Q} = \{2 \quad 1 \quad 1 \quad 0\}$ exists in a 4-dimensional space (actually it exists in a 3-dimensional subspace of that 4-dimensional space, because one component is zero) and the component 2 is a measure of rigidity (or obstruction to change) at the level of $q = 3$. At this level a 3-connection between any pair of T1, T2, and T4 is not possible; this means that no pair share 4 roads. Any traffic (carrying people or goods or messages) which is a function of the road system (in that it needs free access to a variety of roads to connect its various entries and exits) and which requires at least a 3-connection for free-flow is in fact obstructed. This obstruction also manifests itself to an individual person or parcel who uses the traffic set T, in order to move on the road system A. Zero obstruction vector for this person means that all choices are available when it comes to charting a route from entry to exit. As soon as this choice is restricted, as soon as the system is made more rigid, then the obstruction increases – and this is manifest by changes in some of the components of $\hat{Q}$.

2.5 The idea of a pattern on a complex

We can express this idea of an obstruction to something in a mathematical form by trying to be more precise about the 'something'. We do this by introducing the idea of a *pattern* on a complex $K_Y(X; \lambda)$.

Generally we shall use the word 'pattern' to describe a complete set of values attributed to the simplices of a complex. In other words a pattern is to be a set of *co-simplices* on $K_Y(X)$, with values in some appropriate number system like J, $\mathcal{Q}$ (the rationals) or $\mathcal{R}$ (the reals). Such a pattern, say, π, can therefore be expressed as a graded set of co-simplices, one set for each q-value; we shall call a set of co-simplices which are defined on the q-simplices (only) as a *q-pattern* and denote it by π^q. Hence

$$\pi = \{\pi^n, \pi^{n-1}, \ldots \pi^1, \pi^0\}$$

where $n = \dim K$, and where, for each value of q,

$$\pi^q : \{\sigma_q{}^i, \text{ all } i\} \to \text{number system}$$

We now assert that *the obstruction vector is an obstruction to* (an unbiassed) *change in any π on K*.

If the complex is our $K_T(A; \mu_2)$ then π might be a set of numerical values giving, say, the number of people who travel on the system A *via* the simplices T, or the total travel cost of all parcels which travel on A *via* the set T. In this case we are saying that the travelling referred to means that the pattern π under consideration exists on the simplices (the members of T) of $K_T(A; \mu_2)$. Hence any change *via* the values of π (change which is part of a free, uninhibited, unbiassed redistribution of the values of π) effectively mean a free-flow of numbers throughout the complex $K_T(A)$, from one simplex to another. Hence the dimensions of the common faces of two simplices is very important. If the pattern π^q is to change freely then it needs a $(q + 1)$-chain of connection to do so; a q-connectivity will not do. Hence the *number of separate q-components* is an indication of *the impossibility of free flow of any π^q*. These numbers are directly manifest in the obstruction vector $\hat{Q}$. Hence our discussion which suggests that an increase in $\hat{Q}$ indicates an increase in the rigidity, and this can happen at one q-level but not at another. This is why the vector components of $\hat{Q}$ need to be studied separately; it is not helpful to produce a single number out of $\hat{Q}$, like the norm of $\hat{Q}$, $||\hat{Q}||$. Further discussions of the consequences of introducing the notion of patterns is given in Chapter 6 whilst patterns π are discussed more formally in Appendix C.

3 The Game of Chess

3.1 Lasker on chess [37]

Emmanuel Lasker was the world chess champion from the time he defeated Wilhelm Steinitz in 1894 until his own defeat by Raoul Capablanca in 1921, a total reign of twenty-seven years. But his interests were far from narrow. Apart from a creative contribution made to the mathematical theory of primary ideals (he was a close friend of the Noether family) his interest in philosophical matters found a stimulus in the game of chess and led him to think deeply about what he called a philosophy of struggle. The chess-board was not remote from life but, to Lasker, it was a stage which reflects the struggle of life in its purest form — without the muddiness which arises from the injection of personal malice or deceit. 'On the chess-board', he wrote, 'lies and hypocrisy do not long survive. The creative combination lays bare the presumption of a lie; the merciless fact, culminating in a checkmate, contradicts the hypocrite .... and many a man, struck by injustice as Socrates and Shakespeare were struck, has found justice realized on the chess-board and has thereby recovered his courage and his vitality to continue to play the game of Life.' In his generous appraisal of the theories of Steinitz he urged the rational view of the game, the Steinitzian concept of an objective rational structure which was to illuminate the triumphs and the disasters of the earlier combinative master play. He believed that 'reason which governs the world governs also the chess-board', and although writers on chess have often seen in this use of the word 'reason' only a nineteenth century scientific optimism which is out of tune with our own enlightened cynicism, seeing Lasker as (also) a mathematician allows us to read no more into that word 'reason' than Lasker would expect. It is not 'reasonableness' that governs either the world or the chess-board, but simply 'reason' or the rationality peculiar to the human understanding.

In terms of the thesis of this book we can see how the sweet reason of structural analysis in a multi-dimensional pattern of connectivity brings to light a language which talks to us about both of Lasker's philosophical and chess-board struggles.

In that remarkable book *The Chess Mind* by Gerald Abrahams (London: E.U.P., 1951) although it contains some innocent slurs on mathematics, we find the author relating the game of chess to a variety of psychological concepts. Chiefly he writes, 'The most important mental activity in chess is vision, by which is meant the unforced intuition of possibilities by the mind's eye ... the capacity of the mind for making a path through time and

complexity, as the essence and the moving edge of any intellectual process...
in Chess the mind comes as near as possible to pure vision, to that spontaneous
act of intuition which apprehends and controls processes and relationships
without being forced to do so.'

In our Q-analysis of the mathematical relations which exist between the
chess-men and the squares of the chess-board, and which embody the rules
of the game, we are presenting the thesis that chess-masters have a (possibly
subconscious) mental appreciation of the multi-dimensional structures and
that this constitutes their acute assessment of the positional features of the
game.

3.2 Q-analysis for mode [0, 0]

The game of chess is played on a board of 64 squares, the initial position and
notation being already noticed in our previous section 1.7. There we introduced
the specific relations Γ_W and Γ_B which are to provide the substance of our
analysis. For ease of reference we here reproduce Figure 1.2 as Figure 3.1 and
we also repeat the definitions of the mathematical relations Γ_W and Γ_B.

Figure 3.1 Mode [0, 0] in the game of chess

In Figure 3.1 we distinguish the pieces by their initial positions Q-side
(e.g. QR) or K-side (e.g. KB). Figure 3.2 shows the simple numbering of the
squares 1 − 64, used in the computing programmes; thus the Black KB is on
square f8, which equals $6 + (8-1) \times 8 = 62$. Incidentally the initial position

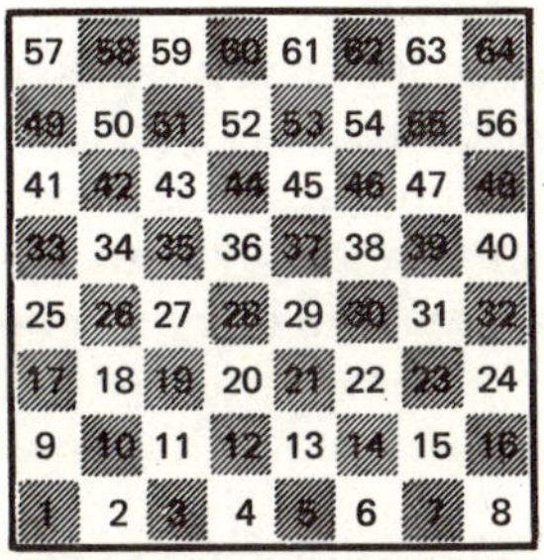

Figure 3.2 The squares of the chess-board

requires the square h1 (8 in Figure 3.2) to be a white square, according to the F.I.D.E. rules.

The world champion Emmanuel Lasker also remarked, 'there are 64 squares on the chess-board; if you control 33 of them you must have an advantage'. This is a gross simplification of the problem but it illustrates the fact that chess-masters have always had a sharp sense of the so-called *'positional'* or *'strategic'* nature of the play. This feature of the game can be seen immediately as an expression of the *mathematical relation* Γ *between the men and the squares*. We therefore consider the two relations Γ_W and Γ_B; Γ_W gives the relation between the White men and the 64 squares, Γ_B that for the Black. Precisely, we define (e.g.) Γ_B by the statement:

> given X = *a piece or pawn,* S = *square on the board,*
>
> then $X \, \Gamma_W \, S$ (or $(X, S) \in \Gamma_W$)
>
> *if and only if* X *attacks* S.

By attacks we mean that *one* of the following holds true:

(1) if it is White's move, and if X_i is not a pawn or the King, then 'X_i–S_j' is a legal move;
(2) if X_i is a pawn then S_j is a capturing square for X_i;
(3) if there is a White man Y on square S then X is protecting Y, in ordinary chess-players' parlance;
(4) if X is the White K then S is an immediate neighbour to the square occupied by X; horizontally, vertically, or diagonally;
(5) if the square S contains a Black piece or pawn Z (other than the K) and if it were White's move than 'X captures Z' is a legal move
(6) the Black K is on square S and is in check to White's X.

Having defined Γ_W and Γ_B, for any position on the board, we therefore have four complexes at our disposal, *viz.*,

$$K_X(S; \Gamma_W), \, K_S(X; \Gamma_W^{-1})$$

and

$$K_X(S; \Gamma_B), \, K_S(X; \Gamma_B^{-1})$$

We shall describe $K_X(S; \Gamma_W)$ as *White's view of Board,* and the conjugate $K_S(X; \Gamma_W^{-1})$ as *Board's view of White*.

In the complex $K_X(S; \Gamma_W)$ each man X is representing a simplex with vertices selected from the 64 squares. If two pieces X_1, X_2 are q-connected in this K then they share $(q + 1)$ squares on the board, that is to say, there exist $(q + 1)$ squares which are attacked by both X_1 and X_2.

In the complex $K_S(X)$ each square S is representing a simplex with vertices selected from the 16 men. If two squares S_1, S_2 are q-connected in this K then they share $(q + 1)$ men, that is to say, there exist $(q + 1)$ men who are attacking both S_1 and S_2.

A particular distribution of men (including both White and Black) on the squares is referred to as a *mode*. A game commences in mode [0, 0]; after

The Game of Chess 49

White's first move the game is in mode [1, 0]; after Black's first move the game is in mode [1, 1]. Figure 3.1 shows mode [0, 0], at the commencement of a game; White to move. In this position the QR-pawn (on a2) is a 0-simplex, since it attacks the one square b3 (number 18), similarly the KR-pawn is a 0-simplex, whereas each of the remaining White pawns is a 1-simplex (e.g. the Q-pawn is the 1-simplex ⟨19, 21⟩). The QR is also a 1-simplex (⟨9, 2⟩) whereas the QN is a 2-simplex (*viz.*, ⟨17, 19, 12⟩). The QB is the 1-simplex ⟨10, 12⟩, the Q is the 4-simplex ⟨3, 11, 12, 13, 5⟩, whilst the K is also a 4-simplex, *viz.*, ⟨4, 12, 13, 14, 6⟩. The Q and K, in mode [0, 0], are therefore 1-connected, with a common face ⟨12, 13⟩; notice however that in Γ_W (or Γ_B) a piece does not attack its own square. This is of practical significance since the pieces and pawns must protect each other by attacking the occupied squares.

We can therefore list the dimensions of and connectivity patterns between White's men when mode [0, 0] (Figure 3.1) applies, as follows:

$K_X(S; \Gamma_W) \equiv$ White's view of Board   (mode [0, 0])

	1	2	3	4	5	6	7	8	9	10	11	12	13	14	15	16		
1	–	–	–	–	–	–	–	–	–	–	–	–	–	–	–	–	1	QR
		2	0	0	0	–	–	–	–	–	–	0	–	–	–	–	2	QN
			1	0	0	–	–	–	–	–	–	–	–	–	–	–	3	QB
				4	1	0	0	–	–	–	–	–	–	–	–	–	4	Q
					4	0	0	–	–	–	–	–	–	–	–	–	5	K
						1	0	–	–	–	–	–	–	–	–	–	6	KB
							2	–	–	–	–	0	–	1	0	7	KN
								1	–	–	–	–	–	–	–	–	8	KR
									0	–	0	–	–	–	–	–	9	QRP
										1	–	0	–	–	–	–	10	QNP
											1	–	0	–	–	–	11	QBP
												1	–	0	–	–	12	QP
													1	–	0	–	13	KP
														1	–	0	14	KBP
															1	–	15	KNP
																0	16	KRP

The values of dim X are in the diagonal of this triangular array; the remaining integers give q-values in the connectivity patterns; the dashes (–) indicated $q = -1$, which means disconnected. The easiest way to read the table is to start at a number in the diagonal and read upwards and then to the left, or to the right and then downwards. Thus:

50 Mathematical Structure in Human Affairs

(1) dim Q = 4   Q is a 4-simplex (5 squares attacked by Q)
and is 0-connected to QB   (via ⟨12⟩)
and is 0-connected to QN   (via ⟨12⟩)
(2) dim QN = 2   QN is a 2-simplex (3 squares attacked by QN)
and is 1-connected to QNP   (via ⟨17, 19⟩)
and is 0-connected to QP   (via ⟨19⟩)
etc.

3.3 Positional motifs and structure

Various positional motifs in master play have an illuminating interpretation in terms of our connectivity patterns.

The modern idea of positional play commenced with Philidor (whom Réti [43] has designated the greatest chess thinker of all time) and subsequently made great advances through the work of Steinitz (a point in time which Emmanuel Lasker [37] described as the greatest landmark in the history of chess), and more latterly through Rubinstein, Nimzowitsch, and then Botvinnik and the modern Russian school, to name only a few.

(1) To Philidor is attributed the sentiment, 'the pawns are the soul of chess', and his own theory and praxis certainly bore witness to this idea. Philidor's main point was to emphasize the idea of unity in play, the co-operation of pieces and pawns in the development of a successful attack on the opponent. This led him to place great emphasis on the 'orderly advance' of a pawn mass — often, in practice, to the neglect of appropriate piece-play behind the pawns. We see at once from our analysis in section 2.1 that a pawn can, at the most, be a 1-simplex in $K_X(S)$; its individual influence (neglecting the queening potential) can therefore be only slight in comparison with a piece. But it follows also that, in mode [0, 0] the *pawns form a connected chain* (at $q = 0$) *in the complex;* their overall power vis-à-vis their power to attack and control squares on the board is considerably enhanced. It is not difficult to see that in mode [0, 0] and in the conjugate complex $K_S(X)$ — that is to say, *Board's view of White* — the pawn subcomplex (which forms a 0-connected chain) is responsible for certain squares being at least 1-simplices. These squares are {18, 19, 20, 21, 22, 23}; for example, in $K_S(X)$ the square 20 represents the simplex ⟨QBP, KP⟩.

Furthermore we see that the q-connected components of $K_X(S; \Gamma_W)$, in mode [0, 0] are as follows:

$Q_4 = 2$ Components are Q and K
$Q_3 = 2$ Components are Q and K
$Q_2 = 4$ Components are Q, K, QN, KN
$Q_1 = 11$ Components are {KN, KNP}, {QN, QNP}, {Q, K}, {QR}, {KB}, {QB}, {QBP}, {QP}, {KP}, {KBP}

and $Q_0 = 3$ Components are {KR}, {QR}, {the rest}

Hence the pawns (*in toto*) are 0-connected to all the pieces except the two Rooks. In this sense we can see that (at the $q = 0$ level) the chain of pawns acts as a support for most of the pieces vis-à-vis the connectivity. It is immediately clear that if the White pawns-and-pieces could advance up the board à la Philidor (in an 'orderly manner') this connectivity structure would be preserved. Indeed such an advance would soon activate the rooks in such a manner that $Q_0 = 1$ so that, at the level of $q = 0$ *White's view of the Board* would be one connected component. The degree of connectivity inherent in $K_X(S)$ is in fact a recurring theme in chess theory, albeit expressed in different terms. Thus, with Philidor, we can see that the pawns exhibit (even in mode [0, 0]) the basic idea of connectivity in their relations with the squares of the board (modulo the rules of the game). If connectivity patterns are at the heart of the game of chess then the pawns can certainly be said to be the soul of the game.

(2) Steinitz introduced the idea of *weak squares* and *strong squares* into chess thinking. He could therefore speak of weak positions or strong positions; he set himself the task of finding the characteristics of position which amounted to an advantage or a disadvantage. By a strong square S he meant a square which is amply controlled by the pieces and pawns so that, for example, it can be safely occupied by a Knight or other piece. It is even stronger if it is well placed, a strong square at 28 is 'stronger' than a strong square at, say, 25. The reasons are clear.

A strong square for White (Steinitz) is a square S such that

$$\dim S \text{ in } K_S(X; \Gamma_W^{-1}) > \dim S \text{ in } K_S(X; \Gamma_B^{-1})$$

— and this is obtained without weighting the vertices of S in any way. If such a square is to be used by White for posting a Knight then it is important for the N (on that strong square) to have maximum affect, to have a maximum dim in $K_X(S; \Gamma_W)$. On S = 28, for example, dim N = 7 since N = ⟨11, 18, 34, 43, 45, 38, 22, 13⟩, whereas on S = 25 we have only dim N = 3.

Powerfully placed pieces are pieces with largest possible values of dim X, in the first place. *General control of the board corresponds to a high-degree of connectivity between powerfully placed pieces.*

Steinitz broadened chess theory to include an appreciation of the *Board's view of White* and urged us to hold it in the mind during the process of controlling *White's view of Board*. He effectively said that not only are White's men co-operating on the Board's squares but equally well are the Board's squares co-operating on White's men. If a square S is a weak square for White then it is a strong square for Black. For example, the *isolated pawn* is a well-known instance in point. If White's QP is isolated on S = 28 then the square S = 36 is weak for White, strong for Black. The advantage for Black is realized when he places a piece (something with a large dim X under these conditions — not a Rook) on S = 36. For White, with respect to the pawn mass, square S = 36 is disconnected ($q = -1$) in $K_S(X; \Gamma_W^{-1})$.

(3) *The relative power* of the pieces is a function of the mode $[I, J]$ of the game (a fact which lies behind every sound Q-sacrifice), but for fixed I, J we must *measure it as the ratio* dim X: dim Y in $K_X(S)$. On this score the wing pawns are bottom of the table, being only 0-simplices. It is not surprising that, for example, Tchigorin (and later, Tartakower) scored many surprises with opening play which consisted in an early advance of the KRP — and its early exchange if possible. Such an advance immediately increased the value of dim KR, giving the Rook a powerful early entry into the game: after only two moves by White (h2–h4 and R–h3) it is possible for the value of dim KR to have increased from 1 to 9. This seems a handsome return for (possibly) sacrificing a wing pawn. It also illustrates much of the positional thinking about opening play and wing gambits in particular.

The elementary discussions of relative strengths of pieces usually suggest what is by-and-large the accepted practical values, *viz.*,

with P = 1 we take B = N = 3, R = 5, Q = 9, K = infinite.

The infinite value for K is not simply a connectivity value but expresses the peculiar role played by the King in that it cannot be captured in any mode $[I, J]$, nor can it be exchanged for any (finite) number of pawns — as, for example, can B or R.

If we leave the King out of account then we can reasonably assess the relative strengths of the Pawns and Pieces in any mode by their dimensions. In mode [0, 0] these are given in the array in section 3.2. After the opening move (1) e2–e4 the game is in mode [1, 0] and it is easy to see that the dimensions of the simplices in $K_X(S; \Gamma_W)$ are unchanged except for the following:

dim Q = 7, dim KB = 5, in mode [1, 0]

whereas   dim Q = 4, dim KB = 1, in mode [0, 0]

This point of view sheds valuable light on that thorny problem of B versus N. There are many positions in which the B is to be preferred to the N, and conversely. The chess-master Rubinstein played those endings involving B versus N with a sound positional judgement. This judgement involved assessing the subsequent structures of $K_X(S)$ from the point of view of controlling the dimensions of the B- or N-simplices. Pawn moves which limit the power of the opponent's B (or N) whilst at the same time extending the power of one's own N (or B) play a crucial role in such situations. Before allowing that type of position to occur it is therefore necessary to see the structural pattern of future complexes $K_X(S)$ and how they can be attained by tactical means. In this respect, the orthodox and rigid valuation of B and N (as equally weighted) is not helpful.

The same reasoning lies behind the notions of *good* B and *bad* B. The latter is one which operates on the same coloured square as most of one's pawns are placed. The relation Γ_W contains this situation and expresses both the fact that the (bad) B is protecting the pawns and the fact that the pawns are restricting the value of dim B, and consequently of its connectivity with other pieces. The malaise is acute when the pawns are relatively fixed in positions, being interlocked with the enemy pawns or blocked by pieces. In such situations the tactical play must be designed to 'free' the position, to change one's bad B into a good B.

In the absence of obstacles on the board the *maximum values* of dim X are given in the list below:

max dim P = 1,	over all possible modes
max dim N = 7,	occurs when N is within the square bounded by S = 43, 46, 22, 19
max dim B = 12	occurs when B is on S = 36, 37, 29, 28
max dim R = 13	occurs when R is on any S
max dim Q = 26	occurs when Q is on S = 36, 37, 29, 28

We notice immediately the importance of the *central squares* 36, 37, 29, 28. These have always played an important part in *opening theory*, since control of these squares gives either player the opportunity of placing his pieces to maximum effect. Whether or not the centre should be occupied by pawns in the first instance is a tactical matter. In contesting that earlier golden rule the *hypermodern school* were making just this point about the wider positional significance of the squares 36, 37, 29, 28. For example, the Réti opening, commencing with (1) N–f3 and (2) c2–c4, amounts to a rapid fight for control of 28, 37, 36 without occupying 28, 29 with pawns. A later fianchetto of the KB by B–g2 increases this pressure on the diagonal central squares 29, 36.

We can also appreciate that school of thought which has claimed that all opening play should be dedicated to the task of bringing the Rooks into play; castling early is a contribution to this and, of course, the classical King's Gambit opening — with an early sacrifice of the KBP — is patently just such a play. Perhaps the style of Morphy exemplified this urge to create open files for the Rooks above all other players. Thus Morphy frequently found himself with a greater command of the board (or of the most significant part of it) than his opponent, with *pieces highly connected in the complex* $K_X(S)$ and *squares* (particularly those in the vicinity of the enemy King) *highly connected in the conjugate* $K_S(X)$. Bringing his Rooks into play so that they enjoyed their maximum dimensions as simplices was often the final touch of disaster for his opponent. Now from section 3.2 we notice that in mode [0, 0] the two Rooks are quite disconnected ($q = -1$) from all other men in $K_X(S)$. Thus arranging for a Rook to move into a more central position will ensure, in an early mode, that it becomes connected in $K_X(S)$. Also in the middle game modes the penetration of the Rook to the enemy's seventh (or eighth) rank — a strategy stressed by Nimzowitsch — is most likely to give a maximum value for dim R, since often the enemy pawns have advanced from the seventh. Since the squares attacked by the R, on the seventh rank, also include significant squares in the vicinity of the enemy King, we expect this invasion to be of great tactical as well as positional value. [56]

3.4 Checkmate

If we consider an easy *checkmate position, viz.*, White's Q on f8 (S = 62), K on g6 (S = 47), and Black's K on h8 (S = 64), then the complexes $K_X(S)$ and $K_S(X)$ for both relations Γ_W and Γ_B are easily found.

$\underline{K_X(S; \Gamma_W)}$ — *White's view of Board:*

        dim Q = 20 and dim K = 7

together with a q-connection between Q and K of q = 4:
precisely   Q = ⟨57, 58, 59, 60, 61, 63, 64, 55, 48, 46,
                  38, 30, 22, 14, 6, 53, 54, 44, 35, 26, 17⟩
and   K = ⟨54, 55, 56, 46, 38, 39, 40, 48⟩
and   Q ∩ K = ⟨54, 46, 38, 55, 48⟩

$\underline{K_S(X; \Gamma_W^{-1})}$ — *Board's view of White:*

        each of the squares 54, 46, 38, 55, 48 is a 1-simplex ⟨Q, K⟩
        the remaining squares are either 0-simplices or not members of
        Γ_W^{-1} in particular 64 = ⟨Q⟩, 63 = ⟨Q⟩, 55 = ⟨Q, K⟩, 56 = ⟨K⟩.

$\underline{K_X(S; \Gamma_B)}$ — *Black's view of Board*

        dim K = 2;
precisely   K = ⟨63, 55, 56⟩

$\underline{K_S(X; \Gamma_B^{-1})}$ — *Board's view of Black*

        each of 63, 55, 56 is a 0-simplex K, the rest are not members of
        Γ_B^{-1}.

Black is in check because his K is on square S = 64 which is a vertex of White's Q in $K_X(S; \Gamma_W)$. The only possible moves for the Black K are the vertices of K in $K_X(S; \Gamma_B)$, *viz.*, S = 63, 55, 56. But the squares 55, 56 are vertices in $K_X(S; \Gamma_W)$ *viz.*, in the simplex K, whilst the vertex 63 is in the simplex Q of the same complex. Hence Black's K has no legal move and is checkmated — a typical player's assessment of the position, since as players we are inclined to think in terms of the complexes $K_X(S)$. But we see now that the *Board's view of White/Black* contains the immediate *checkmate condition*, *viz.*,

        Board's view of Black's K is a subcomplex of
        Board's view of White.

The notation naturally allows us to denote Board's view of Black's K by the subcomplex $K_S(K; \Gamma_B^{-1})$. In this particular illustration we happen to have $K_S(K; \Gamma_B^{-1}) \equiv K_S(X; \Gamma_B^{-1})$ since Black only has one piece. But generally, in other modes, we have

$$K_S(K; \Gamma_B^{-1}) \subset K_S(X; \Gamma_B^{-1})$$

and the *checkmate condition* is now precisely expressed as follows.

Black is checkmated in mode $[I, (I-1)]$ *when the following structure is invariant under all legal transitions to mode* $[I, I]$.

(1) $K_S(K, \Gamma_B^{-1}) \subset K_S(X; \Gamma_W^{-1})$
(2) *with the Black K on square* S_K

$$\langle S_K \rangle \in K_S(X; \Gamma_W^{-1})$$

We notice that this is an economical view of the checkmate condition and is a characteristic of the definitions of the relations Γ_W, Γ_B. Thus, when the condition applies, the Black K cannot move without being in check and it cannot capture the checking piece because the vertices of X do not include the location-square of X. Furthermore, intervention by any other of the Black pieces is ineffective because of the coupling of both modes $[I, (I-1)]$ and $[I, I]$ to the structure.

We can now express, in general terms, the course of a game as the development of the complexes $K(\Gamma_W)$ and $K(\Gamma_B)$, each trying to engulf pieces of (or the whole of) the other. It is rather like two giant amoebae in multi-dimensional space trying to devour each other; each has the ability to grow in unusual ways.

A chess-master normally subordinates his tactical moves to overall positional requirements. When he looks ahead through n moves he is consciously or unconsciously assessing the future structures of all four complexes defined by Γ_W and Γ_B. His tactical analysis only ceases, for some particular n, when he believes the nth structures to be in his favour. Often this belief is based on an intuition developed through years of experience; always it must require an intuitive appreciation of multi-dimensional connectivity patterns; it is not based on linear (network) type structures, except perhaps in the strictly book-keeping sense of tracking the modes from $[I_1, J_1]$ to $[I_n, J_m]$.

3.5 Time in chess

The idea of *time* on the chess-board (players speak of *gain* or *loss* of *tempi*) is an intriguing one. It is discussed at some length by Znosko-Borovsky [56], who builds it into an overall description of positional judgement. Thus it is plausible to think that if White plays (1) e2–e3 and (2). e3–e4, then in some sense he has wasted a tempo, since he could have achieved the same position by (1) e2–e4. Inexperienced players commonly bring the Q out into the centre of the board in the early stages of the game (for example, by playing the Centre Counter Opening). This leads to tactical moves by the opponent which force the Q to retire again – more loss of *tempi*, leaving one player with a superior development (gain of *tempi*). The end result can be a frustrated loser complaining, 'If I had only had one more move I would have been able to force mate!'

This idea of *tempo* is clearly a relation between structure *of the game* and mode $[I, J]$, between $K(\Gamma_W)$, $K(\Gamma_B)$, and $[I, J]$. Thus if White truly wastes a move by (1) e2–e3 and (2) e3–e4, it means that the structure of the game (for White) in mode $[2, 1]$ could have been achieved in mode $[1, 0]$. This situation is felt most acutely in the opening stages of the game before the complexes $K_S(X; \Gamma_W^{-1})$ and $K_S(X; \Gamma_B^{-1})$ are connected. At this stage it is possible for White truly to waste a *tempo* since he is effectively playing without any immediate interaction with Black. Later on, when the forces are obviously joined in combat it is not easy for White to produce identical structures in $[I_2, J_2]$ by different routes from $[I_1, J_1]$. We notice this in chess writers who rightly are unable to sustain an interest in the *tempo*-situation once the game is reaching certain kinds of middle-game structures. It is not therefore surprising that the *tempo*-question arises again in the end-game phase, when most of the pieces and pawns are cleared off the board and the structures $K_S(X; \Gamma_W^{-1})$ and $K_S(X; \Gamma_B^{-1})$ are (often) disjoint, or connected only slightly. Many tactical possibilities arise in end-game modes for a player to deliberately lose a *tempo* in order to recover a certain structure with (or without) the obligation to move. This effectively means that Black is forced to gain a *tempo* vis-à-vis some specific structure — which is advantageous.

Thus in any event the gain or loss of time is only good or bad according to the achievement of desirable structures. If we consider two structural patterns K, K^1 (K denotes $K_X(S; \Gamma_W) \cup K_S(X; \Gamma_W^{-1}) \cup K_X(S; \Gamma_B) \cup K_S(X; \Gamma_B^{-1})$) corresponding to modes $[I, J]$ and $[I^1, J^1]$, then it is reasonable to describe *White's time* with respect to (K, K^1) as $I^1 - I$ and *Black's time* with respect to (K, K^1) as $J^1 - J$. Since K and K^1 both involve four complexes we see that juggling with White's time vis-à-vis Black's time is only part of the struggle to *achieve the structure K^1 with the right to move.*

3.6 The Immortal Game (1851)

A classic game of chess, known in fact as *The Immortal Game,* was that played between Anderssen and Kieseritsky in London (1851). It was a demonstration of Anderssen's remarkable combinational powers and tactical foresight, but it showed too that his instinct for the positional structure was very highly developed. This latter quality of Anderssen's play was regarded as largely magical in his time (twenty years before Steinitz), but without it he would not have been able to produce such elegant and economical tactical play against his adversaries. In 1858 Anderssen was to be soundly defeated in a match with the young Paul Morphy, his equal in tactical imagination but his superior in positional instinct.

The analysis of the game which we now give is based on a Q-analysis produced by the writer's computer program which was run on the PDP-10 at the University of Essex. The program was written in BASYS, an extension of BASIC (BASYS was devised by Brian Gaines and largely developed by Peter Facey), and operates on a Data file which contains the score of the game in the international algebraic notation. After reading a move the program sets up the incidence matrices corresponding to the relations $\Gamma_W, \Gamma_W^{-1}, \Gamma_B, \Gamma_B^{-1}$ and then systematically computes and prints the q-connectivities of the complexes. The four complexes are labelled, for a particular mode $[I, J]$;

$K_X(S; \Gamma_W)$ — White's view of Board
$K_S(X; \Gamma_W^{-1})$ — Board's view of White
$K_X(S; \Gamma_B)$ — Black's view of Board
$K_S(X; \Gamma_B^{-1})$ — Board's view of Black

The score of the game is as follows:

Anderssen v. Kieseritsky (London 1851)

(1)	e2–e4	: e7–e5		(12)	h2–h4	: Q–g6
(2)	f2–f4	: e5*f4		(13)	h4–h5	: Q–g5
(3)	B–c4	: Q–h4+		(14)	Q–f3	: N–g8
(4)	K–f1	: b7–b5		(15)	B*f4	: Q–f6
(5)	B*b5	: N–f6		(16)	N–c3	: B–c5
(6)	N–f3	: Q–h6		(17)	N–d5	: Q*b2
(7)	d2–d3	: N–h5		(18)	B–d6	: Q*a1+
(8)	N–h4	: Q–g5		(19)	K–e2	: B*g1
(9)	N–f5	: c7–c6		(20)	e4–e5	: N–a6
(10)	g2–g4	: N–f6		(21)	N*g7+	: K–d8
(11)	R–g1	: c6*b5		(22)	Q–f6+	: Resigns.

(The symbol for 'captures' is the computer's multiplicative sign *.)

The opening play was a King's Gambit, in the spirit of the times, being an early attempt to create space for White's pieces and in particular for the White KR after the f-file is opened. Black accepts the gambit pawn, brings his Q out for an early check — which loosens the pawn barrier around White's K — and cannot resist capturing the White KB (by (11) ... : c6*b5) which Anderssen deliberately leaves *en prise* (by (11) R–g1). The justification for White's tactical play lies entirely in the structure of the game and the subsequent middle-game possibilities. The character of the game is essentially manifest by the time it is in mode [12, 11]. To investigate this character we therefore commence our analysis in mode [12, 12].

Game in mode [12, 12], following (12) ... : Q–g6

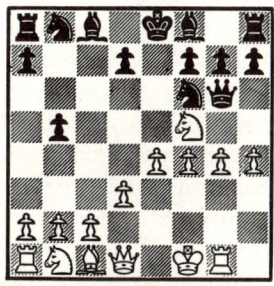

Figure 3.3 Anderssen *v.* Kieseritsky : Mode [12, 12]

58 *Mathematical Structure in Human Affairs*

In White's view of the Board we have the structure vector

$$Q = \{\overset{8}{1} \ 2 \ 2 \ 2 \ 4 \ 5 \ 6 \ 9 \ \overset{0}{5}\}$$

This corresponds to dim Q = 8 — in fact Q = ⟨3, 11, 12, 20, 5, 6, 13, 22, 31⟩ — and includes dim KN = 7, dim K = dim KR = 4, dim QB = 3. The White pieces (excluding the pawns) are not connected until we reach $q = 1$ and then the only pieces which are so connected are Q, K, KR. This is illustrated by the value $Q_1 = 9$. We notice too that the complex consists of 5 separate components at the zero level ($q = 0$).

In Black's view of Board we have the structure vector

$$Q = \{\overset{8}{1} \ 2 \ 2 \ 3 \ 4 \ 4 \ 6 \ 9 \ \overset{0}{5}\}$$

a pattern very similar to White's. But the differences between the positions of White and Black appear in the conjugate complexes. Thus, already, we see that

$$K_S(X; \Gamma_W^{-1}) \cap K_S(X; \Gamma_W^{-1}) \neq \phi; \text{ in fact g7} = \langle KB, Q \rangle \text{ in } K_S(X; \Gamma_B^{-1})$$

and   g7 = ⟨KN⟩ in $K_S(X; \Gamma_W^{-1})$; e7 = ⟨K, KB⟩ in $K_S(X; \Gamma_B^{-1})$

and e7 = ⟨KN⟩ in $K_S(X; \Gamma_W^{-1})$. Squares which are deep inside the Black camp, and close to the K, are already part of the White structure, either as simplices in $K_S(X; \Gamma_W^{-1})$ or as vertices in $K_X(S; \Gamma_W)$. By comparison the White K simplex (in $K_X(S; \Gamma_W)$) is not connected to the Black structure. Furthermore the Black Q is under attack by the White pawns; this is a dangerous situation for Black because, in avoiding further harassment Black must use moves (time) which should be available for strengthening his own structure. In effect, because of the positions of the K-side pawns and the KN, the Black Q acts as if it were a 3-simplex, *viz*., Q = ⟨48, 40, 39, 31⟩. But each of these vertices are in $K_S(X; \Gamma_W^{-1})$, that is to say, the Q cannot move without being captured.

Game in mode [13, 12], following (13) h4–h5.

Black cannot allow the exchange of the Q (a potentially powerful piece with high values of dim Q) for a White pawn (or a R or a N in this position). Hence the Q is driven on to g5; the structure vectors remain almost unaltered, but another square (g6) is attached to $K_S(X; \Gamma_W^{-1})$.

Game in mode [13, 13], following (13) ... : Q–g5

The future possibilities for Black have diminished by this move; even when the KN has moved the value of dim Q can only increase by 2, whereas were the Q still on g6 the increase would have been 5. This cramping effect is manifest in an increase in the structure vector (and therefore in the obstruction vector) for Black. In this mode, in $K_X(S; \Gamma_B)$, we have $Q_2 = 7$ compared with $Q_2 = 6$ in mode [12, 12], the other values of Q_r being unchanged. An advantage for Black lies in the fact that the Q now defends the pawn on f5, but White's next move makes this square into a 1-simplex, f5 = ⟨QB, Q⟩, in $K_S(X; \Gamma_W^{-1})$.

Figure 3.4 Mode [13, 13]

Game in mode [14, 13], following (14) Q–f3

This has increased the value of dim Q from 8 to 12, in $K_X(S; \Gamma_W)$, the new structure vector in White's view of Board being

$$Q = \{\overset{12}{1}\ 1\ 1\ 1\ 1\ 2\ 2\ 2\ 3\ 4\ 4\ 7\ \overset{0}{5}\}$$

In Black's view of Board the max dim X is still $q = 8$, and $Q_2 = 7$ (cf. $Q_2 = 4$ for White) although $Q_0 = 4$. We see also that at the $q = 1$ level there has been an improvement for White ($Q_1 = 7$ against the previous $Q_1 = 9$). Thus we have a tangible sign, *via* the structure vector, that White's game has become more connected (at $q = 1$ and $q = 2$), Black's not so, and the increase in the max dim X for White shows that his game is more open, flexible. For example, apart from the threat of B*f5, White has the tactical possibility of e4–e5, putting dim Q up to 16 and threatening e5*N and Q*R.

Game in mode [14, 14], following (14). . . . : N–g8

Figure 3.5 Mode [14, 14]

This saves the Q by increasing dim Q from 8 to 10, the new structure vector for Black being

$$Q = \{\overset{10}{1}\ 1\ 1\ 1\ 1\ 2\ 3\ 3\ 5\ 8\ 6\}$$

But Q_0 is now 6, due to the retreat of the KN. White will now be able to increase the value of dim QB and to lower the value of Q_2 yet again. The development of the QB will bind even more squares to $K_S(X; \Gamma_W^{-1})$ and, in particular, make d6 a 1-simplex in this complex and c7 a 0-simplex: we notice that, in this mode c7 $\notin K_S(X; \Gamma_W^{-1})$.

Game in mode [15, 15], following (15) B*f5 : Q–f6

Black's structure vector is now

$$Q = \{\overset{17}{1}\ 1\ 1\ 1\ 1\ 1\ 1\ 1\ 1\ 1\ 1\ \overset{5}{2}\ 3\ 4\ 4\ 4\}$$

whilst White's is

$$Q = \{1\ 1\ 2\ 2\ 2\ 3\ 3\ 3\ 4\ 3\ 3\ 7\ 5\}$$

This means the Black's game is being played almost entirely by his Q, the latter only being connected (*via* square e7) at $q = 2$. At this level ($q = 2$) there are 4 components in $K_X(S; \Gamma_B)$ and these are defined by the Black pieces as follows:

$$\{Q, K, KB\}, \{QN\}, \{QB\}, \{KN\}$$

Figure 3.6 Mode [15, 15]

At the $q = 1$ level the pieces fall into 3 components given by

$$\{Q, K, KB, QN, QB, KN\}, \{QR\}, \{KR\}$$

But the squares common to the conjugate complexes $K_S(X; \Gamma_W^{-1})$ and $K_S(X; \Gamma_B^{-1})$ are the following:

$$b8, d6, e5, e7, f5, g5, g6, g7, h4, h6$$

whereas the squares c7, d5 are not in $K_S(X; \Gamma_B^{-1})$ but are in $K_S(X; \Gamma_W^{-1})$. Thus Black is heavily on the defensive and his pieces are spread about in a disconnected way. Kieseritsky now must make every effort to develop his pieces so as to contest key squares and to build up his own complexes again.

Game in mode [16, 16], following (16) N–c3 : B–c5

White's structure vector is now

$$Q = \{\overset{12}{1}\ 1\ 2\ 2\ 2\ 4\ 4\ 5\ 6\ 5\ 2\ \overset{1}{6} = 1 + 5\ 3\}$$

and Black's is

$$Q = \{\overset{16}{1} \ 1 \ 1 \ 1 \ 1 \ 1 \ \overset{10}{2} \ 2 \ 2 \ 2 \ 2 \ 2 \ 3 \ 2 \ 4 \ \overset{1}{4} = 3 + 1 \ 3\}$$

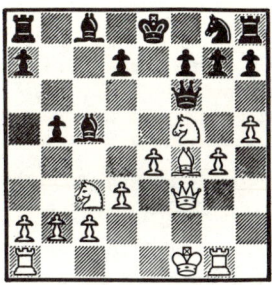

Figure 3.7 Mode [16, 16]

But at $q = 1$ all of White's pieces (excluding pawns) are connected in 1 component whereas Black's pieces form 3 components. At this level ($q = 1$) connection means that at least two pieces control (or attack) the same square. If all the pieces (7 in this case) fall in the same component then there is greater control over a wider portion of the Board. At a higher level (e.g. $q = 7$) the pieces are exerting their (possibly) maximum effect in a disconnected manner. In this case, in White's view of Board, $Q_7 = 4$ and the 4 components are:

$$\{QN\}, \{QB\}, \{Q\}, \{KN\}$$

The level of $q = 2$ can be seen as intermediate in a crucial manner (reviving Nimzowitsch's idea of 'over-protection'?) between the critical $q = 1$ and the higher levels. In White's case we have $Q_2 = 2$, *viz.*,

$$\{QR, QN, Q, K, KR\} \text{ and } \{QB, KN\}$$

In Black's view of Board the Q (dim Q = 16) and KB (dim KB = 10) are in splendid isolation until we reach the low level of $q = 3$. Black's pieces are relatively disorganized therefore, and technically disconnected. Add to this that White's move N–c3 further attacks d5, from where the QN can attack the Q on f6, and we can see that the complex $K_S(X; \Gamma_W^{-1})$ is steadily connecting with the central squares around the Black K.

Game in mode [17, 17], following (17) N–d5 : Q*b2

The structure vector for White is now

$$Q = \{\overset{12}{1} \ 1 \ 2 \ 2 \ 2 \ 4 \ 4 \ 5 \ 6 \ 5 \ 4 \ 5 = 1 + 4 \ \overset{0}{4}\}$$

and for Black,

$$Q = \{\overset{13}{1} \ 1 \ 1 \ \overset{10}{2} \ 2 \ 2 \ 2 \ 2 \ 3 \ 3 \ 5 \ 8 = 5 + 3 \ \overset{0}{3}\}$$

Figure 3.8 Mode [17, 17]

At $q = 1$ all seven of White's pieces fall into 1 component whereas Black's pieces fall into 5 components. Thus Black's 'attacking' play *via* Q*b2 has thrown his own piece structure into disarray. Even at the $q = 0$ level Black's pieces form 2 distinct components. His Q foray has also reduced the connection to his own $K_S(X; \Gamma_B^{-1})$ of the squares d6, d8, e7. These squares are consequently the better attached to $K_S(X; \Gamma_W^{-1})$, the more so since White's move N–d5 has further connected squares c7, e7. For his part Black no doubt thinks that he is threatening to capture either or both of White's Rooks, but at the price of neglecting his own important squares around the K.

Game in mode [19, 18], following (18) B–d6 : Q*a1 +, (19) k–e2

Figure 3.9 Mode [19, 18]

White is offering both Rooks, of course, by (18) B–d6, but in return he has altered the structure so that f7 = ⟨QN, QB, KN⟩ in $K_S(X; \Gamma_W^{-1})$ and f7 = ⟨K, KN⟩ (only) in $K_S(X; \Gamma_B^{-1})$. Thus the Black KB is cut off from the square f7. The situation is serious; if Black rejects the capture of the KR and plays (18)... : B*d6 then (19) N*d6 + : K–d8, (20) N*f7 + : K–e8, (21) N–d6 +: K–d8, (22) Q–f8 mate. The structure vectors are now

for White: $\mathbf{Q} = \{\overset{12}{1} \quad 1 \quad 2 \quad 2 \quad 2 \quad 5 \quad 5 \quad 5 \quad 3 \quad 3 \quad \overset{1}{5} = 1+4 \quad \overset{0}{3} = 1+2\}$

for Black: $\mathbf{Q} = \{\overset{12}{1} \quad 1 \quad 1 \quad 1 \quad 1 \quad 1 \quad 2 \quad 2 \quad 3 \quad 3 \quad 6 \quad \overset{1}{10} = 7+3 \quad \overset{0}{2} = 1+1\}$

The Game of Chess 63

White's pieces form one component at $q = 1$, whilst *Black's form* 7 *components*. Also the high dimensions of White's pieces ($Q_7 = 5$) dominate those of Black's ($Q_7 = 1$). But Black cannot resist capturing the other rook.

Game in mode [20, 20], following (19) ... : B*g1, (20) e4–e5 : N–a6

White's pawn move has finally disconnected the Black Q from square g7, allowing a fatal check by the N on f5. Black's move N–a6 was an attempt to contest square c7, but this is far too late. The flight squares for the Black K, f8, e7, d8, are doomed to be absorbed into the White structure $K_S(X; \Gamma_W^{-1})$ without redress by Black.

The structure vectors show the same pattern; B*g1 has actually increased the number of components as $q = 1$ (piece-wise) to 8 (the maximum number!)

Game in mode [22, 21], following (21) N*g7 + : K–d8, (22) Q–f6 : Resigns

Figure 3.10 Mode [22, 21]

Black can play (22) ... : N*f6 but then he reduces e7 to a 0-simplex only, *viz.*, e7 = ⟨K⟩, and then (23) B–e7 mate; cannot be stopped. Thus Black, very wisely, resigned – just in time to avoid mate.

3.7 Computers and chess

The above analysis of the game Anderssen – Kieseritsky (1851) in its middle-game modes brings out the role of the connectivity pattern in Q-space for both White and Black. The structure vector Q contains much of this pattern, in the first instance. Thus we can see that the level $q = 1$ is crucially important for the *pieces*, and that a first sign of this is a change in the $q = 2$ level. Also the values of Q_t for $t > 3$ are an indication of piece development and board control. High values of (say) Q_5 or Q_6 indicate future possibilities of low values of Q_2 and Q_1. The dimensions of the squares in either $K_S(X; \Gamma_W^{-1})$ or $K_S(X; \Gamma_W^{-1})$ also indicate the contest for control over important parts of the board.

All this would suggest that there is a promising future for computer-chess *via* analyses of structure patterns. The language of connectivity in a multi-dimensional Q-space seems to be naturally suited to a discussion of the game of chess. Furthermore it seems to reflect all the niceties and general truths of the modern sum of class theory. Surely it therefore possesses the ability to more accurately express the way that chess-masters actually think about the game. By 'think' we include, of course, what nowadays often passes for 'instinctive feeling' or 'subconscious appreciation'.

A learning-machine faced with the game of chess should therefore be able to acquire a chess-mastership which is so far denied to the species. Such a project must hopefully throw new light on the structure of the mental processes and the capacities of the human mind.

Much work has already been done in teaching computers to play chess, since an initial stimulus from C. Shannon in an address to the (American) National Institute of Radio Engineers in 1949. An interesting demonstration of the computer-player's ability to conduct a tactical attack was published in the British Chess Magazine of July 1971.

It is in the tactics of formulating the attack that the chess computer programs seem to have been so far largely concentrated. The Russian ex-world champion M.M. Botvinnick has led a strong line of research in this direction for some time [10], aiming at an increasing depth of analysis in the so-called *tree of analysis* (the network which links possible transformations from mode $[I, J]$ to mode $[I', J']$). His method is based on identifying *lines of attack* (and of defense) against a target (an enemy piece) by way of the squares over which the attack can take place. By defining suitable functions (with values in the complex domain) on these squares, which take account of the action of all relevant pieces, he is able to obtain numerical comparisons for the potential successes of White or Black. The analysis is elegantly conceived and mathematically suited to computer programming.

We can see from our analysis however that Botvinnick's mappings are defined on the squares in $K_S(X; \Gamma_W^{-1})$ or $K_S(X; \Gamma_B^{-1})$ and are therefore *cosimplices* (not always 0-cosimplices, as the Russian analysis implies). The connectivity patterns of these complexes should therefore be reflected in the interaction of the various functions and consequently affect the judgement involved in choosing the dynamical tree of analysis. Botvinnick's treatment seems to be particularly primitive (his own word) in assessing the positional features, and this is the area where our connectivity structure seems to be most powerful.

4 Multi-dimensional Art

4.1 A search for structure

Without using any of the formalism of mathematics the artist Piet Mondrian (1871–1944) has left us a view of natural structure, of structure in nature, which transcends the 3-dimensional world-picture of the classical scientist. Even the apparently sophisticated 4-dimensional view which Relativity Theory introduced into the scientist's physical world has been found hereby to be inadequate.

The facts of Mondrian's life and a survey of his artistic progress are to be found in a recent book by Frank Elgar [23]. Eventually abandoning his early naturalistic paintings he sought the essence of structure in his characteristic life's work. Mondrian himself asserted that 'painting offers the artist a means as exact as mathematics of interpreting the essential facts of nature'.

Since each one of us must finally *see* a painting in order to apprehend it (and it is inadequate to talk about seeing, or to listen to an account of another's attempt at seeing it) it is necessary to acknowledge the 'hardware' from which it is constructed. This hardware is also part of our view. One of us might not be able to see all the geometrical shapes which the artist has used in his composition. Another might see the eight colours as if they were only six, and yet another might not see the individual colours at all but see rather an overall unity of pattern — see some relation between a set of colours and a set of pieces of canvas.

But we shall see that however one obtains a view of this picture, there is a multi-dimensional structure (a geometrical space) to go with it. This space is large enough to accommodate all critical views and its description is available in the mathematical language of this thesis. Whether this language is adequate for expressing all that the artist wishes to say cannot be judged in advance; speaking it is the acid test.

We shall examine a single painting by Mondrian, his *Composition, Checkerboard, Bright Colours 1919*.

4.2 Checkerboard, Bright Colours 1919 — Piet Mondrian

We shall reach the conclusion that Mondrian expressed in his abstract painting a sense of multi-dimensional structure which can be found and expressed in our q-connectivity analysis. This particular painting is suitable in an obvious way to our analysis but it should also be clear that other forms would be just as answerable. It will also emerge that the structure which is potentially

66 *Mathematical Structure in Human Affairs*

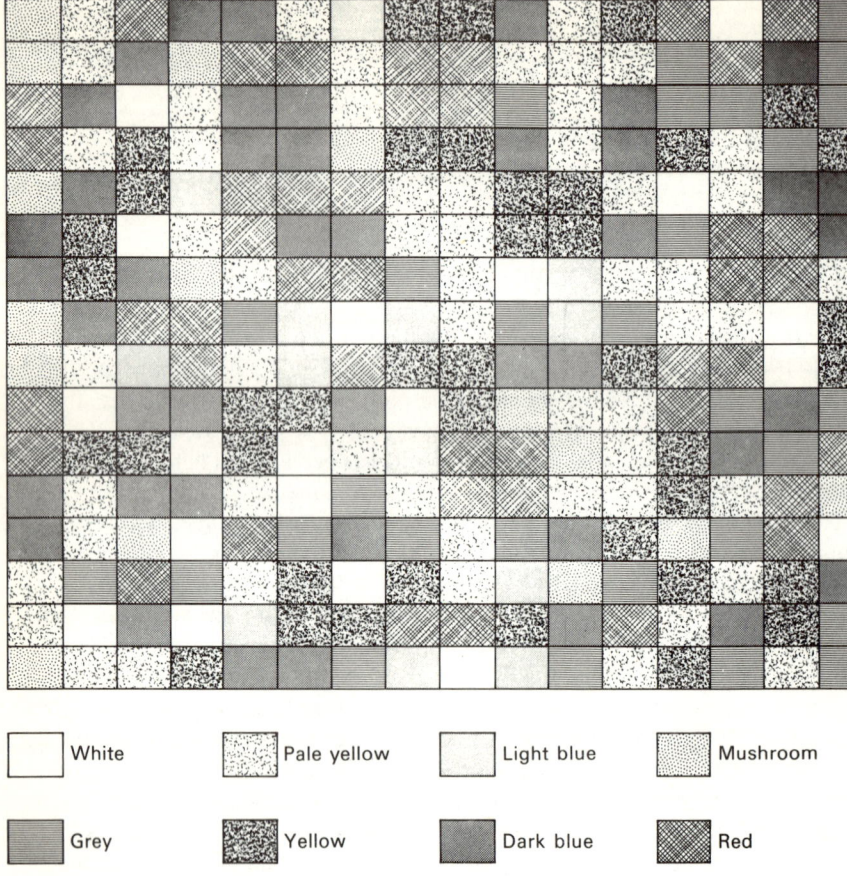

Figure 4.1 *Composition. Checkerboard, Bright Colours, 1919 :* Mondrian

there is very great and diverse and depends very much on the eye of the beholder. Thus, although our analysis is based on various views of the painting each of which is crude and obvious, the method is illustrative of how any view can be so understood. The sensitivity of the artist himself to the inherent structure can thereby be surmised and engenders a deep admiration for his abilities. The plethora of possibilities make reasonable the fact of continuous discussion between viewers of his work.

We begin by noticing that the picture is constructed by the artist allocating one of eight different colours to every one of 256 squares on the canvas. We shall soon be convinced that this allocation is not aimless nor random but that it produces specific structures of a mathematical nature.

We therefore identify a set C of colours which we shall identify by the following list (perhaps the names of the colours illustrate the writer's only excursion into painting, namely home decorating):

$$C = \{C1, C2, C3, C4, C5, C6, C7, C8\}$$

C1 = White   C4 = Yellow   C7 = Mushroom pink
C2 = Grey   C5 = Light blue   C8 = Red
C3 = Pale yellow   C6 = Dark blue

At the same time we visually divide up the canvas into a set of geometrical shapes and we refer to this as the set X. Since the canvas is divided into squares by the artist it is probable that these shapes will dominate our visual response (but it need not). We shall not try to avoid this influence but we shall consider various views which identify the elements of X in rather obvious ways.

4.3   Mondrian picture with card X = 1

In the first place we suppose that we only 'see' one square, the whole canvas, in the set X, as in Figure 4.2, so that card X = 1.

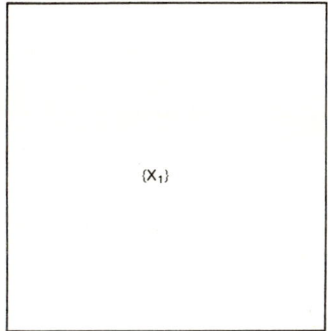

Figure 4.2   Mondrian picture; card X = 1

If we write $X = \{X_1\}$ we obtain a weighted relation $\lambda_1 \subset C \times X$ as follows:

λ_1	X_1
C1	19
C2	29
C3	54
C4	40
C5	13
C6	43
C7	15
C8	43

the total weights adding up to 256; for example, red appears 43 times in X_1. By taking different *slicing parameters* for the colours we obtain a series of complexes $K_C(X; \lambda)$ and $K_X(C; \lambda^{-1})$. Of these $K_C(X; \lambda)$ is particularly simple since no colour can be of greater dimension than zero. But the square X_1 can be of dimension not exceeding 7, depending on the slicing parameter.

Slicing row-wise, at, say, $\theta \geqslant 20$ corresponds to 'seeing' only the colours grey (C2), pale yellow (C3), yellow (C4), dark blue (C6), and red (C8). In other words, only if there are at least 20 occurrences of a colour in X_1 do we see it. The possible analyses for $K_X(C; \lambda^{-1})$ can be listed as follows, for typical slicing parameters.

For each colour	dim X_1	X_1 as simplex
$\theta \geqslant 10$	7	$\langle C1, C2, C3, C4, C5, C6, C7, C8 \rangle$
$\theta \geqslant 20$	4	$\langle C2, C3, C4, C6, C8 \rangle$
$\theta \geqslant 30$	3	$\langle C3, C4, C6, C8 \rangle$
$\theta \geqslant 40$	3	$\langle C3, C4, C6, C8 \rangle$
$\theta \geqslant 50$	0	$\langle C3 \rangle$

In like manner if a viewer 'likes' the colours dark blue, white, and red, then he might see the structure of X_1 by slicing parameters $\theta_1 \geqslant 5, \theta_6 \geqslant 5, \theta_8 \geqslant 5$ and the rest (which he might not want to see?) by $\theta \geqslant 50$. This particular slicing gives

$$X_1 = \langle C1, C3, C6, C8 \rangle \text{ and dim } X_1 = 3$$

Perhaps he would complain 'there is too much C3 (pale yellow)', since he would have liked to see X_1 as the 2-simplex $\langle C1, C6, C8 \rangle$?

4.4 Mondrian picture with card X = 4

If seeing the picture as a single square is too blunt a view then we can try looking at it as 4 quarters, as in Figure 4.3, with the elements of X named as $X_{11}, X_{12}, X_{21}, X_{22}$. Each square (element of X) is made up of 64 of the checkerboard squares, being 8 × 8.

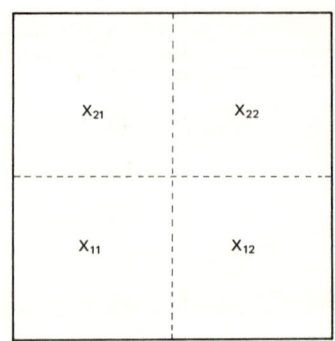

Figure 4.3 Mondrian picture; card X = 4

With this view of the painting we obtain the following weighted relation $\lambda_2 \subset C \times X$.

λ_2	X_{11}	X_{12}	X_{21}	X_{22}
C1	9	3	4	3
C2	7	9	2	11
C3	12	12	12	18
C4	11	12	5	11
C5	5	2	4	2
C6	11	8	15	9
C7	3	5	7	0
C8	7	12	15	9

Slicing the colours at a constant level (the same parameters θ for each row) gives the following set of connectivity patterns in suitable Q-spaces.

(1) Slicing parameter $\theta \geqslant 2$:

$K_C(X)$

C1	C2	C3	C4	C5	C6	C7	C8	
3	3	3	3	3	3	2	3	C1
	3	3	3	3	3	2	3	C2
		3	3	3	3	2	3	C3
			3	3	3	2	3	C4
				3	3	2	3	C5
					2	2	2	C6
						2	3	C7
							3	C8

This has a structure vector

$$Q = \{\overset{3}{1} \ 1 \ 1 \ \overset{0}{1}\}$$

with components:

at $q = 3$ {C1, C2, C3, C4, C5, C6, C8}
at $q = 2, 1, 0$ {all colours}

We notice that every colour possesses zero eccentricity since $\hat{q} = \check{q}$; no colour possesses any individuality.

$K_X(C)$

	X_{11}	X_{12}	X_{21}	X_{22}	
	7	7	7	6	X_{11}
		7	7	6	X_{12}
			7	6	X_{21}
				6	X_{22}

This has a structure vector

$$Q = \{\overset{7}{1} \ 1 \ 1 \ 1 \ 1 \ 1 \ 1 \ \overset{0}{1}\}$$

with components

at $q = 7$ $\{X_{11}, X_{12}, X_{21}\}$
at $q = 6, \ldots, 0$ {all squares}

Again we notice that each square shows top-q = bottom-q; only the square X_{22} is different from the others in that dim $X_{22} = 6$, the others being of dimension 7.

(2) Slicing parameter $\theta \geqslant 4$.

$K_C(X)$

	C1	C2	C3	C4	C5	C6	C7	C8	
	1	0	1	1	1	1	0	1	C1
		2	2	2	0	2	0	2	C2
			3	3	1	3	1	3	C3
				3	1	3	1	3	C4
					1	1	0	1	C5
						3	1	3	C6
							1	1	C7
								3	C8

This has a structure vector

$$Q = \{\overset{3}{1} \ 1 \ 1 \ \overset{0}{1}\}$$

with components

at $q = 3$ {C3, C4, C6, C8}
at $q = 2$ {C2, C3, C6, C8}
at $q = 1, 0$ {all colours}

Although the colours exhibit zero eccentricities at this slicing level the pattern for the conjugate shows that this is not so for the squares.

$K_X(C)$

	X_{11}	X_{12}	X_{21}	X_{22}	
	6	4	5	4	X_{11}
		5	4	4	X_{12}
			6	3	X_{21}
				4	X_{22}

This has a structure vector

$$Q = \{\overset{6}{2}\ 2\ 1\ 1\ 1\ \overset{0}{1}\}$$

with components

at $q = 6$	$\{X_{11}\}, \{X_{21}\}$
at $q = 5$	$\{X_{11}, X_{21}\}, \{X_{12}\}$
at $q = 4$	$\{X_{11}, X_{12}, X_{21}, X_{22}\}$
at $q = 3, 2, 1, 0$	{all squares}

Both X_{11} and X_{21} have non-zero eccentricities with $\check{q} = 5$ and $\hat{q} = 6$; X_{12} shows $\check{q} = 4$ and $\hat{q} = 5$. Now only X_{22} shows zero eccentricity. Thus at this slicing level the squares X_{11}, X_{12}, X_{21}, and X_{22} are exhibiting structural characteristics which were absent at the lower θ-level.

The same kind of distinction between the colours does not arise until we reach a slicing value of $\theta \geqslant 10$.

(3) Slicing parameter $\theta \geqslant 10$.

$K_C(X)$

C1	C2	C3	C4	C5	C6	C7	C8	
–	–	–	–	–	–	–	–	C1
	0	0	0	–	–	–	–	C2
		3	2	–	1	–	1	C3
			2	–	0	–	0	C4
				–	–	–	–	C5
					1	–	0	C6
						–	–	C7
							1	C8

The structure vector is

$$Q = \{\overset{3}{1}\ 1\ 1\ \overset{0}{1}\}$$

with components

at $q = 3$ {C3}
at $q = 2$ {C3, C4}
at $q = 1$ {C3, C4, C6, C8}
at $q = 0$ {C2, C3, C4, C6, C8}

We notice that C1, C5, C7 are not in the structure. Also the colour C3 (pale yellow) possesses non-zero eccentricity with $\hat{q} = 3$ and $\check{q} = 2$.

$\underline{K_X(C)}$

	X_{11}	X_{12}	X_{21}	X_{22}	
	2	1	1	1	X_{11}
		2	1	0	X_{12}
			2	0	X_{21}
				2	X_{22}

giving structure vector

$$Q = \{\overset{2}{4} \ 1 \ 1\}$$

with components

at $q = 2$ $\{X_{11}\}, \{X_{12}\}, \{X_{21}\}, \{X_{22}\}$
at $q = 1, 0$ {all squares}

The four elements of X are now disconnected at $q = 2$; each has top-$q = 2$; and they form a single 1-connected component.

We can see also that the obstruction vectors have ceased to be zero at this slicing level in that, for $K_X(C)$,

$$\hat{Q} = \{3 \ 0 \ 0\}$$

This suggests that 2-connected flow patterns (i.e. change of colour distribution) are obstructed at $\theta \geq 10$. Hence it matters (to the artist) just where the colours are located, at this slicing level.

(4) At a slicing level of $\theta \geq 12$ we obtain:

For $K_C(X)$

$$Q = \{\overset{3}{1} \ 1 \ 1 \ \overset{0}{1}\}$$

with components

at $q = 3$ {C3} $q = 2$ {C3}
at $q = 1$ {C3, C8} $q = 0$ {C3, C4, C6, C8}

Thus the eccentricity of C3 (pale yellow) has increased, with $\hat{q} = 3, \check{q} = 1$.

For $K_X(C)$

$$Q = \{\overset{2}{2} \ 1 \ \overset{0}{1}\}$$

with components

at $q = 2$ $\{\dot{X}_{12}, X_{21}\}$
at $q = 1$ $\{X_{12}, X_{21}\}$
at $q = 0$ {all squares}

Now the only squares with non-zero eccentricities are X_{12} and X_{21}.

4.5 Mondrian picture with card X = 16

Now we look at the painting so that X contains 16 elements (or squares) numbered $X_{11}, \ldots, X_{44}$ as shown in Figure 4.4. Each square contains 16 small checkerboard squares (colour locations).

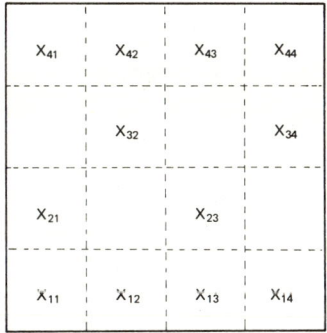

Figure 4.4 Mondrian picture; card X = 16

The corresponding weighted relation $\lambda_3 \subset C \times X$ is the following array.

λ_3	X_{11}	X_{12}	X_{13}	X_{14}	X_{21}	X_{22}	X_{23}	X_{24}	X_{31}	X_{32}	X_{33}	X_{34}	X_{41}	X_{42}	X_{43}	X_{44}
C1	3	1	1	1	2	3	0	1	1	1	1	2	1	0	0	1
C2	2	3	3	4	0	1	0	3	0	2	2	1	0	0	1	7
C3	5	1	3	3	2	4	5	1	1	3	6	5	5	3	6	1
C4	1	4	2	4	2	4	3	3	3	0	4	1	1	2	3	3
C5	0	2	2	0	1	2	0	0	1	2	2	0	0	1	0	0
C6	2	3	2	2	5	1	2	2	5	2	1	3	3	5	4	1
C7	2	0	1	1	1	0	2	1	3	0	0	0	3	1	0	0
C8	1	2	2	1	3	3	4	5	2	6	0	4	3	4	2	3

74 *Mathematical Structure in Human Affairs*

(1) Slicing parameter (by rows) $\theta \geqslant 1$.

$\underline{K_C(X)}$

	C1	C2	C3	C4	C5	C6	C7	C8	
	12	9	12	11	6	12	6	11	C1
		10	10	9	4	10	3	9	C2
			15	14	7	15	8	14	C3
				14	6	14	8	13	C4
					7	7	3	6	C5
						15	8	14	C6
							8	8	C7
								14	C8

with a structure vector

$$Q = \{\overset{15}{1} \ 1 \ 1 \ 1 \ldots 1 \ \overset{0}{1}\}$$

with components

at $q = 15$ {C3, C6}
at $q = 14, 13$ {C3, C4, C6, C8}
at $q = 12, 11$ {C1, C3, C4, C6, C8}
at $q = 10, 9$ {C1, C2, C3, C4, C6, C8}
at $q = 8$ {C1, C2, C3, C4, C7, C8}
at $q = 7, \ldots, 0$ {all colours}

The colours of highest dimension are C3 (pale yellow) and C6 (dark blue); that of lowest dimension is C5 (light blue) with dim C5 = 7. Thus the colour-simplices require a geometrical representation space of at least 15 dimensions. Colours C3 and C6 are identical (maximum) simplices and this simplex ⟨all squares⟩ contains all the other colours as faces; every colour is a polyhedron contained in the 16-vertex polyhedron representing C3 (or C6).

$\underline{K_X(C)}$

X_{11}	X_{12}	X_{13}	X_{14}	X_{21}	X_{22}	X_{23}	X_{24}	X_{31}	X_{32}	X_{33}	X_{34}	X_{41}	X_{42}	X_{43}	X_{44}	
6	5	6	6	5	5	4	6	5	4	4	5	5	4	4	5	X_{11}
	6	6	5	5	6	3	5	5	5	5	5	4	4	4	5	X_{12}
		7	6	6	6	4	6	6	5	5	5	5	5	4	5	X_{13}
			6	5	5	4	6	5	4	4	5	5	4	4	5	X_{14}
				6	5	4	5	6	4	4	4	5	5	3	4	X_{21}
					6	3	5	5	5	5	5	4	4	4	5	X_{22}
						4	4	4	2	4	3	4	3	3	3	X_{23}
							6	5	4	4	5	5	4	4	5	X_{24}
								6	4	4	4	5	5	3	4	X_{31}
									5	4	4	3	3	3	4	X_{32}
										5	4	3	3	3	4	X_{33}
											5	4	4	4	5	X_{34}
												5	4	3	4	X_{41}
													5	3	3	X_{42}
														4	4	X_{43}
															5	X_{44}

This has a structure vector

$$Q = \{\overset{7}{1}\ 1\ 1\ 1\ 1\ 1\ 1\ \overset{0}{1}\}$$

with components

at $q = 7$	$\{X_{13}\}$
at $q = 6$	$\{X_{11}, X_{13}, X_{14}, X_{24}, X_{12}, X_{22}, X_{21}, X_{31}\}$
at $q = 5$	{all except X_{23}, X_{43}}
at $q = 4, 3, 2, 1, 0$	{all squares}

The square X_{13} is therefore the one of highest (maximum) dimension 7; each of the other squares is a face of the X_{13}-simplex. Hence a geometrical representation of $K_X(C)$ can be contained in a 7-dimensional geometrical space.

(2) Slicing at $\theta \geqslant 2$ gives the following Q-analysis.

$K_C(X)$

structure vector

$$Q = \{\overset{12}{1}\ 4\ 3\ 2\ \overset{8}{1}\ 2\ 2\ 1\ \overset{4}{2}\ 1\ 1\ 1\ \overset{0}{1}\}$$

with components

at $q = 12$	{C6}
at $q = 11$	{C3}, {C4}, {C6}, {C8}
at $q = 10$	{C3}, {C4}, {C6, C8}
at $q = 9$	{C3, C6, C8}, {C4}
at $q = 8$	{C3, C4, C6, C8}
at $q = 7$	{C2}, {C3, C4, C6, C8}
at $q = 6$	{C2}, {C3, C4, C6, C8}
at $q = 5$	{C2, C3, C4, C6, C8}
at $q = 4$	{C5}, {C2, C3, C4, C6, C8}
at $q = 3, 2, 1, 0$	{all colours}

The structure vector shows a striking increase in the values of its components and the 4 persistent colours C3, C4, C6, C8 (which we have seen cropping up in the whole analysis so far) are disconnected at $q = 11$. Of these C6 (dark blue) has the highest dimension; each shows non-zero eccentricity; the pairs of extremes being as follows.

Colour	$(\check{q}, \hat{q})$	Colour	$(\check{q}, \hat{q})$
C1	(3, 3)	C5	(3, 4)
C2	(5, 7)	C6	(10, 11)
C3	(9, 11)	C7	(3, 3)
C4	(8, 11)	C8	(10, 11)

With an obstruction vector

$$\hat{Q} = \{3 \; 2 \; 1 \; 0 \; 1 \; 1 \; 0 \; 1 \; 0 \; 0 \; 0 \; 0\}$$

the structure shows a much greater rigidity than at $\theta \geqslant 1$, suggesting that the colour distribution is artistically non-free.

$K_X(C)$

structure vector

$$Q = \{\overset{5}{1} \; 5 \; 3 \; 1 \; 1 \; \overset{0}{1}\}$$

with components

at $q = 5$ $\{X_{13}\}$
at $q = 4$ $\{X_{11}\}, \{X_{12}, X_{13}, X_{32}\}, \{X_{14}\}, \{X_{21}\}, \{X_{23}\}$
at $q = 3$ $\{X_{11}\}, \{X_{22}\}, \{\text{the rest}\}$
at $q = 2, 1, 0$ {all squares}

This shows a significant change in **Q**, as for $K_C(X)$, and the squares with non-zero eccentricities are dominantly along the bottom row of the picture. The obstruction vector has become non-zero, viz.,

$$\hat{Q} = \{\overset{4}{4} \; 2 \; 0 \; 0 \; 0\}$$

as in the conjugate case.

(3) Slicing at $\theta \geqslant 3$ eliminates the colour C5 (light blue) completely and produces the following structure vectors.

For $K_C(X)$:

$$Q = \{\overset{10}{1} \; 1 \; 2 \; 3 \; 4 \; 4 \; 3 \; 2 \; 2 \; 1 \; \overset{0}{1}\}$$

For $K_X(C)$:

$$Q = \{\overset{3}{1} \; 9 \; 1 \; \overset{0}{1}\}$$

The outstanding colour is C3 (pale yellow) and, for example, the three components of $K_C(X)$ at $q = 7$ are $\{C3\}, \{C4\}, \{C8\}$. The other dominant colour C6 has dropped to $q = 6$, where it forms separate components. The 'disconnection' has dropped as low as $q = 2$, the *critical value* of q (at which all the colours form a single component) is now $q = 1$. This means that it is possible to form a chain of connection involving every colour (except C5) and so that each neighbouring pair in that chain share two squares (but not 3 squares). Such a chain is the sequence

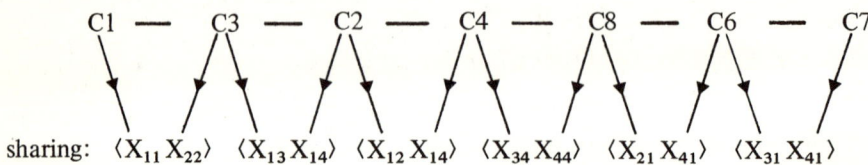

The striking feature of $K_X(C)$ is the increase in Q_2 from 1 (at $\theta \geqslant 2$) to 9 (at $\theta \geqslant 3$). This is a very great increase in the *rigidity of the colour pattern* at the $q = 2$ level (a low level).

(4) Slicing at $\theta \geqslant 4$ eliminates the colours C1, C5, C7 and the square X_{13} (which dominated the complex $K_X(C)$ at $\theta \geqslant 3$). The structure vector became,

For $K_C(X)$:
$$Q = \{\overset{6}{1}\ 1\ 2\ 4\ 4\ 3\ \overset{0}{1}\}$$

For $K_X(C)$:
$$Q = \{\overset{1}{5}\ \overset{0}{1}\}$$

In $K_C(X)$ the critical q-value is now down to 0.

(5) Slicing at $\theta \geqslant 5$ eliminates the colours C1, C4, C5, C7 and the squares X_{12}, X_{13}, X_{14}, X_{22}. The structure vectors become,

For $K_C(X)$:
$$Q = \{\overset{5}{1}\ 1\ 1\ 2\ 3\ \overset{0}{4}\}$$

For $K_X(C)$:
$$Q = \{\overset{0}{4}\}$$

Now we see that, even at the 0-level, both complexes are disconnected; there is no critical value of q (except the formal $q = -1$).

(6) Finally, slicing at $\theta \geqslant 6$ eliminates the colours C1, C4, C5, C6, C7 and all the squares except X_{32}, X_{33}, X_{43}, X_{44}. The structure vectors are now,

For $K_C(X)$:
$$Q = \{\overset{1}{1}\ \overset{0}{3}\}$$

For $K_X(C)$:
$$Q = \{\overset{0}{3}\}$$

The remaining colours are arranged in components in $K_C(X)$ as follows:

at $q = 1$ {C3}

at $q = 0$ {C3}, {C2}, {C8}

whilst, in $K_X(C)$, we obtain

at $q = 0$ {X_{32}}, {X_{33}, X_{43}}, {X_{44}}.

4.6 Mondrian picture with card X = 64

If we finally consider a view of the picture with card X = 64, replacing each of our previous X_{ij} by 4 new squares (each 2 × 2 of the checkerboard

78　*Mathematical Structure in Human Affairs*

squares) then we naturally see the dimensions of the new X_{ij} decrease. Likewise, the dimensions of the colours increase above the optimum situation in the previous section. The new dissection of the painting is shown in Figure 4.5.

X_{51}		X_{83}		X_{85}		X_{87}	
	X_{72}		X_{74}		X_{76}		X_{78}
X_{61}		X_{63}		X_{65}		X_{67}	
	X_{52}		X_{54}		X_{56}		X_{58}
X_{41}		X_{43}		X_{45}		X_{47}	
	X_{32}		X_{34}		X_{36}		X_{38}
X_{21}		X_{23}		X_{25}		X_{27}	
X_{11}	X_{12}		X_{14}		X_{16}		X_{18}

Figure 4.5 Mondrian picture; card $X = 64$

Slicing at $\theta \geqslant 1$ gives the following dimensions for the colours in $K_C(X)$.

dim C1 = 17　　　dim C5 = 11
dim C2 = 23　　　dim C6 = 30
dim C3 = 36　　　dim C7 = 13
dim C4 = 33　　　dim C8 = 30

together with the connectivities below.

C1	C2	C3	C4	C5	C6	C7	C8	
17	6	8	10	2	5	2	8	C1
	23	12	9	5	6	2	11	C2
		36	19	6	12	5	13	C3
			33	5	17	5	10	C4
				11	1	–	4	C5
					30	5	13	C6
						13	5	C7
							30	C8

The structure vector is

$$Q = \{\overset{36}{1}\ \ 1\ \ 1\ \ \overset{33}{2}\ \ 2\ \ 2\ \ \overset{30}{4}\ \ 4\ldots\overset{24}{4}\ \ 5\ldots\overset{20}{5}\ \ 4\ldots\overset{13}{4}\ \ 3\ \ 4\ \ \overset{10}{3}\ldots$$
$$\ldots\overset{7}{3}\ \ 2\ \ 1\ \ 1\ \ 1\ \ 1\ \ \overset{0}{1}\}$$

showing non-zero obstruction at all q-levels from 7 to 33.

Slicing at $\theta \geqslant 2$ produces a drastic change in Q and eliminates a total of 26 squares. The structure vectors are:

for $K_C(X)$:

$$Q = \{\overset{12}{1}\ 1\ 1\ 1\ \overset{8}{2}\ 3\ 3\ 3\ 3\ 3\ 3\ 3\ \overset{0}{3}\}$$

for $K_X(C)$:

$$Q = \{\overset{1}{5}\ 3\}$$

The dominating colours are C3 ($q = 12$), C6 ($q = 8$), and C8 ($q = 7$).

4.7 Forces inherent in a change of view

We can interpret a change of view by representing any one such view in terms of the ring of polynomials discussed in Appendix D. To remind ourselves of the colours we can introduce algebraic variables c_i, $i = 1, \ldots 8$, whence (e.g.) the case of card X = 4 (section 4.4) and the slicing level of $\theta \geqslant 2$ is represented by a pattern polynomial

$$\pi_2 = c_1 c_2 c_3 c_4 c_5 c_6 c_8 + c_1 c_2 c_3 c_4 c_5 c_6 c_7 c_8$$

corresponding to $\quad\quad\quad X_{22} \quad\quad + \text{ the remainder}$

This pattern describes the backcloth (the simplicial complex) at this particular slicing level. It is a graded pattern, being

$$\pi_2 = \pi_2^6 + \pi_2^7$$

If we now change the view, for example by slicing at the level of $\theta \geqslant 10$, then we obtain a new pattern which defines the structure, viz.,

$$\pi_{10} = c_3 c_4 c_6 + c_3 c_4 c_8 + c_3 c_6 c_8 + c_2 c_3 c_4$$

representing $\quad\quad X_{11}\ +\ X_{12}\ +\ X_{21}\ +\ X_{22}$

with a grading $\quad\quad\quad \pi_{10} = \pi_{10}^2$

This change of view of the picture is equivalent to the experience of a change of pattern, viz., $\Delta\pi$ where

$$\Delta\pi = \pi_{10} - \pi_2$$

with grading $\quad\quad \Delta\pi = \pi_{10}^2 - \pi_2^6 - \pi_2^7$

We can interpret this experience as the combination of

> a 7-force of repulsion from X_{11}, X_{12}, X_{21}, together with
>
> a 6-force of repulsion from X_{22}, and
>
> a 2-force of attraction towards each of the four squares X_{ij}.

These forces exist in the complex $K_X(C; \lambda^{-1})$, that is to say, in the abstract geometrical space representing the two relations produced by the slicing. They refer to the 'stresses' which are involved in adjusting one's view of the squares so that, with respect to the set of colours, they change their connectivities from a geometry with the obstruction vector

$$\hat{Q}(\theta \geqslant 2) = \{\overset{7}{0}\ 0\ 0\ 0\ 0\ 0\ 0\ \overset{0}{0}\}$$

to a geometry with obstruction vector

$$\hat{Q}(\theta \geqslant 10) = \{\overset{7}{0}\ 0\ 0\ 0\ 0\ \overset{2}{3}\ 0\ \overset{0}{0}\}$$

Since, at $\theta \geqslant 2$, the squares X_{11} and X_{12} are identical simplices (being the simplex containing all the 8 colours) they must be 7-connected. Thus there is zero obstruction to the shuffling of the colours between these two squares — such a shuffling being a mental image process which might be part of our visual awareness of the picture. The zero obstruction vector expresses this fact. In a similar way, because the square X_{22} is a 6-face of X_{11} these two squares are 6-connected. There is therefore zero obstruction to the (mental) movement of the seven colours in X_{22} and X_{11}. These imaginary movements may themselves be regarded as dynamic patterns on the basic geometry. For example, we might consider the pattern

$$\pi = 3\langle X_{22}\rangle + 4\langle X_{11}\rangle$$

defined on the complex represented by π_2. The numbers 3 and 4 might be weightings, or rankings, which we wish to give to the separate squares (as pieces of the canvas) due to the presence of their colours. Now any change which adjusts these weightings — like, subtracting 2 from the 4 and adding it to the 3 — is a change of pattern, *viz.*,

$$\Delta\pi = +2\langle X_{22}\rangle - 2\langle X_{11}\rangle$$

resulting in the new 'square awareness',

$$\pi = 5\langle X_{22}\rangle + 2\langle X_{11}\rangle$$

This kind of dynamic change, against the static geometry defined by π_2, is free, unobstructed, 'allowed' by the geometry inherent in π_2. Notice, of course, that the dynamic movement involved cannot include any change of awareness with regard to the colour C7, which plays no part in this 6-connection.

If we move to geometry associated with π_{10} we see at once that there is a non-zero obstruction at the level of $q = 2$. This means that the best we can say of the squares X_{ij} is that they are 1-connected; they share pairs of colours; they do not share triples of colours. There cannot therefore be any 'free' colour dynamics between the parts X_{ij} of the picture which involves movements of triples. This kind of pattern change $\Delta\pi$ is obstructed by the inherent geometry — which allows movements of pairs however. It seems then that we must attribute to the artist this very intention of creating geometrical structure, *via* the use of colours on the canvas, which possesses definite properties. The obstruction vector is a measure of those properties: when it is zero the colours are 'fluid' in the sense that they might be anywhere on the canvas. But when it is non-zero then it means that the colour distribution is relatively rigid. In other words we must pay the artist the compliment of assuming that he knew what he was doing, and the complexity of what that was is manifest in a geometrical space of high dimensions.

We have merely indicated fairly obvious ways of carving up the basic shape of the canvas to obtain a selection of views, but the method gives a clear indication of the fact that the total number of possible views, the total number of all the possible geometrical structures which have been built into it by the artist, is a staggering number. Would Mondrian have been intrigued by the thought that every one of these possible views has a unique representation by a mathematical polynomial in a rather specialized algebra?

5 Space is Full of Holes

5.1 Real-space and actual-space

In the broad spectrum of human affairs, particularly during the last 150 years, the physical scientist has come to play an ever-increasing role. So much so that every style of thinker, wishing to claim intellectual respectability, has sought to be 'scientific' in the same way. If the physicist (to use a generic word) convinces himself that the objective world should be described in terms of words like 'electron', 'gravitational field', 'probabilistic laws', etc. then so must the scientific-psychologist or the scientific-sociologist describe his world. But the undoubted triumphs of the physicist-type thinking, which have led us to outstanding technological achievements, are peculiarly anchored in that strange desert of the inanimate world. This has resulted in a great blockage in the mind of the youthful (and very animate) scholar in that his intuition runs away from the thought that, as individual people, we can be adequately described as so many interacting electrons and protons or that we can be bounced around like a handful of dice in some mad gambler's universe. But if there is madness here, which we cannot hope to understand, there is also method, which we must understand whether we wish to nurture it or to retard it.

The thesis of this book is that the heart of the scientific method, and of all rational study of any human activity, lies in the process of identifying sets and of understanding the structural properties of relations between sets. The physicist is dedicated to identifying his sets under controlled conditions so as to eliminate spurious and non-essential phenomena. This naturally involves an interaction between himself and not-himself, between the observer and the observed, and ultimately this means that he must use his physical senses. Nature, in all her infinite goodness, has provided us with a selection of *signals*, or seeing-agents, for just this purpose — what the writer has previously referred to as *base-elements* [2]. And with such a signal the observer explores the world around him, finding his sets and relations.

One would suppose therefore that the first thing our observer had to do was to set about identifying the sets and relations which constitute the idea of *space*, but the history of the subject strongly suggests that this has been heavily glossed over. It is essentially a Newtonian *idea* (rather than an observation) that space is something *a priori,* a sort of thing *wherein objects are found*. We move around and have our being *in space;* we are not a structural part of that thing space. On the other hand it is essentially a Leibnitzian view that our idea of space is a concomitant of the relations between objects. In other words, Leibnitz sought for the meaning of the word 'space' in relations between observed sets (of objects) and not as an unobservable prerequisite for observed sets.

The difference is clearly profound and turns out to be important in the form and content of physical theories about all phenomena set against a backcloth of the thing called 'space'. The Newtonian view, which is probably the orthodox view, results in a phrase like 'the geometry of space' being nothing but a tautology: it only means 'the geometry of geometry' because of the historical fact of the identification of the classical Euclidean geometry with (what was hoped was) the physics (observation-wise) of space. This particular move was initiated by Descartes and when he married the geometry of Euclid to the algebra of the reals $\mathcal{R}$ (the real number system) he gave momentum to a revolution in mathematical and scientific thinking which has lasted for four hundred years. More precisely, he postulated that the space of our physical experience (the so-called real-space) can be identified with the 3-dimensional geometry of Euclid. Furthermore he implied that the symbolism of elementary algebra provided a complete structural framework for that space. This meant that the points of real-space were to be set into a (1–1) 'onto' correspondence with elements of the algebraic structure $\mathcal{R} \oplus \mathcal{R} \oplus \mathcal{R}$; where $\mathcal{R}$ denotes the set of all real numbers and $\oplus$ denotes the algebraic direct sum. Since the backbone of this correspondence lay in the concept of the Pythagorean metric (the assertion of the truth of Pythagoras' theorem amounts to the completion of the rationals by adjoining the irrationals) it amounted to defining the real-space in the following topological-cum-algebraic way.

Real-space is a set of entities called *points* $\{P\}$ together with

(1) a *bijective map* $\rho: \mathcal{R} \times \mathcal{R} \times \mathcal{R} \to \{P\}$, $\mathcal{R}$ denoting the continuum of the real numbers,

(2) the *Pythagorean metric map* $d: \mathcal{R} \times \mathcal{R} \times \mathcal{R} \to \mathcal{R}$, viz.,

$$d(x, y, z) = +\sqrt{(x^2 + y^2 + z^2)}$$

This map ρ then provides an algebraic structure for $\{P\}$ *via* the induced isomorphism $\rho^*: \{P\} \cong \mathcal{R} \oplus \mathcal{R} \oplus \mathcal{R}$, whilst the metric d provides a topological structure $\{P\}$ *via* the natural *metric topology*.

The complete collection of structures on the set $\{P\}$ is what we now mean by Euclidean 3-space and which we denote by E^3. We shall try to avoid confusion by allowing this to be called real-space (because of the role of the real-number system) but by coining the term *actual-space* for what we can observe (by whatever means).

Thus Descartes made the astonishing claim that

actual-space is E^3

and this idea has dominated physical theories to the present day, certainly to the beginning of the twentieth century. With the honourable exceptions of Leibnitz, Hamilton, Cayley, and Clifford, the eighteenth and nineteenth century mathematicians pursued this Cartesian assumption with an uncritical faith which finally killed the revolution and set up its own establishment of reaction; as one would expect. Finally, the facts of physical observations led to the fundamental rethinking of, on the one hand, Einstein's relativity theory and, on the other hand, Quantum theory.

But the Pythagoreans knew that irrational numbers – as predicted by Pythagoras' theorem – are not observable quantities. The latter are rational numbers (or the *ratio* of integers) only; $\sqrt{2}$ is not a number of the form p/q, p, q positive integers (without common factors). Why was this piece of ancient Greek knowledge the only piece which the scientists chose to ignore?

The argument that the physicist cannot measure, say $\sqrt{2}$, in the laboratory is countered, at the elementary level, by saying that it is possible to construct an isosceles right-angled triangle with equal sides of length 1. Then, by *Pythagoras' theorem*, the hypoteneuse *must be* of length $\sqrt{2} = \sqrt{(1^2 + 1^2)}$. But this clearly begs the question since Pythagoras' theorem can only be appealed to in actual-space if some successful measuring process has already established its validity. If the hypoteneuse is actually measured by the same devices as are used to measure the other two sides then the result will not be $\sqrt{2}$ – in the sense that the mathematician understands that symbol.

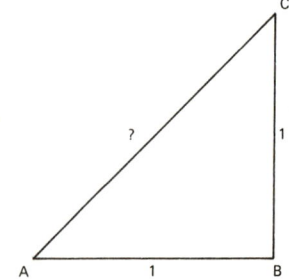

Figure 5.1 The Pythagorean dilemma

Admittedly the measurement of AC in Figure 5.1 by progressively sophisticated rulers might give the rational numbers 14/10, 141/100, 1414/1000, etc., but the 'etc.', is only a *finite set* of rationals.

As the ancient Greeks well-knew, AC in actual-space (in the physical laboratory) is a rational number. Hence Pythagoras' theorem cannot be regarded as a law of (observable) nature.

In mathematics (of a certain specified kind) the assertion of Pythagoras' theorem is permissible; it is part of a theoretical abstract structure. But in physics the assertion of *Pythagoras' Law* is not permissible.

But of course it is very tempting to 'save the day' by pointing out that the act of measurement of the length AC at least gives us an approximate value and that, for *all practical purposes,* the degree of approximation is perfectly adequate: we can 'get as close as we need to' in measuring AC. So why not accept this approximation argument and use the reals $\mathcal{R}$ in our description of nature?

Although this might well do for measuring bits of string and sealing wax we know, to our cost, that the necessary pursuit of fine detail in physical observation has led us to abandon the reals for measurements at the atomic level. Thus no physicist would claim today that there is any point in contemplating an atomic energy level with value $h\sqrt{2}$, h being the rational number known as Planck's constant. There are many fundamental observations in which we must now assert the paramountcy of the rationals (actually, the integers) and the irrelevancy of the irrationals.

But, in addition to this, the idea that a rational number q is 'close to' an irrational number ψ is itself dependent on the fundamental topological assumptions of the space $\{P\}$, v. Hu [34]. The Cartesian postulate has conditioned our minds to think in terms of the metric topology induced by the Pythagorean law — we might refer to it as the *Pythagorean topology* of the set $\{P\}$. Thus 'near to' means 'sharing a Pythagorean open set' in the metric topology on $\{P\}$. But if our actual-space consists of an observation of the points $\{P\}$ in it then if we assume the Pythagorean topology we must admit that between our rational q and irrational ψ there exists (for observation purposes) an infinity of points $\{P\}$, however 'near' they are.

What if we observed points in a plane by instruments which allowed us to see only infinite strips (of varying width) parallel to the y-axis? Then the topology would no longer be Pythagorean (based as that is on the observation of circular discs) but would be an example of what is called a non-Hausdorff topology. Now points P_1, P_2 are 'near' to each other if they share an observable strip. All points P_i on the same 'vertical' line are equally near to each other; they are 'coincident'.

Thus 'nearness' is not only a topological (mathematical) concept but is also deeply embedded in the process of observation. What kind of topology, of nearness, would we ascribe to real-space if we observed it by touch, or by probing it with feather dusters? And if we altered the topology in some such way would we find any significant role for the number system to play?

In fact *our physics is a light-based physics;* all our observations are subject to the light signal; we *see* the actual-space, literally. All our sophisticated instruments use the light signal for the final transmission of information to the observer. Thus the topology of actual-space must be determined by the relation between our sensory organs and the light signal. It has been shown (see e.g. Zeeman [54]) that we only educate ourselves into the Pythagorean topology, and however convenient it might be for us all to be conditioned in the same way, we must admit that the metric topology is not a fundamental *a priori* absolute of the actual-space.

In the laboratory (by which I mean to include the world of everyday experience) an observation of actual-space must be the observation of 'real' things, of objects, of particles. We must therefore adopt, as the foundation of physics, the Leibnitzian view that *actual-space is the set of relationships between objects;* we cannot take as fundamental the Newtonian-Galileian view that *actual-space is absolute and real objects are observed in it*. The latter view is unrealistic as a description of the *physics* of space, however fascinating it might be as a point of philosophic discussion.

An observer who sets out to identify sets of things he wishes to call geometrical points (or points of actual-space) must do it by relating one such point to another, and each point is an actual-object 'place' observed (or *seen)* by the aid of a signal. This idea, which is Leibnitzian in its implications, is surely the idea behind all that well-known talk about 'measuring rods', 'clocks', and 'light signals' which endless popular discussions of relativity theory have already made familiar. When our observer collects up his measuring rods and light signals and goes out into the desert to observe his geometry of space, he does not in fact observe the Cartesian E^3 with its Pythagorean metric and its continuum of the real numbers. On the contrary, he obtains a *discrete mesh of points* packed together, more or less closely, according to the set of rods he possesses and the particular pair of spectacles he is wearing. In any event he obtains a *finite set* of things he will call points; perhaps if he is so inclined he might allow himself the luxury of supposing that the set is potentially infinite (if he is potentially infinite) but even then his idealized set will be *countable,* there will not be more than there are integers in the set J.

In the midst of our observer's expedition, as he is busy connecting up his points by laying out an elaborate mesh of rods, he suddenly comes to a large boulder – being a scientist he calls it an object, not a point. Now this object can only be mapped by identifying points on its surface; the light signal enables him to notice the coincidence of points at the ends of the measuring rods and points on the boulder's surface. This restriction is a property of the light-signal-plus-rods, we say that the light signal cannot penetrate the object, the 'interior' of the object is opaque to the signal, there is no observable interior for this boulder. But this means that the object has the effect of creating a large *hole* in the mesh of points which we could have constructed if the boulder were not there. Every such object that we can observe in our actual-space can therefore be regarded as a hole in some structure which the *signal enables us to identify.* Such an interpretation is strongly suggestive of the idea of non-bounding *homological cycles* (*v*. Appendix C) in a *simplicial complex* whose vertices are the points of the mesh.

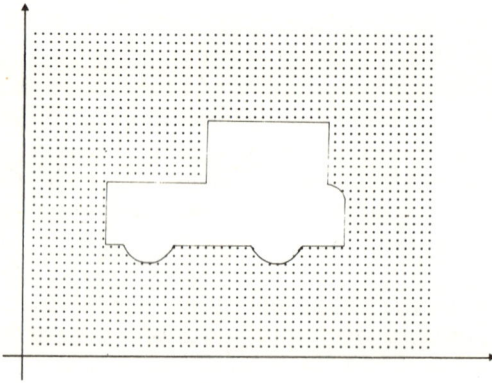

Figure 5.2 Each object is a hole in actual-space

Naturally enough, if the signal changes then the holes change, the objects change. What is opaque to one signal need not be to another. As observers we seem to be able to combine the observations of objects in different actual-spaces, that is to say, in actual-spaces which are observed by different signals. Thus we know that the window-pane is not an object for the light signal (we say it is transparent) but it is an object for the touch-signal. But the housefly seems unable to reconcile these two different views of the window-pane and appears to persist in believing that the glass is a not-object. In like manner we have learned that the X-ray signal extends our actual-space mesh of points further than the light-signal and nuclear physicists assure us that the neutrino-signal cannot even 'see' the earth as an object but goes straight through it as if it were not there — as indeed it is not, for the neutrino-signal actual-space mesh of points!

The idea that we can allow the concept of actual-space to be a part of a physical theory based on identifying (finite) sets and relations between them extends the thinking that began with Einstein relativity — where the significance of the light signal was first built into a mathematical theory. But now we must allow for the signal being varied and able to give a *characteristic homological structure* to the *physical objects* it can 'see' (or allow us to see) in its own actual-space mesh. In any particular pattern of observations there will therefore be a peculiar set of phenomena A (peculiar to the signal, or base-element) which will identify the points of the mesh {P} together with a specific relation λ which expresses the structure of the mesh points (modulo A). Hence we have the structure

$$\lambda \subset A \times P$$

and

$$K_A(P; \lambda); \quad K_P(A; \lambda^{-1})$$

as basic to this signal-oriented actual-space; objects (observed by this signal) being identified as *generators* of non-bounding *homological cycles* in $K_A(P; \lambda)$.

The idea that the physical universe is in some sense rigid and unchangeable is an expression of the attempt to believe that $K_A(P; \lambda)$ is quite independent of the observer and a characteristic of the base-element (say) ξ_0. On the other hand we have seen that, in a social context, structures exist which can presumably be free to change 'from the inside', since people can create new vertices and destroy old ones. Also we have so far been primarily concerned with the local structure of the 'social' complexes $K_Y(X; \lambda)$ not with this apparently cruder global idea of homological cycle.

But an emphasis on the cycle, for observations in physics, as opposed to the chains of connectivity, must surely be a reflection of the exclusive concern of the base-element ξ_0 for the objects *qua* objects. Then presumably if an object is to be seen as a p-cycle by ξ_0, p must be a function of ξ_0. If we change the nature of the signal we shall possibly change the nature of the object; a 2-cycle object might become a 3-cycle object, and this must have profound effects on any mathematical theories which relate to the objects.

5.2 The idea of the cocycle law

So the process of observing an actual-space goes something like the following.

(1) Select a base-element (seeing-agent) ξ_0.
(2) Take a basic set of objects (such as the ends of some measuring-rods-kit) and map out a mesh of actual-space points, in the light of ξ_0.
(3) The process under (2) creates a relation $\lambda(\xi_0)$ between a set of phenomena A and a set of things called mesh points P.
(4) The homological structure $H_.(K_A(P); J)$ of $K_A(P; \lambda)$, or $H_.(K_P(A); J)$ of $K_P(A; \lambda^{-1})$, now contains the totality

(actual-space) ∪ (all observed objects)

(5) Every object can be identified with a non-bounding p-cycle, Z_p, in $K_A(P; \lambda)$ for a suitable value of p.

Firstly, we notice the role which is now played by the theorem, due to Dowker [20], that the two homological structures mentioned above are *isomorphic*; $H_.\{K_A(P); J\} \cong H_.\{K_P(A); J\}$.

Secondly, it now follows that if we wish to begin to build up a physics around properties of the objects seen by ξ_0 we normally, and traditionally, map these properties into a number system. Since the properties so observed (like mass, speed, charge, length, etc.) are clearly manifest in actual-space *via* the objects themselves, such a physics amounts to setting up a *cohomology structure* for the *conventional measurements* of the properties. Since we are also asserting that 'counting' is the only sort of measurement which is reliable the coefficient group for the cocycle groups must be taken as the integers J, or some subset of (say) ℜ which is isomorphic to J. For example,

mass of *object* equals *number*

describes the cocyle mapping

$$z^p : z_p \to J$$

where z_p is the p-cycle in $K_A(P)$ which represents the object as seen by ξ_0, and the word 'number' means an integral number of some arbitrary unit — this integral number being in J.

We therefore expect *mathematical theories of bodies in actual-space* to be expressed in a *cohomology theory* and that every observable (which the physicist claims to be of significance in his theory) *must be* expressed in a *cocycle law*

$$\delta z^p = 0$$

for a suitable value of p.

If, furthermore, we attempt to set up *observables attributed to individual points* P in our actual-space then we are in effect shifting from the complex $K_A(P; \lambda)$ to its conjugate $K_P(A; \lambda^{-1})$. But in $K_P(A; \lambda^{-1})$ every point P is a simplex and therefore its boundary is a cycle (trivially). It follows that associating an observable with a single point (such as is involved in the traditional thinking of 'particle' or 'field theory') contains the possibility of its expression as a trivial cocycle (a cobounding cocycle) *via*

$$\delta z^p = 0$$

because

$$z^p = \delta c^{p-1}$$

This c^{p-1} is a cochain defined on the $(p-1)$-face of the p-simplex representing the point P in $K_P(A; \lambda^{-1})$; z^p is the coboundary of this c^{p-1}, under an appropriate operator δ. Such a situation is to be found as a constant theme running through modern theoretical physics, from the apparently 'elementary' macrophysics of the text-books to theories based on differential equations, relativity formulations, and quantum mechanics.

We shall illustrate these instances in the subsequent sections but prior to this we can make the following general points.

In building a mathematical physics on what we might call 'point-theories' we are committing ourselves to the trivial cocycle law and possibly to missing the significance of the global structure of $K_P(A; \lambda^{-1})$. If this structure (of non-bounding homological cycles) intrudes into our observational system then we shall be obliged to introduce special laws (properties of our pseudo-point-objects) to account for it.

We shall also need to construct a convenient mathematical frame-work to carry the observational *simplex structure* of each point P in $K_P(A; \lambda^{-1})$. This can mean that formally the coboundary operator δ is a function of each choice of P, and sometimes not. Generally we shall see that the simplest kind of representative mathematical structure which can carry the simplex and also contain the formalism needed to define $H.(P; J)$ is one based on an *exterior algebra (v.* [13] and Appendix C). This most naturally contains the possibility of orientation, desirable for the set-up of the boundary and coboundary operators ∂ and δ.

We can illustrate this observational simplex structure at a point P in the following way. Suppose the mesh points P of actual-space are identified by the phenomena of flashing lights (ξ_0) and that conditions of the observations are such that neighbouring pairs $\langle P_i P_j \rangle$ are observable, each such pair corresponding to an element in the set A. Then our conventional 3-space

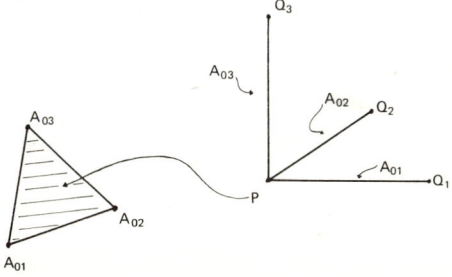

Figure 5.3 P is a simplex in $K_P(A; \lambda^{-1})$

corresponds to $K_P(A; \lambda^{-1})$ in which each point P is related to 3 A's, say A_{01}, A_{02}, A_{03}, as shown in Figure 5.3. This makes P a 2-simplex in $K_P(A)$ and the edges of this 2-simplex must play the role of the 1-face on which some c^{p-1} is to be defined. The conventional axes of co-ordinates at the point P are a *geometric* representation of this 1-face, of these A_{01}, A_{02}, A_{03}. Representing them, further, by the *algebraic* symbols u_1, u_2, u_3 (called vectors) and forming the exterior products

$$u_1 \wedge u_2 \quad u_2 \wedge u_3 \quad u_3 \wedge u_1 \quad u_1 \wedge u_2 \wedge u_3$$

now provides us with all the simplicial complex structure needed to formally derive $H_p = \ker \partial / \operatorname{im} \partial$.

5.3 The cocycle law in macrophysics

It has been argued in a recent research paper [2] that the natural laws for macrophysics can all be encompassed within the idea of a bilinear (1-1) correspondence over an algebraic division ring F. In its historical associations with projective geometry such a bilinear relation is called an homography [42], and when it is symmetrical it is known as an *involution*.

An important example of such a homography is provided by a non-metrical formulation of Special Relativity theory. If point-particles are ascribed a co-ordinate called *velocity*, say, in an assigned direction, and if we contemplate two possible observers measuring the velocity of a single particle (ξ_0 being the light signal), then the Theory is based on two assumptions. The first is that if observer S attributes a velocity v (ϵ F) to the particle then observer S' attributes a *unique* velocity v' (ϵ F) to the same particle. The second is that when S attributes a velocity V to S' then $v = v'$ if and only if $v = v' = c$, where c is the velocity that either attributes to the light signal ξ_0. This is all contained in a postulated homography, say

$$Avv' + Bv + Cv' + D = 0 \qquad 5.3(1)$$

with A, B, C, D, 0 ϵ F.

Since we know two pairs (v, v') in this relation, viz., $(V, 0)$ and $(0, -V)$, 5.3(1) becomes

$$Avv' + C(v' - v) + CV = 0 \qquad 5.3(2)$$

Now the characteristic feature of the theory, the second assumption, supposes that a *double point* of 5.3(2) is provided by

$$v = v' = c$$

whence we obtain

$$Vvv' + c^2(v - v') - c^2 V = 0 \qquad 5.3(3)$$

and this constitutes the kinematics of Special Relativity Theory. It is certainly worthy of note that the assumption that $c \to \infty$ reduces 5.3(3) to

$$v' - v + V = 0$$

which is the kinematics of Galileo-Newton.

Making 5.3(3) homogenous by the substitution $v = x/t$, $v' = x'/t'$ gives us
$$Vxx' + c^2(xt' - x't) - c^2Vtt' = 0$$
which is also
$$x'(Vx - c^2t) + ct'(cx - cVt) = 0 \qquad 5.3(4)$$

Since each observer can choose his co-ordinates in a selfish and arbitrary manner we must suppose from 5.3(4) that there exists a separation constant β, independent of v, v' (but not necessarily of V, c) such that
$$\beta(ct - \frac{Vx}{c}) = ct'$$
and
$$\beta(x - Vt) = x'$$
It is usual to introduce the 4-vector $\mathbf{r} = (x\ y\ z\ ct)$ whence
$$\mathbf{r'} = \mathbf{Lr} \qquad 5.3(5)$$
where L is the matrix operator
$$\mathbf{L} = \mathbf{L}(V) = \begin{pmatrix} \beta & 0 & 0 & -\beta V/c \\ 0 & 1 & 0 & 0 \\ 0 & 0 & 1 & 0 \\ -\beta V/c & 0 & 0 & \beta \end{pmatrix}$$
Since we expect the roles of S and S' to be interchanged when V is replaced by $-V$ we can take
$$\mathbf{L}^{-1} \equiv \mathbf{L}(-V)$$
so that
$$\mathbf{L}(-V)\mathbf{L}(V) = \mathbf{I}_4$$
which gives
$$\beta^2(1 - V^2/c^2) = 1 \qquad 5.3(6)$$
This condition, which is derived without any appeal to a metric or a pseudo-metric, ensures that 5.3(5) represents the usual Lorentz-Einstein transformations.

Another important homography expresses the scalar gravitational (or electrostatic) potential energy in its relation to the radial distance r. If the potential energy is denoted by V the homography is simply
$$Vr + \mu = 0 \qquad 5.3(7)$$
where μ is some constant in F (usually F is taken as $\mathfrak{R}$). This homography is equivalent to the inverse square law of force.

If we take the general form of the homography, over F, as
$$axy + bx + cy + d = 0$$

and re-write the symbols x, y as the ratios $x/t, y/s$ respectively — so as to make the form homogeneous — we obtain the basic equation

$$axy + bxs + cyt + dst = 0 \qquad 5.3(8)$$

This is characterized by the 2 × 2 matrix M,

$$M = \begin{pmatrix} a & b \\ c & d \end{pmatrix}$$

since 5.3(8) is a scalar condition on a 2-dimensional vector space $V(F)$. That is to say, 5.3(8) is the condition

$$X M Y^T = 0 \qquad 5.3(9)$$

where X is the vector $(x\ t)$ in V and Y is the vector $(y\ s)$ in V, Y^T denoting the transpose vector $\begin{pmatrix} y \\ s \end{pmatrix}$. The condition for 5.3(8) to be non-degenerate is now det $M \neq 0$, which is $ad - bc \neq 0$.

We can now associate the homography 5.3(8) with the exterior product space

$$\Lambda V_2 = \Lambda^0 V_2 + \Lambda^1 V_2 + \Lambda^2 V_2$$

in which $\Lambda^0 V_2 = F$.

If V_2 is spanned by the basic vectors

$$\mathbf{u}_1 = (0\ 1) \text{ and } \mathbf{u}_2 = (1\ 0)$$

then, since $\Lambda^1 V_2 = V_2$, $\Lambda^2 V_2$ is a 1-dimensional vector space spanned by the basis vector $\mathbf{u}_1 \wedge \mathbf{u}_2$. The elements of $\Lambda^2 V_2$ are *pseudoscalars* and so we may regard the symbol 0 (zero) in 5.3(8) as a member of $\Lambda^2 V_2$. We can then express the homography 5.3(8) as a 1-cocycle statement in a cohomology theory obtained by identifying the boundary operators δ_0, δ_1 in the sequence:

$$\Lambda^0 V_2 \xrightarrow{\delta_0} \Lambda^1 V_2 \xrightarrow{\delta_1} \Lambda^2 V_2$$

with $\delta_1 \cdot \delta_0 = 0$ (nilpotency).

We do this defining a matrix $\overset{+}{M}$ by

$$M \overset{+}{M} = (\det M) \begin{pmatrix} 0 & -1 \\ 1 & 0 \end{pmatrix}$$

so that $\overset{+}{M}$ 'sees' the space ΛV_2 from 'the other end', the matrix $\begin{pmatrix} 0 & -1 \\ 1 & 0 \end{pmatrix}$ being a representation of the basis $\mathbf{u}_1 \wedge \mathbf{u}_2$ of $\Lambda^2 V_2$.

This gives $\overset{+}{M} = \begin{pmatrix} -b & -d \\ a & c \end{pmatrix}$, and we then define $\delta_1 \equiv \delta_1^X$ by putting

$$\delta_1^X = (\overset{+}{M} X^T) \wedge$$

the homography 5.3(8) is then the result of operating on the vector Y ($\epsilon \Lambda^1 V_2$) with this wedge operator $\delta_1{}^X$, viz.,

$$\delta_1{}^X Y \equiv (\overset{+}{M} X^T) \wedge Y = 0$$

Defining $\quad \delta_0 \equiv \delta_0{}^X \quad$ by $\quad \delta_0{}^X : k \to k\,(\overset{+}{M}\,X^T)$

where $k \in F \;(\equiv \Lambda^0 V_2)$, ensures the nilpotent condition.

We can now see that the homography 5.3(8) says:

> *given a vector* X, *the corresponding vector* Y *is such that* Y *is a 1-cocycle in the cohomology on* ΛV_2.

Furthermore it is not difficult to show that if the homography is non-degenerate then the cohomology is trivial, and conversely. Thus the idea of a natural law as a non-degenerate homography is equivalent to finding a 1-cocycle which is also a 1-coboundary.

This is the statement of the cocycle law in the macrophysics governed by the homography.

We notice here, as mentioned in the previous section, that the coboundary operators (δ_0 and δ_1) are functions of X (of the selection of the point P in the complex $K_P(A; \lambda^{-1})$ — which here corresponds to the 1-simplex $\langle A_{0x}, A_{0t} \rangle$ identifying this vector X).

5.4 The cocycle law in classical mechanics

The classical mechanics governed by Hamilton's canonical equations was first expressed in the form of the cocycle law, in 1815, by Pfaff *via* his first differential form [53]. If the classical system is defined by the n independent co-ordinates $q_1, q_2, \ldots q_n$ and the conjugate momenta $p_1, p_2, \ldots p_n$, then the system of Hamiltonian equations which describe the dynamical motions are

$$\frac{dp_r}{dt} = -\frac{\partial H}{\partial q_r} \quad (r = 1, \ldots n) \qquad 5.4(1)$$

$$\frac{dq_r}{dt} = +\frac{\partial H}{\partial p_r}$$

t being the time co-ordinate and $H(q, p, t)$ being the Hamiltonian of the system. [35]

The cohomology is set up at a mesh point P in terms of the exterior derivative on the graded wedge space ΛV_{2n+1}, where V_{2n+1} is spanned by the basis $\{dq_1 \ldots dq_n, dp_1 \ldots dp_n, dt\}$. In other words the classical equations 5.4(1) are equivalent to the cocycle law expressed *via* the De Rham cohomology (*v.* Appendix C); of course, classically the mesh points form a continuum and this is expressed in terms of the limiting notions involved in defining the differentials. To obtain 5.4(1) we take the differential 1-form $\theta^1 \in \Lambda^1 V_{2n+1}$, viz.,

$$\theta^1 = p_1\,dq_1 + \ldots + p_n\,dq_n - H dt$$

and assert the cocycle law

$$\delta\theta^1 = 0 \qquad 5.4(2)$$

where δ is the exterior derivative. This gives the statement

$$\delta\theta^1 = \theta^2 = \sum_{j=1}^{n}\sum_{i=1}^{n}\left(\frac{\partial p_i}{\partial g_j} - \frac{\partial p_j}{\partial q_i}\right) dq_j \wedge dq_i + \sum_{j=1}^{n}\sum_{i=1}^{n}\frac{\partial p_i}{\partial p_j} dp_j \wedge dq_i$$

$$+ \sum_{i=1}^{n}\frac{\partial p_i}{\partial t} dt \wedge dq_i - \left(\sum_{i=1}^{n}\frac{\partial H}{\partial q_i} dq_i + \frac{\partial H}{\partial p_i} dp_i\right) \wedge dt$$

$$- \frac{\partial H}{\partial t} dt \wedge dt$$

$$= 0 \in \Lambda^2 V$$

Since the p's and the q's are treated as independent variables in V_{2n+1} it follows that $\partial p_i / \partial q_j = 0$ (for all i, j) and since also

$$\frac{\partial p_i}{\partial p_j} = \delta_j^i \text{ and } \frac{\partial p_i}{\partial t} = \frac{dp_i}{dt}$$

we obtain

$$\sum_{i=1}^{n}\{dp_i \wedge dq_i + \frac{dp_i}{dt} dt \wedge dq_i + \frac{\partial H}{\partial q_i} dt \wedge dq_i - \frac{\partial H}{\partial p_i} dp_i \wedge dt\}$$

$$= 0, \ \epsilon \Lambda^2 V$$

This means that

$$\frac{dp_i}{dt} = -\frac{\partial H}{\partial q_i} \qquad i = 1, \ldots n$$

and

$$\frac{dq_i}{dt} = +\frac{\partial H}{\partial p_i} \qquad i = 1, \ldots n$$

which is the set 5.4(1).

We expect, furthermore, that the classical point-object (at the mesh point P) results in the trivial cohomology. If we also assert therefore that θ^1 is also a coboundary we must demand the existence of a function $W(q, p, t) \in \Lambda^0 V$ such that

$$\theta^1 \equiv \delta W$$

This requires that

$$\left(\sum_{i=1}^{n} p_i \, dq_i\right) - H dt \equiv \sum_{i=1}^{n}\left(\frac{\partial W}{\partial q_i} dq_i + \frac{\partial W}{\partial p_i} dp_i\right) + \frac{\partial W}{\partial t} dt$$

so that
$$p_i = \frac{\partial W}{\partial q_i}, \quad i = 1, \ldots n$$

$$0 = \frac{\partial W}{\partial p_i}, \quad i = 1, \ldots n$$

and
$$H + \frac{\partial W}{\partial t} = 0.$$

The second of these conditions means that W is a function of $q_1, \ldots q_n, t$ only. It is usual then to write the third condition as

$$H\{q_i, \frac{\partial W}{\partial q_i}, t\} + \frac{\partial W}{\partial t} = 0 \qquad 5.4(3)$$

and this is the well-known Hamilton-Jacobi equation of classical dynamics.

This derivation illustrates the fact that Hamiltonian dynamics is a theory expressed in terms of the cocycle law in a trivial cohomology — due to the association of the observable co-ordinates with a single mesh point P in the complex $K_P(A; \lambda^{-1})$.

5.5 The cocycle law in Maxwell field theory

As in the case of classical mechanics, but more recently, the Maxwell equations of the electromagnetic field can be seen as a statement of the cocycle law [26]. If we introduce the electric and magnetic field vectors **E, B, H, D** these equations are normally written as follows:

$$\text{curl } \mathbf{E} = -\frac{1}{c}\frac{\partial}{\partial t}\mathbf{B}, \qquad \text{div } \mathbf{B} = 0 \qquad 5.5(1)$$

$$\text{curl } \mathbf{H} = \frac{4\pi}{c}\mathbf{J} + \frac{1}{c}\frac{\partial \mathbf{D}}{\partial t}, \qquad \text{div } \mathbf{D} = 4\pi\rho \qquad 5.5(2)$$

$$\text{div } \mathbf{J} + \frac{\partial \rho}{\partial t} = 0 \qquad 5.5(3)$$

$$\mathbf{E} = \text{grad } A_0 - \frac{1}{c}\frac{\partial \mathbf{A}}{\partial t}, \qquad \mathbf{B} = \text{curl } \mathbf{A} \qquad 5.5(4)$$

where **J** is the current density vector,

ρ is the static charge density,

A_0 is the electrostatic scalar potential,

and $\mathbf{A} = (A_1, A_2, A_3)$ is the magnetic vector potential

These observables are referred to a 4-dimensional space at any point P of the mesh, the four variables being the Euclidean spatial x_1, x_2, x_3 whilst the fourth variable is $x_4 = ct$, c being the velocity of the light signal and t being a time co-ordinate. Again we obtain equations 5.5(1) to 5.5(4) as expressions of a cocycle law in a trivial De Rham cohomology over ΛV where V is spanned by $\{dx_1, dx_2, dx_3, dx_4\}$.

Firstly, we introduce the 2-cocycle θ^2 and 3-cocycle θ^3 defined by

$$\theta^2 = E_1\, dx_1 \wedge dx_4 + E_2\, dx_2 \wedge dx_4 + E_3\, dx_3 \wedge dx_4$$
$$+ B_1\, dx_2 \wedge dx_3 + B_2\, dx_3 \wedge dx_1 + B_3\, dx_1 \wedge dx_2$$

and

$$\theta^3 = \frac{4\pi}{c} \{J_1\, dx_2 \wedge dx_3 \wedge dx_4 + J_2\, dx_3 \wedge dx_4 \wedge dx_1$$
$$+ J_3\, dx_4\, dx_1\, dx_2 - \rho\, dx_1 \wedge dx_2 \wedge dx_3\}$$

If we now assert that θ^2 is a cocycle, so that $\delta\theta^2 = 0$, δ denoting the exterior derivative, we obtain the equations 5.5(1). Similarly the assertion that θ^3 is a 3-cocycle, so that $\delta\theta^3 = 0$, gives us the equation 5.5(3). If we also demand that θ^2 should be a coboundary then there must exist a $\theta^1 \in \Lambda^1 V$ such that

$$\theta^2 = \delta\theta^1 \qquad \qquad 5.5(5)$$

This can be identified as the 1-cochain

$$\theta^1 = A_1\, dx_1 + A_2\, dx_2 + A_3\, dx_3 + A_0\, dx_4$$

whence 5.5(5) is equivalent to the set 5.5(4). Demanding also that θ^3 should be a coboundary requires us to identify a 2-cochain, say, ϕ^2 such that

$$\theta^3 = \delta\phi^2. \qquad \qquad 5.5(6)$$

This is provided by the 2-cochain

$$\phi^2 = H_1\, dx_1 \wedge dx_4 + H_2\, dx_2 \wedge dx_4 + H_3\, dx_3 \wedge dx_4$$
$$- D_1\, dx_2 \wedge dx_3 - D_2\, dx_3 \wedge dx_1 - D_3\, dx_1 \wedge dx_2$$

The condition 5.5(6) now provides the set of equations 5.5(2), the whole trivial cohomology being provided in the following scheme.

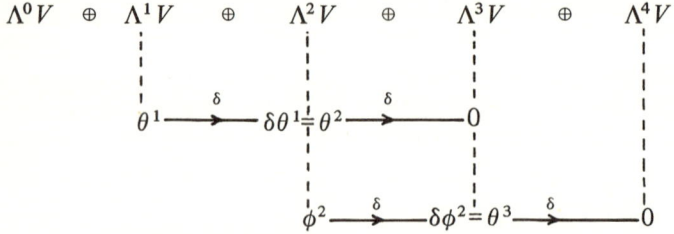

The relation between the De Rham differential forms and the simplex representation of the point P in $K_P(A; \lambda^{-1})$ is illustrated in Figures 5.4 and 5.5.

Space is Full of Holes 97

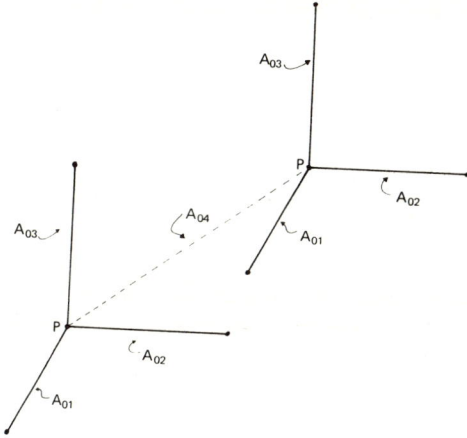

Figure 5.4 The mesh point P related to $\{A_{0i}\}$

In Figure 5.4 we see the mesh point P related to the phenomena $A_{0i} \in A$ (*via* base element ξ_0); the dotted line A_{04} represents the observation of time interval at the (geometrical) point P. These phenomena A_{01}, A_{02}, A_{03}, A_{04} form the vertices of the P-simplex (a 3-simplex) in the conjugate complex $K_P(A; \lambda^{-1})$ shown in Figure 5.5.

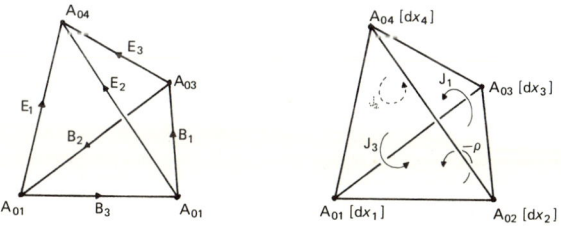

Figure 5.5 Mesh point P as 3-simplex $\langle A_{01}, A_{02}, A_{03}, A_{04} \rangle$

In Figure 5.5 we see how the various cocycles (θ^2 and θ^3) are defined on the faces of the simplex in $K_P(A; \lambda^{-1})$. The exterior product space ΛV, where $V = \{dx_1, dx_2, dx_3, dx_4\}$, is a sufficient mathematical model of the oriented simplex with vertices A_{0i} (or dx_i). The characteristic antisymmetric product of ΛV, for example $dx_1 \wedge dx_2 = -dx_2 \wedge dx_1$, provides the orientation on the P-simplex. The cocycle θ^2 is a cochain (of *order 2 in the De Rham theory* but of *order 1 on the P-simplex*) on the *edges* of $\langle A_{01}, A_{02}, A_{03}, A_{04} \rangle$. The cocyle θ^3 is a cochain (of *order 3 in the De Rham theory* but of *order 2 on $K_P(A; \lambda^{-1})$*) defined on the 2-faces of the P-simplex. This difference in order is not of substantive significance, being a feature of the mathematical model only.

98 Mathematical Structure in Human Affairs

We notice that our discussion emphasises that the key equations in the Maxwell set are 5.5(1) and 5.5(3), not 5.5(1) and 5.5(2) as conventionally assumed. Thus it selects the observational basis of the theory as the *field vectors* E and B together with the 'substance' vector J and scalar charge ρ.

5.6   The transition to quantum theory

Quantum theory begins with the requirement that *action* (energy × time) *must be quantized*. This means that action must take values nh, where h is a universal constant (Planck's constant) and n is a positive integer. This means, in its turn, that if action is to be a cocycle then it is a mapping with values in J — since the subset of $\mathcal{R}$ consisting of numbers nh can be regarded as isomorphic to J.

Since classical mechanics is normally formulated in the continuum of the reals $\mathcal{R}$, *via* the cocycle θ^1 of section 5.4, it was historically a dilemma for physicists to preserve $\mathcal{R}$ and yet restrict values to the discrete and countable set J. It was achieved in an intriguing way by replacing $\mathcal{R}$ by the complex domain $\mathbf{C}$ and an argument which we can express in the following cohomological manner.

Firstly, we notice that the classical dynamics is based on the trivial cohomology and therefore expressed, as we have seen, by the Hamilton-Jacobi equation

$$H\{q_i, \frac{\partial W}{\partial q_i}, t\} = -\frac{\partial W}{\partial t}$$

where $W(q_i, t)$ is a scalar function in $\Lambda^0 V$. This means that, because of the trivial cohomology, the variables p_i and H act as the operators $\partial/\partial q_i$ and $-\partial/\partial t$ on this function W. We therefore write this Hamilton-Jacobi equation in the operator form

$$HW = -\frac{\partial W}{\partial t}$$

where H is now the formal $H\{q_i, \partial/\partial q_i, t\}$. Thus we can say that there is a *Hamiltonian operator H* which is *cohomologous* to $-\partial/\partial t$, as well as a *momentum operator* p_i cohomologous to $\partial/\partial q_i$.

Now we extend the field $\mathcal{R}$ to the complex plane $\mathbf{C}$ and suppose that W is now a function defined on variables which are in $\mathbf{C}$. To avoid confusion we replace the symbol W by the symbol Ψ, and this is to become known as the wave function of the system. But before we can claim to have properly arrived at the historical point of the formulation of quantum mechanics (or wave mechanics) we must build in the characteristic integral values for the action.

Since our Hamilton-Jacobi equation is now written as

$$H\{q_i, \frac{\partial}{\partial q_i}, t\} \Psi = -\frac{\partial}{\partial t} \Psi \qquad 5.6(1)$$

and all the variables are in $\mathbb{C}$, we notice that values of action (action is a quantity like $H\,dt$) would be values of the contour integral

$$\int_\Gamma H\,dt = -\int_\Gamma d\Psi/\Psi$$

where Γ is a closed contour enclosing the origin in the Ψ-plane. But the contour integral

$$\int_\Gamma d\Psi/\Psi = 2\pi i \quad (i^2 = -1)$$

and since the value of

$$\int_\Gamma H\,dt$$

must equal h we can introduce the factor $h/2\pi i$ into 5.6(1) and rewrite it as

$$H\left\{q_i, \frac{h}{2\pi i}\frac{\partial}{\partial q_i}, t\right\}\Psi = -\frac{h}{2\pi i}\frac{\partial}{\partial t}\Psi \qquad 5.6(2)$$

where we now say that, in quantum theory, the *classical variables* p_i and H are *cohomologous* to

$$\frac{h}{2\pi i}\frac{\partial}{\partial q_i} \quad \text{and} \quad -\frac{h}{2\pi i}\frac{\partial}{\partial t}$$

respectively. This ensures the quantized condition provided the theory of the cocycle θ^1 is extended from a De Rham cohomology with $\Lambda^0 V = \mathfrak{R}$ to one with $\Lambda^0 V = \mathbb{C}$.

Equation 5.6(2), with this understanding, is what began as the *Schrödinger wave equation*. The somewhat strange requirement that old-fashioned classical variables should be replaced by certain differential operators is not so strange when we view it from the point of view of cohomology. Thus Schrödinger's equation 5.6(2) expresses the same trivial cohomology, over $\Lambda V(\mathbb{C})$, as does the Hamilton-Jacobi equation over $\Lambda V(\mathfrak{R})$. As a differential equation 5.6(2) is separable and Ψ can be written as $\Psi = \Psi(q)\exp(-[2\pi i/h]\,Et)$ where E, the separation constant, becomes the energy value of H and the equation becomes

$$H\Psi = E\Psi \qquad 5.6(3)$$

giving the stationary states of the system. The countable eigen-functions $\{\Psi_n\}$ of this equation may be regarded as providing a complete set of 0-cochains, in $\Lambda^0 V(\mathbb{C})$, such that $\theta^1 = d\Psi_n$.

5.7 Quantum theory and special relativity

If p_1, p_2, p_3 are the non-relativistic classical momenta of a single particle at the point $P(x, y, z)$ in orthodox real-space E^3, it is not difficult to show from the Lorentz-Einstein transformations of section 5.3 that the 4-vector representing momentum must be

$$\{\beta_0 p_1, \beta_0 p_2, \beta_0 p_3, \beta_0 mc\}$$

where, the particle possessing velocity components v_1, v_2, v_3,

$$\beta_0^2 \{1 - (v_1^2 + v_2^2 + v_3^2)/c^2\} = 1$$

This would suggest that, with $x_1 = x, x_2 = y, x_3 = z, x_4 = ct$, the classical 1-cocycle

$$\theta^1 = p_1 \, dx_1 + p_2 \, dx_2 + p_3 \, dx_3 - \frac{H}{c} \, dx_4$$

should be replaced by the relativistic 1-cocycle

$$\theta^1 = \beta_0 p_1 \, dx_1 + \beta_0 p_2 \, dx_2 + \beta_0 p_3 \, dx_3 - \beta_0 mc \, dx_4$$

to obtain relativistic mechanics. From the point of view of our cohomological view of physics we would expect that θ^1 and ϕ^1 should be cohomologous, since we do not expect the relativistic view to create or destroy actual objects in our actual-space.

Demanding that θ^1 and ϕ^1 be cohomologous therefore requires that they differ, at the worst, by $d\theta^0$ where $\theta^0 \equiv \theta^0(x_1, x_2, x_3, x_4) \in \Lambda^0 V(\mathcal{R})$. Thus, in general, we could require

$$\beta_0 p_i = p_i + \frac{\partial \theta^0}{\partial x_i} \quad \text{and} \quad \beta_0 mc = \frac{H}{c} + \frac{\partial \theta^0}{\partial x_4}$$

It is therefore a sufficient condition for $\theta^1 \sim \phi^1$ that

$$H = \beta_0 mc^2 \qquad 5.7(1)$$

and this is the accepted expression for the relativistic Hamiltonian, in the absence of a potential field. Writing $p_4 = mc$ (m is here the rest mass) we can express 5.7(1) as

$$H = c \{p_1^2 + p_2^2 + p_3^2 + p_4^2\}^{1/2} \qquad 5.7(2)$$

and this is the form which will presumably allow us to rewrite the Hamilton-Jacobi equation in a relativistically significant form. The result of so doing is to produce the Dirac equation [18],

$$H\Psi = E\Psi \qquad 5.7(3)$$

where Ψ is a 4-vector and H is a linear operator expressed in a Clifford algebra with a basis of 16 dimensions. Precisely,

$$\frac{H}{c} = p_1 \alpha_1 + p_2 \alpha_2 + p_3 \alpha_3 + p_4 \alpha_4$$

where

$$\alpha_1^2 = \alpha_2^2 = \alpha_3^2 = \alpha_4^2 = 1$$

and
$$\alpha_r \alpha_s + \alpha_s \alpha_r = 0, \quad r \neq s$$

and the Clifford algebra $\mathbb{C}$ is formed over a vector space $V(\mathbb{C})$ spanned by $\alpha_1, \alpha_2, \alpha_3, \alpha_4$.

It is relevant here to note that the Dirac equations 5.7(3) are not, strictly speaking, a rewrite of the Schrödinger wave equation. The latter is a statement to the effect that θ^1 is a 1-coboundary in $\Lambda V(\mathbb{C})$ and the *Dirac equations are a condition on* $\{p_1, p_2, p_3, p_4, E/c\}$ *to ensure that* θ^1 *and* ϕ^1 *describe the same cohomology*.

The Clifford algebra can be seen as equivalent to a certain exterior algebra, by noticing that $u_1 = \alpha_1 + i\alpha_2$ and $u_2 = \alpha_3 + i\alpha_4$ act as elements in a ΛV_2, since $u_1^2 = u_2^2 = 0$ and $u_1 u_2 = -u_2 u_1$. Similarly, for $v_1 = \alpha_1 - i\alpha_2$ and $v_2 = \alpha_3 - i\alpha_4$, which are the complex conjugates of u_1 and u_2. We therefore suppose that $\{u_1, u_2\}$ (or $\{v_1, v_2\}$) span a 2-dimensional vector space $V_2(\mathbb{C})$ and form the exterior product space

$$\Lambda V_2 = \Lambda^0 V_2 \oplus \Lambda^1 V_2 \oplus \Lambda^2 V_2$$

The members of ΛV_2 are to be called *spinors* (v. [12]) and are defined in association with so-called isotropic vectors (that is, vectors of zero norm) in E^N. In this case the isotropic vectors E^5 are those whose components are $p_1, p_2, p_3, p_4, E/c$ and such that

$$\mathbf{X}^2 \equiv \left(\frac{E}{c}\right)^2 + p_1^2 + p_2^2 + p_3^2 + p_4^2 = 0 \qquad 5.7(4)$$

With this condition 5.7(4) we obtain a *nilpotent* operator $M(\mathbf{X})$ such that the spinors of ΛV_2 lie in the kernel of $M(\mathbf{X})$. The operator $M(\mathbf{X})$ is given by

$$M(\mathbf{X}) = \begin{pmatrix} E/c & 0 & p_3 + ip_4 & p_1 - ip_2 \\ 0 & E/c & p_1 + ip_2 & -p_3 + ip_4 \\ p_3 - ip_4 & p_1 - ip_2 & -E/c & 0 \\ p_1 + ip_2 & -p_3 - ip_4 & 0 & -E/c \end{pmatrix}$$

and, since $M^2 = 0$, this defines a cohomology on the sequence

$$\Lambda V_2 \xrightarrow{M} \Lambda V_2 \xrightarrow{M} \Lambda V_2$$

Again we see that, given $\mathbf{X} = \{p_1, p_2, p_3, p_4, E/c\}$ at a mesh point P, we obtain a coboundary operator specific to P, viz., $M(\mathbf{X})$, and that the Dirac equations 5.7(3) are equivalent to the cocycle law

$$M(\mathbf{X}) \phi = 0 \qquad 5.7(5)$$

where $\phi = \{\phi_0, \phi_1, \phi_2, \phi_3\}$

and where
$$\phi_0 \in \Lambda^0 V_2 (\mathbb{C})$$
$$\phi_1, \phi_2 \in \Lambda^1 V_2 (\mathbb{C})$$
$$\phi_3 \in \Lambda^2 V_2 (\mathbb{C})$$

The ϕ's can be seen as linear combinations of the Dirac ψ's (v. [12]).

The Dirac equations 5.7(3) exhibit the property of intrinsic spin for the particle under consideration, specifically the value of spin ½, where the unit is taken as $h/2\pi$. Particles of spin 0 are associated with the *Klein-Gordon equation*, viz.,

$$\frac{h^2}{4\pi^2}\left(\frac{\partial^2}{\partial x_1^2} + \frac{\partial^2}{\partial x_2^2} + \frac{\partial^2}{\partial x_3^2} - \frac{\partial^2}{\partial x_4^2}\right)\Psi = m^2 c^2 \Psi \qquad 5.7(6)$$

and may be seen as the equation obtained from 5.7(2) by squaring and making the transformations

$$p_i \to \frac{h}{2\pi i}\frac{\partial}{\partial x_i} \quad i = 1, 2, 3$$

$$\frac{E}{c} \to -\frac{h}{2\pi i}\frac{\partial}{\partial x_4}$$

It is not surprising that each component of the Dirac 4-vector ψ satisfies 5.7(6). We see too that the Klein-Gordon equation is equivalent to the assertion that the classical θ^1 and the relativistic ϕ^1 (modified to incorporate the quantization condition) describe cohomologous cocycles.

5.8 The direct use of the cocycle law by Bohr

We can find in the theory propounded by Niels Bohr [9] a direct appreciation of the homological (or topological) nature of the problems posed by quantization. He obtained a remarkably effective theory of the hydrogen atom by regarding the motion of the electron around the nucleus as a circular orbit under the Coulomb law and, in addition, postulating the quantization of the orbital angular momentum (which is 'action'). The circular orbit is shown in Figure 5.6, where q is the angular co-ordinate, mv is the tangential (linear) momentum, r is the radius of the circle, and e is the numerical value of the electron (or proton) charge.

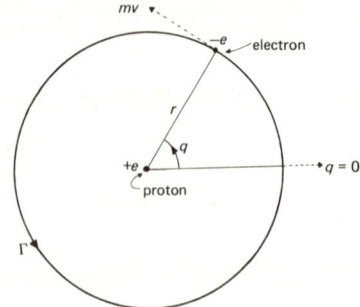

Figure 5.6 The Bohr picture of the H-atom

The Bohr theory argued in classical mechanical terms as follows. The electrostatic Coulomb energy is $-e^2/r$ and because the motion is circular the Coulomb attraction to the centre must be equal to mv^2/r so that

$$\frac{mv^2}{r} = \frac{e^2}{r^2}$$

Since $v = r\dot{q}$ ($\dot{q}$ means dq/dt) this gives

$$mr\dot{q}^2 = \frac{e^2}{r^2}$$

Also the angular momentum is instantaneously given by

$$p = mvr$$

which gives

$$p = mr^2\dot{q},$$

and this is a constant of the motion. He now introduced a *quantization postulate* to the effect that the total angular momentum in the orbit must be nh where n is a positive integer and h is Planck's constant. This he expressed in the form

$$\int_\Gamma p\, dq = nh \qquad 5.8(1)$$

Since p is constant this gives

$$p \int_0^{2\pi} dq = 2\pi p = nh$$

and then

$$p = mr^2\dot{q} = \frac{nh}{2\pi}$$

gives us, with the previous equations,

$$r = \frac{n^2 h^2}{4\pi^2 me^2}$$

and

$$E = \text{energy} = -\frac{2\pi^2 me^4}{n^2 h^2} \qquad n = 1, 2, \ldots$$

We see from the above that the crucial point of the argument lies in what we might call the *Bohr condition*, 5.8(1). This asserts that the *hydrogen atom is effectively a hole in space* (a hole in Descarte's E^2) and that the circle Γ is the edge of that hole. Associated with that 1-cycle (which is what Γ really is) is a thing called angular momentum denoted by a symbol p. The observable angular momentum is therefore a 1-cocycle with integral values (in J) on this 1-cycle.

The expression of this fact is the Bohr condition 5.8(1) since

$$(z_1, z^1) = \int_{z_1} z^1 = \int_\Gamma p\, dq = nh$$

This Bohr picture of the H-atom was therefore an attempt to go straight to the homological hub of the problem, it was not an attempt to set up a mathematical structure (like ΛV) to simulate the complex at a point P of the continuum E^3. We can therefore see the Bohr theory as a recognition of the apparent fact that when we try to look at a hydrogen atom by means of our usual base elements ξ_0 we only succeed in seeing a structured complex with

$$H_0 \cong J \text{ because of arc-wise connectedness}$$

and

$$H_1 \cong J \text{ because of the cycle } \Gamma.$$

A weakness of the Bohr theory must surely lie in the restriction of the discussion to a 1-hole in E^2. Presumably the H-atom must exist in the physicist's E^3, if it is in any E^N. But that would suggest that we can only know that the atom is in E^3 if we see it as a 2-hole as well. Perhaps then we might consider an extension of the Bohr intuition to the following:

(1) the hydrogen atom exhibits properties compatible with an actual-space whose homology is (at least)
$$H_0 \cong J;\ H_1 \cong J;\ H_2 \cong J$$

(2) the orbital angular momentum is a 1-cocycle defined on the generator (Γ) of H_1 by
$$\int_\Gamma z^1 = nh$$

(3) there will be an observable quantity, which is the counterpart to orbital angular momentum, which will be represented by a 2-cocycle z^2 with integral values (mh) on the generator (z_2) of H_2. If we call this z^2 the *spin* (because it is a quantizable action) its basic (smallest) value is its value on z_2 (which is the unit sphere). Hence we get this smallest value as $\hat{z}^2$ where

$$\int_{z_2} \hat{z}^2 = \hat{z}^2 \ \{\text{surface area of unit sphere}\}$$
$$= \hat{z}^2 \cdot 4\pi$$
$$= h$$

Hence the unit of 'spin' must be $\tfrac{1}{2} \cdot \dfrac{h}{2\pi}$.

6 Urban Structure

6.1 Multi-dimensional town

If we look at a conventional map of a town it is very natural for us to take it as a serious representation of the physical backcloth of the community. By 'serious' we mean to imply that it contains the essential substance and structure of the town. After all, the map is a detailed description of the land-use — which can include a great deal of information about the social and economic activities associated with the buildings, the plots of land, and the road system of communications. But the reader will not now be surprised if we emphasize, as a point of criticism, that the representation is (only) a two-dimensional picture. Admittedly, of course, it is not difficult to include with the map a mental image of the town which is 3-dimensional — allowing for the heights of buildings and the contours of the earth's surface. Trying to make the most of this elementary geometrical view of an urban area led the pioneers of the Chicago school of social scientists, men like Park, Burgess, and McKenzie, to experiment with 2-dimensional circular zones as a means of describing the urban structure vis-à-vis population densities. Such beginnings of what was to be called the *ecological view* of an urban community, embracing ultimately the geographical, sociological, psychological, and economic factors inherent in the structure, were already a sign of the research for an overall *structural* view of the community. The essence of the problems facing research workers in this field is discussed in an illuminating way in a recent book by B. T. Robson [44]. The fact that the general ecological view of an urban area is inevitably a mass of mathematical relations, being recognized, has not always been helpful, because of the obvious complexity of the problem. But even so, it has been recognized, and in various areas of mathematical social science has resulted in the emergence of research which has made use of networks (or graph theories). In the purely sociological field, for example, this kind of analysis is well illustrated in the work of Abell [1], Barnes [8], Flament [25], and McGinnis [40], a useful discussion in this field is provided in Doreian's book on the mathematics of social relations [19]. In the field of physical and human geography an important contribution has been made by Haggett; see, for example, his use of network ideas in recent books [27, 28].

In the light of the discussion in this book it should be clear that interpreting a mathematical relation $\lambda \subset Y \times X$ in terms of a network (or linear graph) amounts to taking the 1-*dimensional skeleton* of the complexes $K_Y(X; \lambda)$ and $K_X(Y; \lambda^{-1})$. The result is that the maximum connectivity which is comprehensible is that of zero order, $q = 0$. If we wish to interpret the relevant

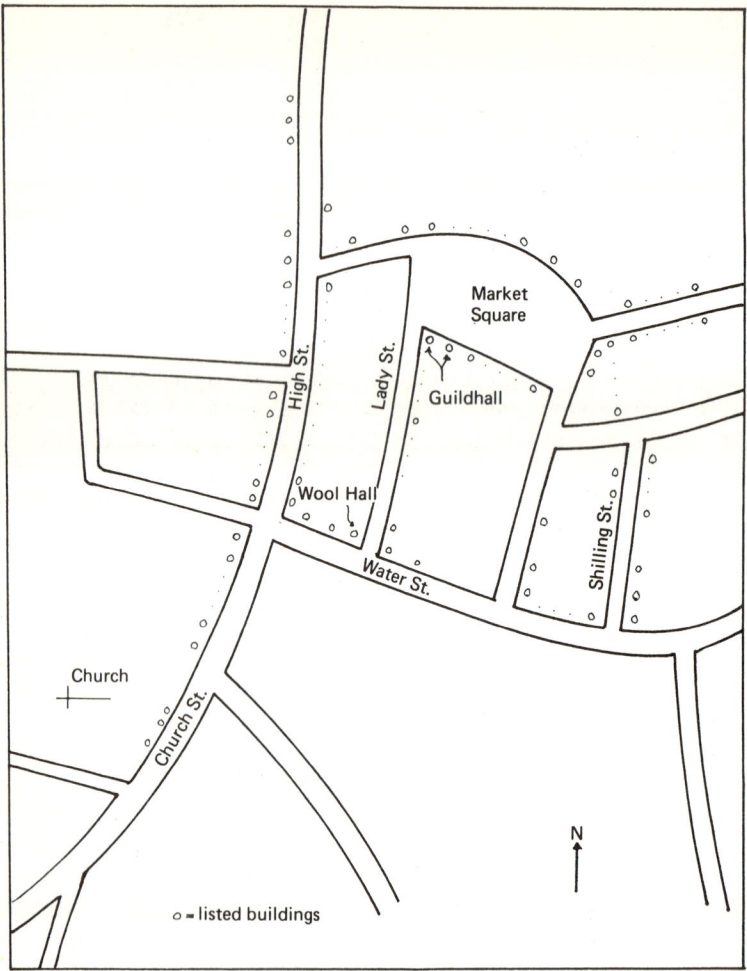

Figure 6.1 The centre of Lavenham, West Suffolk

mathematical relations in the multi-dimensional spaces occupied by the complexes $K_Y(X; \lambda)$ and $K_X(Y; \lambda^{-1})$ then naturally we must be prepared to see the town, the urban community, as a *dynamic structure* in a multi-dimensional space. More precisely, it will be many such structures corresponding to the many relations λ and the many sets X and Y. The *functioning* of the town, its life and fever, must be grasped by obtaining an understanding of the interaction of those relations, their dependence and influence one upon the other. When we then return to the town map and see it as a network of lines joining points we must be able to see the points (the network nodes) as collapsed simplices (of various orders) and the lines as collapsed chains of q-connection (for various values of q). Also, of course, there will be many complexes which never appear on the town map representation; they refer to intangibles in the life of the community or to non-static physical entities which cannot be frozen into a

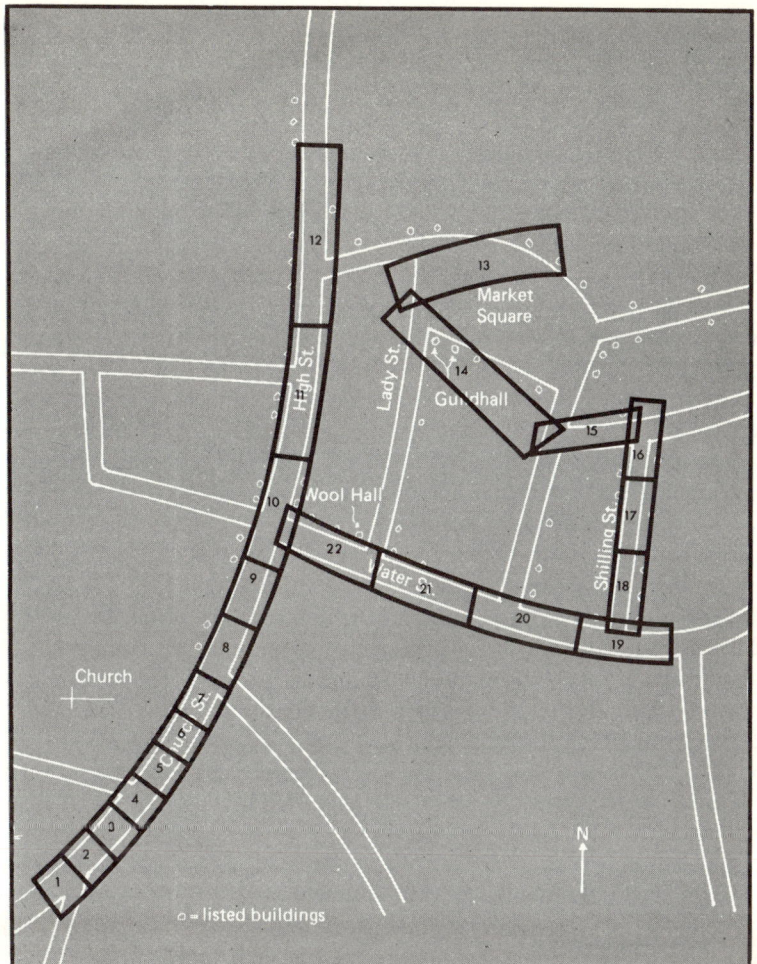

Figure 6.2 Cover-set for Lavenham

2-dimensional network. But nevertheless such complexes form a significant part of the life of the town, preserving the town, or destroying — none of these things can be adequately described by drawing red lines on the 2-dimensional town map. Thinking otherwise can be equivalent to letting a small boy repair the TV set with a big bag of nails and a bright shiny hammer.

6.2 A Tudor village in Q-space

Before we can know enough about a town to do our shopping there, or to direct strangers down the wrong street, we obtain a first impression — a *visual* impression — of its buildings and streets, as we come to it and move through it. This impression gives us an immediate feeling for the town; it might in fact be

108 Mathematical Structure in Human Affairs

so favourable in its impact as to cause a visiting motorist to consider seriously the possibility of parking his car. It is one of the intangible relations which we keep with us as a memory long after the mere things we might have bought there have crumbled away.

In the counties of East Anglia (England) there are many surviving buildings from the prosperous days of the wool trade of the Middle Ages. A small town which more than any other exemplifies this survivial is Lavenham, in West Suffolk. Its buildings, both residential and official, are predominantly Tudor; naturally its biggest problem is the ever-present anxiety as to whether its character can survive the twentieth century traffic. The visual impact of Lavenham lies in the sight of Tudor plaster and beams and the strangely non-Euclidean shapes which result from the battle between these and the gravitational pull of the earth. The core of this visual image is contained in a set of 'listed buildings' (listed, that is, by the responsible civic authorities of West Suffolk) — which are mostly Tudor but which contain some Georgian, some just mongrel-ancient, and many of them of a functional historic significance; for example, the fine church, the Guildhall (Moot Hall) in the Market Square, or the Wool Hall (now part of the Swan Inn). Some idea of the distribution of these listed buildings is given by the sketch map reproduced in Figure 6.1. The analysis which we shall consider in this section is based on a choice of one-hundred listed buildings and whether they can be seen from any one of twenty-two possible locations — on a typical journey round the town. These locations, or pieces of area, are indicated in Figure 6.2. The relation between these 'lozenges' (a word which roughly describes the shapes of the areas) and the listed buildings, that is to say, a relation λ between sets L = {lozenges} and B = {buildings}, can then be represented in the usual mathematical way, using an incidence matrix.

We propose therefore to consider the complexes $K_L(B; \lambda)$ and $K_B(L; \lambda^{-1})$ corresponding to this relation $\lambda \subset L \times B$ and, from this point of view, obtain an interpretation of the connectivity pattern of the *visual-image complex* for Lavenham. The listed buildings are numbered B1 to B100 and the lozenge-areas L1 to L22. The Q-analyses, given below, were produced on the PDP-10 computer at the University of Essex using a program 'Q5 BA' written in BASYS.

The Q-analysis of $K_L(B; \lambda)$, the listed buildings being the vertex set and the lozenges L_i being represented by simplices, is as follows.

$K_L(B, \lambda)$

q-value	q-connected components	value of Q_q
18	{L10}	1
17	{L10}	1
16	{L10}	1
15	{L10}	1
14	{L10}, {L14}	2

Urban Structure 109

q-value	q-connected components	value of Q_q
13	{L10}, {L14}	2
12	{L10}, {L14}	2
11	{L10}, {L11}, {L13}, {L14}, {L19}	5
10	{L10}, {L11}, {L13, L14}, {L19}	4
9	{L10}, {L11}, {L13, L14}, {L19}	4
8	{L8}, {L10}, {L11}, {L13, L14}, {L19}	5
7	{L8}, {L10, L11}, {L12}, {L13, L14}, {L19}, {L22}	6
6	{L8}, {L10, L11}, {L12}, {L13, L14}, {L19}, {L21}, {L22}	7
5	{L6}, {L8}, {L9}, {L10, L11}, {L22}, {L13, L14}, {L19}, {L21}, {L22}	9
4	{L5}, {L6}, {L8}, {L9}, {L10, L11}, {L12}, {L23, L14}, {L16}, {L19}, {L20}, {L21}, {L22}	12
3	{L5, L6}, {L8}, {L9}, {L10, L11, L21}, {L12}, {L13, L14}, {L16}, {L17}, {L19}, {L20}, {L22}	11
2	{L3}, {L5, L6, L7}, {L8}, {L9}, {L10, L11, L21, L22}, {L12}, {L13, L14}, {L26}, {L17}, {L18}, {L19, L20}	11
1	{L2, L3, L4, L5, L6, L7, L8, L9, L10, L11, L12, L21, L22} {L13, L14}, {L15}, {L16}, {L17, L18}, {L19, L20}	6
0	{all}	1

We notice that the structure vector is

$$Q = \{\overset{18}{1}\ 1\ 1\ 1\ \overset{14}{2}\ 2\ 2\ \overset{11}{5}\ 4\ 4\ 5\ \overset{7}{6}\ 7\ 9\ \overset{4}{12}\ 11\ 11\ 6\ \overset{0}{1}\}$$

with a consequent obstruction vector

$$\hat{Q} = \{\overset{14}{1}\ 1\ 1\ 4\ 3\ 3\ 4\ \overset{7}{5}\ 6\ 8\ 11\ 10\ 10\ 5\ \overset{0}{0}\}$$

The lozenge L10 is the largest simplex, of dimension 18. Figure 6.3 shows the visual record of this 18-simplex. This geographical point in Lavenham (the junction of Church Street and Water Street) is therefore the optimal point for an experience of the visual Tudor-image of the town.

The next highest lozenge is L14, which is along one side of the Market Square. This contains the many fine Tudor buildings in the square, including the large and well-preserved Guildhall. At $q = 11$ we find the lozenges L11, L13, L19 coming into the structure and forming, with the initial L10 and L14, five separate 11-connected components. The details of Figure 6.2 show that these five components encompass the heart of the town. The lozenges L13, L14 are the first simplices to be connected (at $q = 10$), which is probably not surprising since they border the Market Square. The simplex L19 is shown in Figure 6.4; this is a view along the sequence L19, L20, L21, L22, being the sequence of our journey round the town.

Figure 6.3 A visual 18-simplex
Figure 6.4 A visual 11-simplex

Figure 6.5 A visual 5-simplex
Figure 6.6 A visual 8-simplex

112 *Mathematical Structure in Human Affairs*

A typical low $\hat{q}$-value occurs with L5, coming into the structure at $q = 4$; as a visual feature it is shown in Figure 6.5; this is a view down the hill in Church Street, towards the High Street (which begins at L10). By comparison, as we approach closer to the centre, L8 is an intermediate 8-simplex, and is shown in Figure 6.6. The *pairs of extremes* for each lozenge are listed as follows:

Simplex	$(\check{q}, \hat{q})$
L1	(0, 0)
L2	(1, 1)
L3	(1, 2)
L4	(1, 1)
L5	(3, 4)
L6	(3, 5)
L7	(2, 2)
L8	(1, 8)
L9	(1, 5)
L10	(7, 18)
L11	(7, 11)
L12	(1, 7)
L13	(10, 11)
L14	(10, 14)
L15	(0, 1)
L16	(0, 4)
L17	(1, 3)
L18	(1, 2)
L19	(2, 11)
L20	(2, 4)
L21	(3, 6)
L22	(2, 7)

This list shows that $(\hat{q} - \check{q})$ is greatest for L10 (value is 11) with L19 (value is 9) and L8 (value is 7) following closely behind. The high value for the eccentricity of L10 suggests that this location presents us with a characteristic view of Lavenham which is unique and outstanding, although L8 and L19 give strong visual support. In fact, only four out of the twenty-two lozenges possess zero eccentricity, viz., L1, L2, L4, and L7. Each of these four simplices is associated with the entrance to the town, down Church Street and, as it happens, down a hill turning into the centre.

The high values of Q_q, and consequently the high values of the components of the obstruction vector $\hat{Q}$, show that a journey through Lavenham is full of surprises; the view-simplices being disconnected to a very large degree down to the value of $q = 1$. The vector $\hat{Q}$ can therefore be regarded as a measure of the town's visual-image rigidity, at various q-values. It is therefore necessary to move completely round the town in order to fully experience the visual images. The component values of $\hat{Q}$ could be reduced greatly by knocking down some of the listed buildings, for example, the Swan Inn in lozenges L10 and L22. Removing this building (which is actually about three of our listed buildings) would immediately connect the simplices L9, L10, L11, L21, L20, L19, L14, L13, L15 at values of q greater than $q = 1$. Consequently it would produce a drop in the component values of $\hat{Q}$; the obstruction to a free view of Lavenham, from any geographical point, would be greatly reduced. Such a macabre suggestion, as the destruction of the Swan Inn, illustrates forcibly the role of the obstruction vector as a characteristic measure of the connectivity pattern of this visual-image complex.

The high values of the components of $\mathbf{Q}$, particularly at the low-q end, also helps to account for the characteristic non-zero eccentricities of most of the simplices. As we have seen, once we are down the hill in Church Street all the simplices possess non-zero eccentricities. This means, yet again, that each lozenge-view must be experienced if Lavenham is to be experienced. In some sense therefore, the eccentricities of the simplices contain in them an overall 'feel' of the visual-image complex. This sense can probably be interpreted by an induced mathematical relation μ which is derived in the following way.

Since the values of $\check{q}$ range from 0 to 10 and those of $\hat{q}$ range from 0 to 18 we can regard the actual pairs of extremes as the members of a relation $\mu_0 \subset Y \times X$, where $Y = \{0, 1, \ldots, 10\}$ and $X = \{0, 1, \ldots, 18\}$. The symbol μ can then be reserved for the weighted relation which represents the number of occurrences of the actual 'co ordinates' $(\check{q}, \hat{q})$ in $K_L(B; \lambda)$. This μ is represented in Figure 6.7 and its associated matrix is given by M.

M	X_0	X_1	X_2	X_3	X_4	X_5	X_6	X_7	X_8	X_{11}	X_{14}	X_{18}
Y_0	1	1	0	0	1	0	0	0	0	0	0	0
Y_1	0	2	2	1	0	1	0	0	1	0	0	0
Y_2	0	0	1	0	1	0	0	1	0	1	0	0
Y_3	0	0	0	0	1	1	1	0	0	0	0	0
Y_7	0	0	0	0	0	0	0	0	0	1	0	1
Y_{10}	0	0	0	0	0	0	0	0	0	1	1	0

If we slice this weighted relation μ at $\theta \geq 1$ (for all rows or columns) we obtain the following Q-analysis for the two complexes contained in

M	X
Y	(μ_{ij})

114 Mathematical Structure in Human Affairs

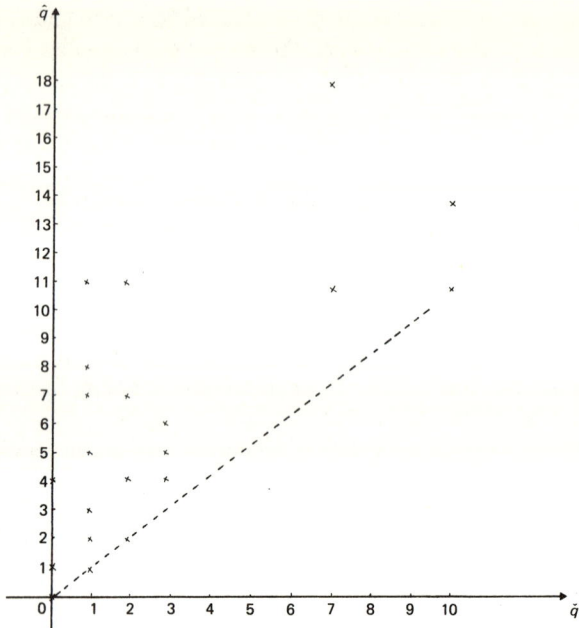

Figure 6.7 Eccentric relation for $K_L(B; \lambda)$

For $K_Y(X; \mu)$:

Y_0	Y_1	Y_2	Y_3	Y_7	Y_{10}	
2	0	–	0	–	–	Y_0
	4	0	0	–	–	Y_1
		3	0	0	–	Y_2
			2	–	–	Y_3
				1	0	Y_7
					1	Y_{10}

with the following components:

at $q = 4$ $\{Y_1\}$
at $q = 3$ $\{Y_1\}, \{Y_2\}$
at $q = 2$ $\{Y_0\}, \{Y_1\}, \{Y_2\}, \{Y_3\}$
at $q = 1$ $\{Y_0\}, \{Y_1\}, \{Y_2\}, \{Y_3\}, \{Y_7\}, \{Y_{10}\}$
at $q = 0$ {all}

For $K_X(Y; \mu^{-1})$:

X_0	X_1	X_2	X_3	X_4	X_5	X_6	X_7	X_8	X_{11}	X_{14}	X_{18}	
0	0	–	–	0	–	–	–	–	–	–		X_0
	1	0	0	–	0	–	–	0	–	–	–	X_1
		1	0	–	0	–	–	0	–	–	–	X_2
			0	–	0	–	–	0	–	–	–	X_3
				2	0	0	0	–	–	–	–	X_4
					1	0	–	0	–	–	–	X_5
						0	–	–	–	–	–	X_6
							0	–	0	–	–	X_7
								0	–	–	–	X_8
									2	0	0	X_{11}
										0	–	X_{14}
											0	X_{18}

with the following components:

at $q = 2$ $\{X_4\}, \{X_{11}\}$
at $q = 1$ $\{X_1\}, \{X_2\}, \{X_4\}, \{X_5\}, \{X_{11}\}$
at $q = 0$ $\{all\}$

The structure vector for $K_{\tilde{q}}(\hat{q}; \mu)$ is therefore

$$Q = \{\overset{0}{1}\ 2\ 4\ 6\ \overset{0}{1}\} \qquad 6.2(1)$$

and for $K_{\hat{q}}(\check{q}; \mu^{-1})$ it is

$$Q = \{\overset{2}{2}\ 5\ 1\} \qquad 6.2(2)$$

The interpretation of 6.2(1) gives us an overall view of the *connections between the connections* in the original $K_L(B; \lambda)$. The one $\{Y_1\}$, at $q = 4$, means that there is one 4-simplex of lozenge which possess a bottom-q value of $\check{q} = 1$. This 4-simplex is actually $\langle X_1, X_2, X_3, X_5, X_8 \rangle$, in other words, it is the 5-vertex polyhedron defined by the top-q values of $\hat{q} = 1, 2, 3, 5, 8$. The new component $\{Y_2\}$, at $q = 3$, is a 3-simplex of lozenges with bottom-q value of $\check{q} = 2$. This 3-simplex is $\langle X_2, X_4, X_7, X_{11} \rangle$ which is therefore 0-connected to Y_1, *via* the 0-simplex $\langle X_2 \rangle$. This means that the 'bottom-q value of 1' is 0-connected to the 'bottom-q value of 2' *via* a 'top-q value of 2'. Indeed we see that the bottom-q simplices are only connected at the 0-level *via* any top-q values. Hence we notice that the *critical value* q_c of $K_{\tilde{q}}(\hat{q}; \lambda)$ is

$$q_c = 0$$

this being the level at which *all* the bottom-q simplices fall into one connected component. The vector 6.2(2) exhibits the same property, *viz.*, the critical value, at which all the top-q simplices fall into one connected component, is $q_c = 0$. Hence, in either case, the simplices are hinged together at vertices (only); this is a characteristic of the original complex $K_L(B; \lambda)$. It could have been otherwise, for example, if $K_L(B; \lambda)$ had contained a simplex L_k with a pair of extreme (2, 3), for then the relation μ would have contained a 1 in the location (Y_2, X_3); this could have resulted in Y_1 and Y_2 being 1-connected, and the presence of other suitable simplices in L would have ensured $q_c = 1$.

Slicing the weighted relation μ at $\theta \geqslant 2$ also illustrates a higher critical q-value since it gives the very simple complex $K_{\tilde{q}}(\hat{q}; \mu)$ which consists of a single 1-simplex $Y_1 = \langle X_1, X_2 \rangle$. Thus the structure vector is

$$Q = \{1 \quad 1\}$$

Turning our attention to the conjugate visual-image complex $K_B(L; \lambda^{-1})$ we obtain, from the computer, the following analysis.

$K_B(L; \lambda^{-1})$

q-value	q-connected components	value of Q_q
4	{B1}	1
3	{B1}, {B3}, {B17}	3
2	{B1, B3}, {B6}, {B7, B8}, {B17}, {B18, B19}, {B36}, {B50}, {B51}, {B63}, {B78}	10
1	{B1, ..., B8}, ..., {B90}, {B91}	11
0	{all}	

In the eleven 1-connected components there is a total of forty-five buildings. The structure vector is

$$Q = \{\overset{4}{1} \quad 3 \quad 10 \quad 11 \quad 1\}$$

and obstruction vector

$$\hat{Q} = \{\overset{3}{2} \quad 9 \quad 10 \quad 0\}$$

The low q-values of the buildings reinforces the interpretation of $K_L(B; \lambda)$, showing that the visual features are not accessible from many common locations. The building of highest dimension is B1, which happens to be the church; B17 is the Swan Inn at the junction of Church Street and Water Street. The critical q-value is 0, and generally the picture of Lavenham building-wise is a repeat and a reinforcement of that based on our discussion of the conjugate complex, lozenge-wise.

6.3 A general analysis for a town

In the previous section we have seen how our intuitive sense of structure, expressed in connectivity language, can be studied even in relation to the intangible visual-image of a town. But, of course, the functioning of a town involves very much more than this, and it is therefore necessary for us to consider how to deal with the many relations which are relevant to a complete study of an urban community.

We shall suppose that, as before, we can cover the town map with a set of pieces of area — which we shall refer to generally as lozenges. It is not essential for the whole Euclidean map to be covered, rather is it important to cover the relevant public access areas — such as streets, open spaces, public parks — having in mind the pedestrian public. The Euclidean sizes of any one lozenge-area (or even its peculiar shape) are important but can be initially arbitrary. What matters most about the lozenge sizes is that they be sufficiently small to allow for future amalgamation into larger lozenge-areas. It is reasonable that, along the streets, the smallest lozenges need be no smaller than that which just covers the length of one building. Having produced a set $L = \{L_i\}$ where the L_i are the smallest lozenge areas to be used in the subsequent analysis we shall refer to *that lozenge-cover and that associated analysis* as the *hierarchical level N*. Subsequent to this stage of the study we shall be able to refer to hierarchical levels $(N-1)$ and to $(N+1)$. By the $(N-1)$-level we shall mean the adoption of a new set $L^- = \{L^-_j\}$ in which every L^-_j is properly contained in some L_i at the N-level, that is to say, the lozenge-areas have been reduced in size, but always in such a manner as to ensure that each L_i (at the N-level) is an integral number of the L^-_j (at the $(N-1)$-level). By the $(N+1)$-level we shall mean the adoption of a new set $L^+ = \{L^+_k\}$ where each L^+_k is an integral number of the L_i (at the N-level). In other words, we are making the lozenge-areas, at the $(N+1)$-level, larger units by amalgamating the areas at the N-level. The whole scheme is illustrated in Figure 6.8.

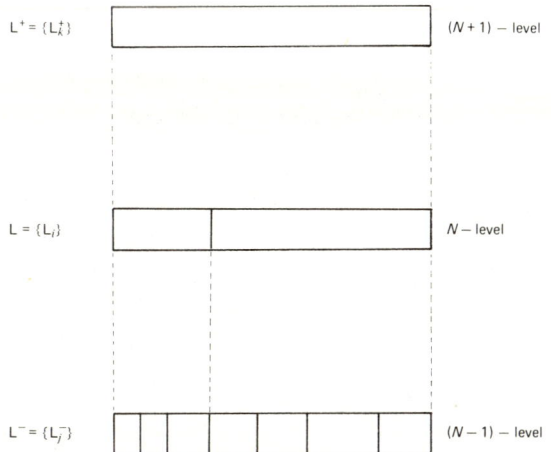

Figure 6.8 Hierarchical levels of analysis

This notion of the hierachy corresponds acutely to the philosophy of our thesis, which may be summarized in the following terms.

Sets of elements are defined at the N-level, the structure of relations at the N-level is intuitively appreciated at the (N + 1)-level.

We need only concentrate our discussion at a convenient level which we naturally regard as the N-level (N for normal, natural, necessary — although not necessarily sufficient) — and at that level we can suppose that we are equipped with a lozenge-cover set $L = \{L_i\}$. This set L is a geographical entity and, commencing with it, we now must associate additional sets of features and activities, both tangible and intangible, which go to make up our sense of the urban community. To avoid searching for descriptive nouns for these *sets* we shall refer to them all as *activities* (even though some of them, seen as human actions, are passive rather than active) and denote them by their mathematical names A1, A2, A3, ... AM, M being some integer which is large enough for everyone's taste. When referring to a general one of these sets we shall denote it by AJ, and imagine that J can take any one of the values 1, 2, ..., M. We do not, incidentally, allow any AJ to represent the set L, this latter set is to play a basic role as a physical reference for all the AJ. Whereas L is a geographical-geometric entity, A1 might be aesthetic (like our visual images of the previous section), A2 might be commercial-economic (like the set of all retail trades to be found in the town), and so on.

Examples of the possible kinds of sets AJ which interest us, and some idea of their extent (their cardinalities), are provided in the following lists — some of which are currently being used in the Urban Structure Research Project at the University of Essex, (*v.* also [7]).

A1 — *Retail trading activities*

Butcher	Confectioner	Fish-and-chips	Dry cleaning
Baker	Footwear	Off-licence	D.I.Y.
Greengrocer	Ironmonger	Wine merchant	Photography
Fishmonger	Electrical goods	Flowers	Art supplies
Grocery provisions	Radio, TV	Toys	Sports shop
Dairy	Electrical machinery	Antiques	Betting shop
Specialist foods	Household hardware	Auction room	Newsagent
Supermarket	Furniture	Haberdasher	Launderette
Hairdresser — Male	Soft furnishings	Music — instruments	Optician
Hairdresser — Female	Garage	Music — records	
Tailor	Car sales	Jewellers	
Clothing — Male	Car accessories	Leather goods	
Clothing — Female	Bookshop	Fancy goods	
Clothing — Children	Chemist — drugs	Office equipment	
Tobacconist	Chemist — cosmetic	Department store	

A2 – Types of residential property

Detached house	Institutional housing	Garden – secluded
Semi-detached house	Private estate	Garden – open plan
Terraced house	Local authority estate	Garden – no
Self-contained flat	Owner-occupied	
High-rise	Rented – furnished	
Low-rise	Rented – unfurnished	
Hotel	Garage – attached	
Boarding house	Garage – space	

A3 – Cultural amenities

Museum	Special school	Art school
Art gallery	Nursery school	Youth club
Exhibition hall	Primary school	Church
Theatre	Secondary school	Amateur societies
Concert hall	Technical college	Social societies
Library	Polytechnic	Political societies
Club	University	
Cinema	Training college	

A4 – Private and public services

Water supply	Bus service	Medical practitioner
Sewage disposal	Train service	Dental practitioner
Refuse collection	Sea port	Solicitor
Electricity supply	Airport	Accountant
Gas supply	Local market	Insurance
Telephone	Police	Banking
Post Office	Fire service	Finance
Social security	Hospital	

A5 – Outdoor recreational activities

Gardening	Golf	Skating	Bowls
Sailing	Fishing	Football – soccer	Croquet
Flying	Bird watching	Football – rugger	Archery
Motoring	Water skiing	Cricket	Athletics
Walking	Children's playground	Netball	
Riding	Swimming	Hockey	

together with similar sets, for example,

A6 — *Light manufacturing*

A7 — *Heavy industry and chemicals*

A8 — *Agricultural and market gardening*

A9 — *Visual features of facades*
(types of doors, windows, finishes, colours, etc.)

A10 — *Lists of companies' activities*
(commerce, directors, turnover, capital assets, etc.)

A particularly important set (or set of sets) will describe the state of the *vehicular traffic* on the set L. Since this is likely to vary a great deal with the time of day and day of the week, we would expect to find a weighted relation between L and sets (which we can call) AT1, AT2, etc. where the 1, 2, ... refer to time intervals (of say half-an-hour) specified throughout a period of time which could be arbitrary (depending on the point of the study). Common to all these ATJ we would expect a minimum list of types of vehicles, something like,

Private car	Bus — single deck	Moped
Small commercial van	Bus — double deck	Bicycle
Large commercial van	Taxicab	
Lorry	Minicab	
Heavy lorry — articulated	Emergency vehicles	
Heavy lorry with trailer	Motor cycle	

Here the idea would be that the weighted relation μ, between L and AT1, would tell us how many of the vehicular types were to be found in the L_i during the specified interval 1 (which might be the period 0800–0830 on Monday the 19th June, 1973). The consequences of this kind of data will be discussed more fully in a later section; something of its flavour has already been met with in section 2.4.

Commencing with a typical list of sets AJ, such as those specified above, we need to obtain the data which will allow us to identify *weighted relations* $\mu_j \subset L \times AJ$ (where $j = J$). Then the set of $\{\mu_j\}$, together with any meaningful slicing parameters θ, provides us with a set of simplicial complexes,

$$K_L(AJ: \mu_j; \theta) \text{ and their conjugates } K_{AJ}(L; \mu_j^{-1}; \theta)$$

This set of structured complexes provides us with a *structural backcloth* (or system) S, a *basic structural pattern* which *supports the urban community* under discussion. This backcloth S, is also a function of the hierarchical level N and, because of that, it would be preferable to write it as S(N). If then, it is important for us to change our view from the level N to the level N' we can conveniently do so symbolically by changing S(N) to S(N'). Of course, we only have in mind the two possibilities $N' = n - 1$ and $N' = n + 1$.

Having obtained our backcloth S(N) we can now obtain a composite view of the town in various ways. Naturally, an obvious way is to combine all the sets AJ into one new set, say, A and then to look at $K_L(A)$ and $K_A(L)$. This is equivalent to defining a single relation μ which is the union of the separate μ_j. In this way the system S(N) becomes a single complex, instead of a number (M in fact) of complexes. The reason why it is unlikely to be helpful, at the intuitive interpretative level, is the size of its dimensions. Also, the spread of activities over A1 to AM is intuitively difficult to grasp when q-values run very high.

At this stage in the development of the language, and its application to urban structure, it seems more fruitful to search for ways of combining the many complexes in S(N) so as to retain the maximum possibility of sound intuitive interpretations. With this in view we can proceed in some such way as follows.

The *system of complexes* at the N-level, S(N), are all referred to a common lozenge-cover L = {L_i}, hence we can select a particular L_i, say L_1, and obtain a view of it from each complex $K_L(AJ; \mu_j) \in S(N)$. Since its connectivity is the first thing we want to understand we can find the M pairs of extremes $(\check{q}, \hat{q})_j$, for $j = 1, 2, \ldots$ M, one for L_1 in each sliced weighted relation μ_j. If we contemplate, for whatever reason, k_j possible slicings for μ_j and if we list all the possible pairs of extremes for L_1 obtained thereby, we end up with a total of

$$k_1 + k_2 + \ldots + k_M$$

points $(\check{q}, \hat{q})$ for L_1 in (what is effectively) Q × Q – space. We therefore have a weighted relation $\mu_0 \subset Q \times Q$ which represents the connectivity-extremes of this particular lozenge L_1, as we roam all over the backcloth system S(N). This relation μ_0 must therefore contain an overall view of the way L_1 fits into the connectivity structures generated by the various activities A1, ..., AM. We must therefore look for this view in the complexes

$$K_{\check{q}}(\hat{q}; \mu_0) \text{ and } K_{\hat{q}}(\check{q}; \mu_0^{-1})$$

for various slicing parameters. Notice that, contrary to the example of the previous section, $K_{\check{q}}(\hat{q}; \mu_0)$ is not the eccentric relation of all lozenges over one complex but it is the relation of one lozenge over all complexes. We shall refer to μ_0 as the *anchored eccentric relation*, since it is anchored on one lozenge L_1, and when we want the notation to reflect the particular L_1 we can write the relation as $\mu_0(L_1)$. Thus, out of the anchored eccentric relation $\mu_0(L_1)$ we derive the two conjugate complexes

$$K_{\check{q}}(\hat{q}; \mu_0(L_1)) \text{ and } K_{\hat{q}}(\check{q}; \mu_0(L_1)^{-1})$$

whose structures represent the connectivity role of L_1 throughout the backcloth generated by A1, ..., AM. Any adjustment of the relations μ_j which relate the sets L and AJ, will now be reflected in the structures of these two complexes. Any proposal for a change (such as the 'change of user' involved in a butcher's shop being converted into a fishmonger's shop) can be monitored by studying the connectivity patterns of these complexes. In practice, if the monitoring shows no effect whatsoever then it is not manifest at this particular hierarchical level. Moving from S(N) to S(N + 1) and interpreting L_i as L_k^+, where $L_i \in K_l^+$, will increase the possibility of detecting the effect of the proposal.

Since L is a set common to all the complexes of $S(N)$ it also serves the purpose of allowing a reference of an element in A1 to an element in A2. We can, in effect, find a new relation (say) $\mu_{12} \subset (A1 \times A2) \times L$ which is the intersection of the two relations μ_1 and μ_2. Precisely, we can define μ_{12} by saying that, if $x \in A1$ and $y \in A2$, then:

$((x, y), L_i) \in \mu_{12}$ if and only if there exists an L_i such that $(L_i, x) \in \mu_1$ and $(L_i, y) \in \mu_2$.

Notice that the same L_i must work for both μ_1 and μ_2; if x and y are found in the same L_i then they are related by μ_{12} to this L_i. For example, if x and y are both found in the same three lozenge-areas L_1, L_2, L_3 the pair (x, y) will be a 2-simplex, viz., $\langle L_1\ L_2\ L_3 \rangle$, in $K_{A1 \times A2}(L; \mu_{12})$. It must have been, therefore, that x was at least a 2-simplex in $K_{A1}(L; \mu_1^{-1})$ as must y have been in $K_{A2}(L; \mu_2^{-1})$. The 2-simplex $\langle L_1\ L_2\ L_3 \rangle$ must be common to these two complexes. It follows that our μ_{12} identifies the intersection $K_{A1} \cap K_{A2}$ of K_{A1} and K_{A2}. This intersection is a subcomplex of either K_{A1} or K_{A2}.

We are therefore saying that we can compare the two sets A1 and A2 (or relate their connectivity roles with respect to L, in $S(N)$) by studying the intersection $K_{A1} \cap K_{A2}$, using the original μ_1 and μ_2. It follows that we can compare the sets A1, A2, A3 in the same way by studying the intersection $K_{A1} \cap K_{A2} \cap K_{A3}$ and so on. This is particularly easy to follow through as we move from one hierarchical level to another; an alteration of the set L produces new complexes $K_{AJ}(L'; \mu_j^{-1})$, where $L' = L^-$ or L^+, and the intersections of these follow at once.

We notice too that there is an *array of filtrations* (v. Appendix D) which applies to these intersections. If we use the notation K_{12} to mean $K_{A1} \cap K_{A2}$, with similar extensions, we get the following array

$$K_1 \supset K_{12} \supset K_{123} \supset \ldots \supset K_{12\ldots M}$$
$$K_1 \supset K_{13} \supset K_{134} \supset \ldots \supset K_{13\ldots M}$$
$$\vdots$$
$$K_1 \supset K_{1M}$$
$$K_2 \supset K_{23} \supset K_{234} \supset \ldots \supset K_{23\ldots M}$$
$$\vdots$$
$$K_2 \supset K_{2M}$$
$$\vdots$$
$$K_{M-1} \supset K_{M-1,M}$$

We can speak of K_{A1} being *filtered by* A2, A3, ... AM when we mean to refer to the top row of this set of filtrations; notice that, because $K_{12} = K_{21}$, it is only necessary to list $K_{ij...h}$ with $\{i, j, \ldots h\}$ forming an increasing sequence of integers. If α and β are two such sequences of integers and if $\alpha \subset \beta$, then $K_\alpha \supset K_\beta$. Figure 6.9 illustrates a simple case of two complexes K_1, K_2 and their intersection $K_1 \cap K_2 = K_{12}$.

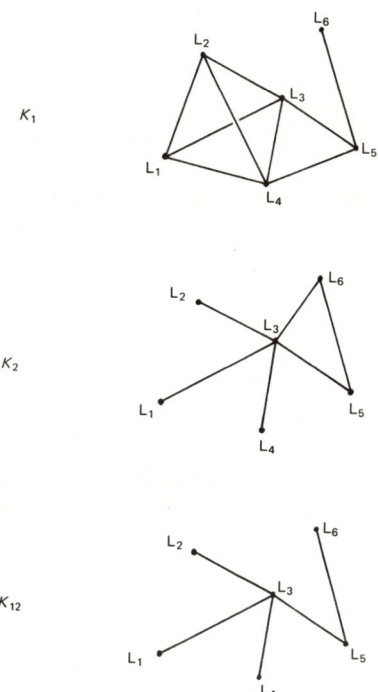

Figure 6.9 $K_1, K_2,$ and $K_{12} = K_1 \cap K_2$

Suppose, for example, that $K_1 \equiv K_{A1}(L)$, $K_2 \equiv K_{A2}(L)$, and that A1 = $\{X_1, X_2, X_3, X_4, X_5\}$, A2 = $\{Y_1, Y_2, Y_3, Y_4, Y_5, Y_6\}$, with the simple identification:

$$X_1 = \langle L_1\, L_2\, L_3\, L_4 \rangle$$
$$X_2 = \langle L_3\, L_4\, L_5 \rangle, \quad X_4 = \langle L_1\, L_2\, L_4 \rangle$$
$$X_3 = \langle L_5\, L_6 \rangle, \quad X_5 = \langle L_3\, L_4 \rangle$$

and

$$Y_5 = \langle L_3\, L_5\, L_6 \rangle$$
$$Y_1 = \langle L_2\, L_3 \rangle, \quad Y_2 = \langle L_1\, L_3 \rangle, \quad Y_3 = \langle L_1\, L_4 \rangle,$$
$$Y_4 = \langle L_3\, L_5 \rangle, \quad Y_6 = \langle L_3\, L_6 \rangle.$$

Then, *relative to the intersection* $K_1 \cap K_2 = K_{12}$, the A1-set can be regarded as (only) the set X_1, X_2, X_4, since the other two, X_3, X_5, are in K_{12}. With this interpretation K_2, relative to K_{12}, is reduced to the three simplices Y_3, Y_5, Y_6.

We can therefore use K_{12} as a base, or a sink, which effectively, for comparison purposes, removes some of the activities from A1 and A2. When we are comparing K_1 and K_2 in this way we shall use the notation (e.g.)

$$K_1 \text{ (mod } K_{12}), \text{ or } K_1/K_{12}$$

to indicate that we are removing from K_1 any of its activity-simplices which are wholly contained in K_{12}. (Notice that this is not the same thing as merely eliminating a simplex $\langle L_i\ L_j \rangle$ etc. since such a process might well result in the structure, viz., $K_1 - K_{12}$, not being a simplicial complex.)

This process of forming an intersection K_{12} therefore results in two possible comparisons of the structural roles of A1 and A2. These are:

(1) a view of $K_{12} = K_1 \cap K_2$ itself, which represents the simplex identities between A1 and A2;
(2) a view of K_1 (mod K_{12}) and of K_2 (mod K_{12}), which represent the simplices of K_1 (or of K_2) which stand out from the intersection.

By these means — forming the anchored eccentric relations and forming the intersections $K_i \cap K_j \cap$ etc. — we can begin to take into account the whole backcloth, or system, of complexes $S(N)$ at the N-level. In connection with this system $S(N)$ we can then contemplate the introduction of *additional information* about the *dynamics of the community*, and we can do this by the introduction of patterns of *cosimplices* π — as already mentioned in section 2.5. A pattern is defined in the following way (*v*. Appendix D):

A pattern π, associated with a complex $K_Y(X)$, is a set of cosimplices $\sigma_i^p : Y_i \to R$, where R is a suitable arithmetic structure.

Each pattern π can therefore be graded and written

$$\pi = \pi^0 \oplus \pi^1 \oplus \ldots \pi^t \oplus \ldots \oplus \pi^N$$

where $N = \dim K$, and where π^t consists of t-cosimplices only.

The role of the backcloth system $S(N)$ is parallel to the role of the backcloth complexes (actual-space) $K_A(P)$ and $K_P(A)$ of the physical sciences. Just as the dynamics of physics is manifest through cocycles z^p defined as $K_P(A)$ so do the patterns π (on $S(N)$) define the dynamics of the social sciences.

Some typical quantities which will give rise to expression as patterns on $S(N)$ are the following:

(1) population on the L_i, restricted by age-brackets;
(2) population distribution on L_i, by income-brackets;
(3) employment distribution, by various categories;
(4) consumer-goods spending, by specified time intervals;
(5) vehicle journeys in the L_i, by vehicle types;
(6) capital investment, distribution over the L_i;
(7) immigration into areas L_i, various ethnic groups;
(8) political voting distributions, with respect to party politics.

In each of these possibilities, the patterns π will be defined on complexes

$K_L(AJ)$, for some suitable set AJ which forms part of the backcloth at the N-level. Changing from $S(N)$ to $S(N-1)$ is equivalent to providing more detailed data for the patterns; it corresponds in the physical sciences to taking a microscopic (as opposed to a macroscopic) view. In urban studies it can clearly correspond to taking successive views down the sequence: region, town, area, street, house. Moving up this sequence corresponds to changing from $S(N)$ to $S(N+1)$, successively.

A particular t-pattern π^t requires $(t+1)$ vertices (from the set AJ) for its definition, being defined on the t-simplices of the complex. We can therefore suppose that, in the absence of any other constraints, a *necessary condition* for a *free change* in π^t (by *free* we mean that it is *structurally free* — there is enough 'geometry' to carry it) is that the $\sigma_t{}^i$ be t-connected. This situation, which we naturally refer to as zero obstruction to $\Delta \pi^t$, will certainly arise if all the $\sigma_t{}^i$ are faces of some σ_p, with $p > t$. It is this consideration which gave rise to our concept of *obstruction vector* $\hat{Q}(K)$. If there are two distinct t-simplices σ_t^1 and σ_t^2 which are not t-connected then we expect the obstruction to $\Delta \pi^t$ (obstruction to a change in π^t) to be non-zero. Hence, generally, we assert:

> the obstruction vector $\hat{Q}(K)$ provides a measure of
> the effective obstruction to any change $\Delta \pi$ in a
> pattern π; if π^t is a component of π then $Q_t \in \hat{Q}$
> measures the obstruction to $\Delta \pi^t$.

The definition of $\hat{Q}$ ensures that zero obstruction corresponds to the case when $K =$ a single N-simplex, giving zero obstruction to $\Delta \pi^t$ for all values of t from 0 to N.

We must stress that this is a notion of necessity, not sufficiency; the peculiarities of some particular pattern π might well involve constraints on the actual (inner) chains of connection within a single connected component which place additional obstacles in the way of the change $\pi \to \pi + \Delta \pi$. Our *obstruction* is specifically related to the underlying structural geometry of the complex; zero obstruction is a sign of a *static backcloth without stress*, under changes symbolized by Δ.

For example, ideas of conservation (comparable to the idea of the conservation of energy etc., in physical science) might affect the role of the obstruction vector. Conservation in this sense might be manifest by requiring, for example,

$$\pi^t = \{\pi^t_i, i = 1, 2, \ldots k_t\}$$

and that $\Delta \pi^t$ must be compatible with

$$\sum_{i=1}^{k_t} \pi^t_i (L_i) = C, \text{ a constant.}$$

Then the changes in π^t must be such that

$$\sum_{i=1}^{k_t} \Delta \pi^t_i = 0$$

6.4 Patterns and *t*-forces on an anciente towne

To illustrate the basic notion of a pattern we need to look at an urban community which is not too complicated, so that the analysis can be done without the aid of a computer; and it would also be interesting to see how a little data can be put to effective use. A community which is relatively stable, where change can be manifest and comprehended on a time scale which does not leave the observer breathless, could also be desirable for illustrative purposes. We shall therefore have a look at what is known of the urban town of Saffron Walden, in the county of Essex, around the year 1600 A.D. The proposed map is that shown in Figure 6.10 and is reproduced by permission of the Essex Records Office and Mrs D. Cromarty. The lozenge-cover which we propose to use is shown in Figure 6.11, covering most, if not all, of the heart of the town.

The population of the market town of Saffron Walden in 1600 A.D. was something in the region of 1000 – 1500. With such a population it naturally needed at least one whipping post or ducking stool (cucking-stole), although serious crime and offenders were dealt with in the town of Colchester – where the Gaoler was better equipped to keep rogues and vagabonds in a different kind of custody. The industry which gave the town its name was the manufacture and use of dyes, notably saffron – the deep yellow derived from the stamens of the yellow crocus flower (*Crocus aureus*), so that the mercers' guild, whose members practised the trade of silks and fabrics, must have been a prosperous one – as its members practised in the centre of the town. The trade in saffron brought rich merchant travellers to Saffron Walden, mostly from London, and it is not surprising that the town was therefore well provided with inns for that (and other) purposes. Brewing was clearly an important activity, by the number of malt houses, and must have resulted in a large malt trade to the 'outside'.

We take a simple view of the town activities at the N-level (that defined by the set L, with card L = 18) and identify three sets A1, A2, and A3, under the broad headings of Trade, Public Administration, and Buildings. Some of the categories must be guessed at, as must the weighted relations which we use, but the data is not a luxury so long as it appears only plausible. Perhaps the methods illustrated might encourage more serious students of history to use more reliable and informative data.

Set A1 = $\{X_1, X_2, X_3, X_4, X_5, X_6, X_7\}$ with

X_1 = Inn
X_2 = Malthouse
X_3 = Leather, harness, etc.
X_4 = Butcher
X_5 = Dairy produce
X_6 = Mercers, cloth, dyes, etc.
X_7 = Household pots, pans, etc.

Set A2 = $\{Y_1, Y_2, Y_3, Y_4, Y_5\}$ with

Y_1 = School
Y_2 = Church
Y_3 = Guildhall
Y_4 = Welfare
Y_5 = Penal

Set A3 = {Z_1, Z_2, Z_3, Z_4, Z_5} with

Z_1 = Large household (merchant class)
Z_2 = Medium (artisan)
Z_3 = Small (labourer)
Z_4 = Commercial building
Z_5 = Almshouses

We take the weighted relation $\mu_j \subset L \times AJ$ to be that contained in the table below.

μ	X_1	X_2	X_3	X_4	X_5	X_6	X_7	Y_1	Y_2	Y_3	Y_4	Y_5	Z_1	Z_2	Z_3	Z_4	Z_5
L_1	0	0	0	0	0	0	0	0	0	0	0	0	0	0	12	0	0
L_2	0	0	0	0	0	0	0	1	1	0	0	0	6	3	0	0	0
L_3	0	1	0	0	0	0	0	0	1	0	0	0	7	3	2	2	0
L_4	0	0	0	0	0	0	0	0	1	0	1	0	1	0	10	0	0
L_5	1	1	0	0	0	0	0	0	1	0	0	0	5	0	0	0	0
L_6	1	0	0	0	0	0	0	0	0	0	0	0	3	4	0	2	0
L_7	0	1	0	0	0	0	0	0	0	1	0	0	2	0	8	2	0
L_8	1	0	0	0	0	0	0	0	0	0	1	0	0	9	15	0	12
L_9	0	0	0	0	1	0	0	0	0	0	0	0	2	10	2	4	0
L_{10}	0	0	3	0	1	4	0	0	0	1	0	0	0	3	0	12	0
L_{11}	1	0	0	2	0	0	0	0	0	0	0	0	0	2	0	3	0
L_{12}	0	0	0	2	0	3	2	0	0	0	0	0	0	8	4	10	0
L_{13}	2	0	0	0	1	0	0	0	0	1	0	0	0	3	0	8	0
L_{14}	1	0	0	0	0	0	1	0	0	0	0	0	0	3	6	2	0
L_{15}	0	0	0	0	0	0	1	0	0	0	0	0	5	2	2	0	0
L_{16}	1	1	0	0	0	0	0	0	0	0	0	1	4	10	4	2	0
L_{17}	0	0	0	0	0	0	0	0	0	0	0	0	6	0	0	0	0
L_{18}	0	0	0	0	0	0	0	0	0	0	0	1	0	0	12	0	0

If we consider the structure of this hierarchical N-level the backcloth system of complexes is

$$S(N) = \{K_L(AJ), K_{AJ}(L), \text{ with various slicing parameters}\}$$

An incomplete view of the backcloth is provided by the following structures, each of which follows from the sliced weighted relations μ_j.

$K_L(A1)$, sliced at $\theta \geq 2$ (both rows and columns):

$$Q = \{\overset{2}{1} \ \overset{1}{2} \ \overset{0}{2}\}$$

128 *Mathematical Structure in Human Affairs*

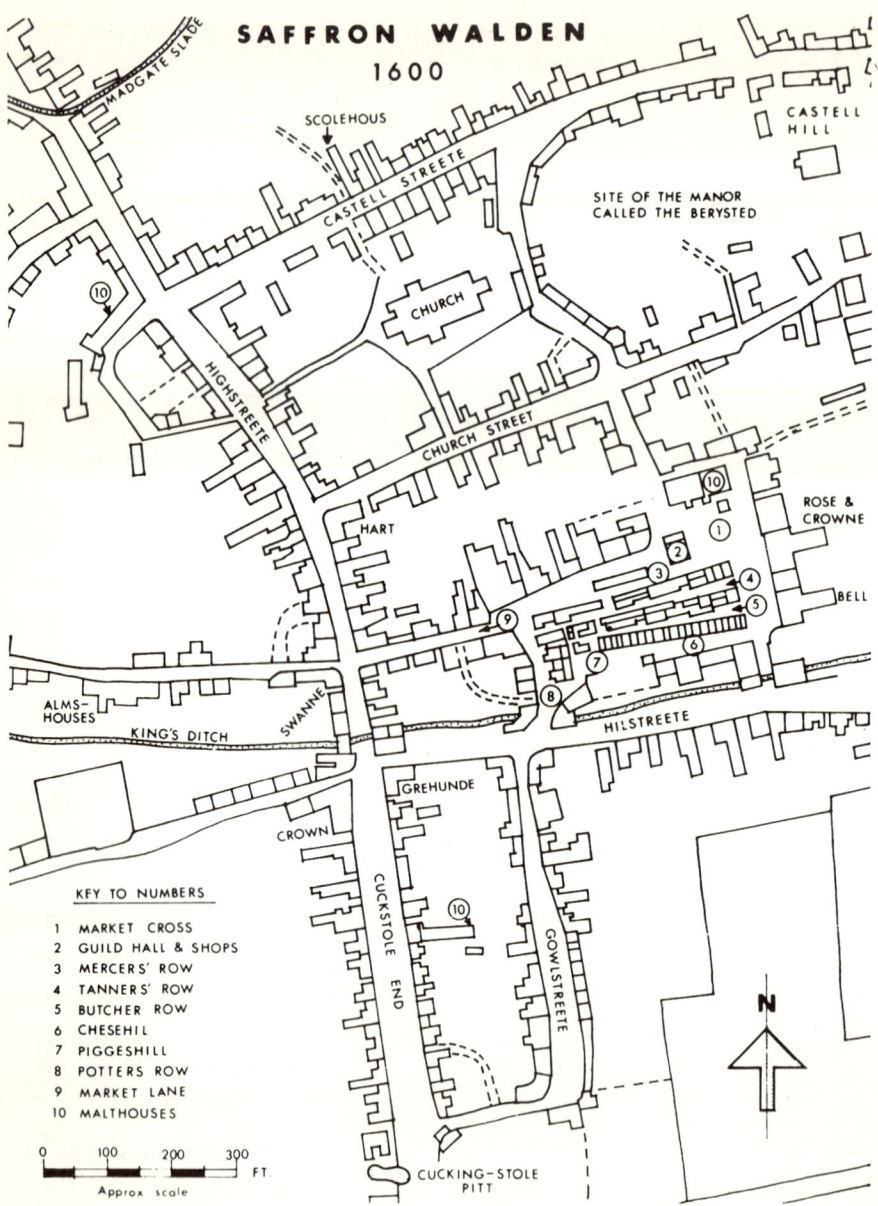

Figure 6.10 Reconstruction of Saffron Walden in 1600 A.D.

Urban Structure 129

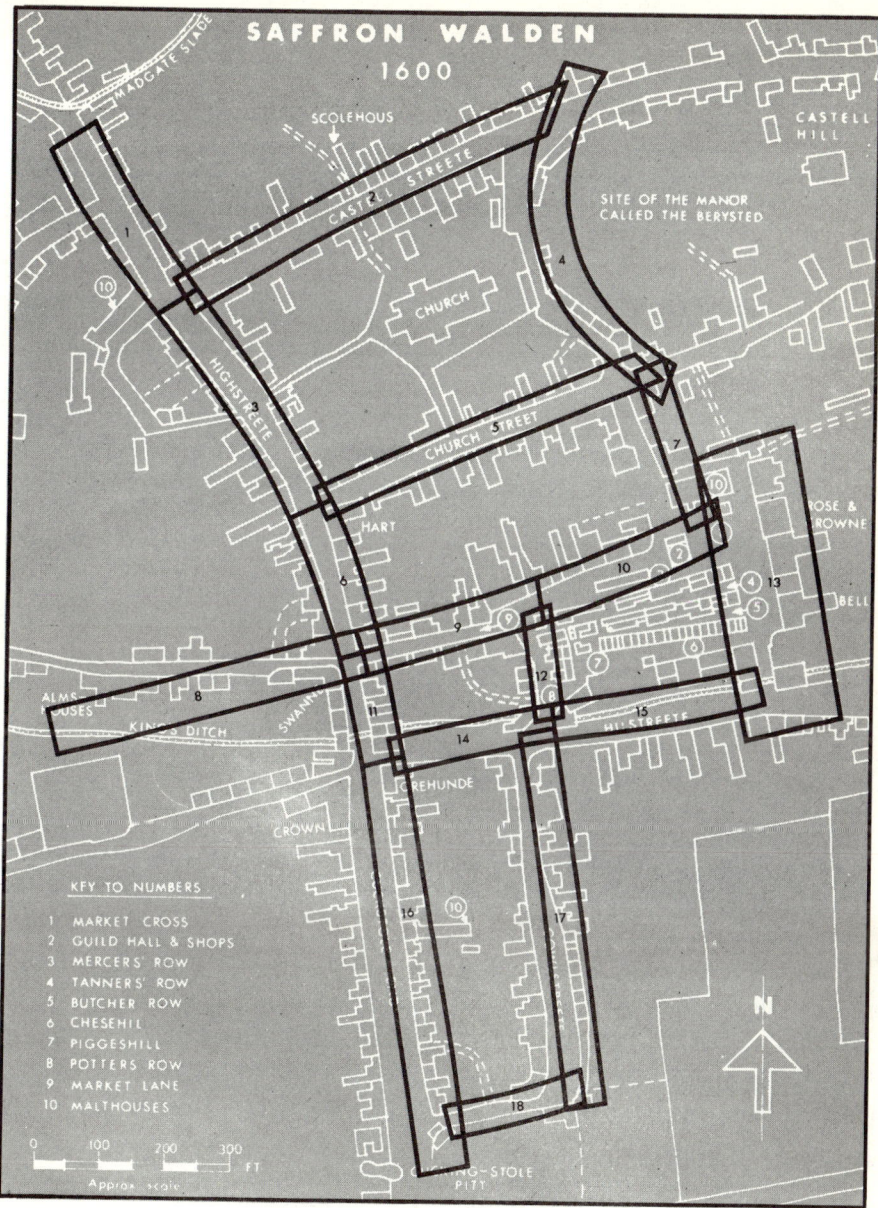

Figure 6.11 Cover-set for Saffron Walden

with components

at $q = 2$ $\{L_{12}\}$
at $q = 1$ $\{L_{12}\}, \{L_{10}\}$
at $q = 0$ $\{L_{10}, L_{11}, L_{12}\}, \{L_{13}\}$

This analysis identifies the trade centre (shopping centre?) as the lozenge-areas $L_{10}, L_{11}, L_{12}, L_{13}$ — suitably connected. With it we get the conjugate, $K_{A1}(L)$, sliced at $\theta \geq 2$:

$$Q = \{\overset{1}{2} \; \overset{0}{2}\}$$

with components

at $q = 1$ $\{X_4\}, \{X_6\}$
at $q = 0$ $\{X_1\}, \{X_3, X_4, X_6, X_7\}$

Slicing at $\theta \geq 1$ (both rows and columns) we get,

$K_L(A1)$,

$$Q = \{\overset{2}{2} \; \overset{1}{7} \; \overset{0}{1}\}$$

with components (e.g.)

at $q = 1$ $\{L_5\}, \{L_{10}\}, \{L_{11}\}, \{L_{12}\}, \{L_{13}\}, \{L_{14}\}, \{L_{16}\}$

$K_{A1}(L)$,

$$Q = \{\overset{6}{1} \; 1 \; 1 \; \overset{3}{2} \; 4 \; \overset{1}{4} \; \overset{0}{1}\}$$

with components (e.g.)

at $q = 6$ $\{X_1\}$
at $q = 2$ $\{X_1\}, \{X_2\}, \{X_5\}, \{X_7\}$

The other sets give us structures as follows.

$K_L(A2)$, sliced at $\theta \geq 1$,

$$Q = \{\overset{1}{2} \; \overset{0}{3}\}$$

with components

at $q = 1$ $\{L_2\}, \{L_4\}$
at $q = 0$ $\{L_2, L_3, L_4, L_5\}, \{L_7, L_{10}, L_{13}\}, \{L_{16}, L_{18}\}$

$K_{A2}(L)$, sliced at $\theta \geq 1$,

$$Q = \{\overset{3}{1} \; 2 \; 3 \; \overset{0}{3}\}$$

with components (e.g.)

at $q = 3$ $\{Y_2\}$
at $q = 1$ $\{Y_2\}, \{Y_3\}, \{Y_5\}$

$K_L(A3)$, sliced by columns at $\theta_j \geqslant 6$ for $j = 1, \ldots 5$.

$$\mathbf{Q} = \{\overset{2}{1} \ 2 \ \overset{0}{2}\}$$

$K_{A3}(L)$, sliced by $\theta_j \geqslant 6$ for $j = 1, \ldots 5$.

$$\mathbf{Q} = \{\overset{5}{1} \ 1 \ 2 \ 4 \ 4 \ \overset{0}{2}\}$$

with components (e.g.)

at $q = 5$ $\{Z_3\}$
at $q = 2$ $\{Z_1\}, \{Z_2\}, \{Z_3\}, \{Z_4\}$

$K_L(A3)$, sliced by $\theta_j \geqslant 3$ for $j = 1, \ldots 5$

$$\mathbf{Q} = \{\overset{2}{2} \ 1 \ \overset{0}{1}\}$$

with components (e.g.)

at $q = 1$ $\{L_2, L_3, L_6, L_8, L_9, L_{10}, L_{12}, L_{13}, L_{14}, L_{16}\}$

$K_{A3}(L)$, sliced by $\theta_j \geqslant 3$,

$$\mathbf{Q} = \{\overset{9}{1} \ 1 \ 2 \ \overset{6}{3} \ 3 \ 4 \ \overset{3}{1} \ 1 \ 1 \ \overset{0}{1}\}$$

with components (e.g.)

at $q = 9$ $\{Z_2\}$
at $q = 6$ $\{Z_1\}, \{Z_2\}, \{Z_3\}$
at $q = 3$ $\{Z_1, Z_2, Z_3, Z_4\}$

$K_L(A3)$, sliced by $\theta_j \geqslant 1$,

$$\mathbf{Q} = \{\overset{3}{1} \ 2 \ 1 \ \overset{0}{1}\}$$

with components,

at $q = 3$ $\{L_3, L_9, L_{16}\}$
at $q = 2$ $\{L_3, L_6, L_7, L_9, L_{12}, L_{14}, L_{15}, L_{16}\}, \{L_8\}$
at $q = 1$ $\{L_2, L_3, L_4, L_6, L_7, L_8, L_9, L_{10}, L_{11}, L_{12}, L_{13}, L_{14}, L_{15}, L_{16}\}$
at $q = 0$ $\{\text{all}\}$

$K_{A3}(L)$, sliced by $\theta_j \geqslant 1$,

$$\mathbf{Q} = \{\overset{11}{1} \ 2 \ \overset{9}{4} \ 3 \ 3 \ 2 \ \overset{5}{1} \ 1 \ldots \overset{0}{1}\}$$

with components,

at $q = 11$ $\{Z_2\}$
at $q = 9$ $\{Z_1\}, \{Z_2\}, \{Z_3\}, \{Z_4\}$
at $q = 7$ $\{Z_1\}, \{Z_2, Z_4\}, \{Z_3\}$
at $q = 5$ $\{Z_1, Z_2, Z_3, Z_4\}$
at $q = 0$ $\{\text{all}\}$

These structures, as a description of S(N), contain a great deal of interpretative detail.

Slicing $K_L(A3)$ by columns at $\theta_j \geq 6$ identifies the richer housing of the town and the value of $Q_0 = 2$ shows that this style of living occurred in two disconnected areas, whereas the value of $Q_5 = 1$ (in $K_{A3}(L)$) shows that the largest connection occurs through the presence of the smaller labourers' cottages – so that the poor were ubiquitous. As we lower the slicing parameter to $\theta_j \geq 3$ we naturally obtain a higher connectivity, in particular Q_0 drops to 1 and the greatest q-value in $K_A(L)$ increases from 5 to 9. This is not achieved through Z_3 but through the presence of Z_2 – houses occupied by the artisan class. Comparison between $\theta_j \geq 6$ and $\theta_j \geq 3$ shows that the artisan class are more scattered, in smaller amounts, than are the labourers – who dominate the scene at the higher slicing values. When θ_j is dropped down to $\theta_j \geq 1$ this new dominance by Z_2 persists in $K_{A3}(L)$ where the maximum q-value is $q = 11$. The simplex with the lowest dimension is Z_5 (a 0-simplex), representing the almshouses (for the deserving aged and poor). We notice too that Z_2 and Z_4, the artisan-type housing and buildings used for trade and commerce, are the first to be connected at $q = 7$; not, perhaps, surprising.

It is only relevant to slice $K_L(A2)$ at $\theta \geq 1$, and the value of $Q_0 = 3$ shows that the public administration exists in three disconnected portions of the town; no one can be unaware of its existence. The highest q-value in $K_{A2}(L)$ is at $q = 3$, occurring with Y_2 – the Church. The next highest order simplex is Y_3, the Guildhall, being centred (v. Figure 6.11) in the trading heart of the town. This supports too the idea that the political influence in the town, insofar as it was democratically based, centred on the merchant and would-be merchant class in L_{10}, L_{13} whilst, at the other end of the town, the Church and Manorial squire represented what we would now call the Establishment's influence – based on L_2, L_3, L_4, L_5.

We have already noticed the significance of slicing $K_L(A1)$ at $\theta \geq 2$, identifying the commercial centre of the town. Slicing at $\theta \geq 1$ gives a large increase in Q_1 from 2 to 7, and since $Q_0 = 1$, we get associated with the complex $K_L(A1)$ an obstruction vector

$$\hat{Q} = \{1 \quad 6 \quad 0\}$$

whilst $K_{A1}(L)$ provides

$$\hat{Q} = \{1 \quad 3 \quad 3 \quad 0\}$$

This suggests that changes in patterns π, defined on $K_L(A1)$, are highly obstructed at $q = 1$; patterns defined on $K_{A1}(L)$ are less obstructed at $q = 1$ but threefold obstructed at $q = 2$. The highest order simplex in $K_{A1}(L)$ is X_1 (inn) with $\hat{q} = 6$, the next one below this being X_2 (at $q = 3$), malthouse. It looks therefore as if brewing and hostelry are widespread throughout the town, compared with other trades. The comparison is numerically contained in the eccentricities of X_1 and X_2 via the top-q and bottom-q values, viz.,

$$X_1 = (\check{q} = 1; \hat{q} = 6)$$
$$X_2 = (\check{q} = 1; \hat{q} = 3)$$

Now we can illustrate the idea of a pattern by considering the distribution of population, at the N-level, relative to the complex $K_L(A3)$. The data must be a plausible guess, consistent with the known overall total of between 1000 and 1500. We propose therefore the pattern of mappings $\pi : L \to J$ as follows.

	L_1	L_2	L_3	L_4	L_5	L_6	L_7	L_8	L_9
$\pi(L_i)$:	51	75	84	66	50	54	58	160	72

	L_{10}	L_{11}	L_{12}	L_{13}	L_{14}	L_{15}	L_{16}	L_{17}	L_{18}
$\pi(L_i)$:	18	9	48	14	44	62	94	64	56

and from this we shall deduce a pattern $\pi : K_L(A3) \to J$. The total number of people in this part of town is, on this count, 1079. The plausible guessing simply consists in giving a crude average for different types of houses (for example, a large household is unlikely to have fewer than ten occupants, counting servants) and adding them up. The point we want to bring out is the nature of the t-connectivity's influence on a pattern π and this is not to be confused with although it is related to, the method of arriving at the value of π on L_i.

Now we have seen in the previous section that a pattern π can be graded so that it consists of $\pi^0 + \pi^1 + \ldots + \pi^t + \ldots$ and that, when it is so graded, the index t is an indication of the connectivity required for a free change π^t in π^t. Thus, in the numerical case above, $\pi(L_3)$ is a number obtained as a linear combination over Z_1, Z_2, Z_3, Z_4 (which is why L_3 is a 3-simplex) and because of this we shall say that $\pi : L_3 \to J$ is to be regarded as a π^3. This decision about the value of t, in the notation π^t, will now determine the effect of the q-connectivities (among the L_i) on changes in π^t. Thus we are claiming that *changes* in π^t require q-values which need not be immediately obvious from those required in the definition of π^t. The difference is comparable to that between velocity **v** and acceleration d**v** in physics; changes in **v** amount to acceleration d**v**, and these are dependent on a thing called force in a way which **v** is not. Pursuing the analogy further, if **v** is a cosimplex (pattern) on $K_A(P)$ — actual space — then it is defined on a 1-simplex $\langle P_1 P_2 \rangle$ and can exist (even) in a 0-connected complex; acceleration d**v** will generally require a 2-simplex $\langle P_1 P_2 P_3 \rangle$, and thereby provides a 1-connection between the **v**'s. We can therefore take our cue from this physical example and contemplate a change of pattern π as a new pattern $\Delta\pi$ and expect to find it associated with the connectivities in the following specific way.

When we know that $\pi = \pi^t$ we shall assert that $\Delta\pi$ exists freely, without internal constraints, only if the structure is at least $(t + 1)$-connected.

If the above population distribution pattern π is a π^0 then $\Delta\pi$ is unobstructed on simplices L_i provided they are at least 1-connected in $K_L(A3)$, with similar interpretations in the event that $\pi = \pi^1, \pi^2$, etc. Generally, we would expect a pattern π to be a linear combination (with coefficients 0 or 1) of a set of patterns π^t, π^r, π^s etc.

The existence of non-free changes $\Delta\pi$, due to the presence of constraints can be illustrated by considering the single 3-connected component of $K_L(A3)$, viz., $\{L_3, L_9, L_{16}\}$. The total population on this component is

$$84 + 72 + 94 = 250$$

and since we can easily see (from the relation which defines $K_L(A3)$) that each of these lozenge-areas represents the same simplex, viz., $\langle Z_1\ Z_2\ Z_3\ Z_4 \rangle$, we shall take 250 *as the value of π on this simplex.* Since there is no 4-simplex in the complex there can be no free change in π on this particular 3-simplex. Hence we have a situation which is similar to a principle of conservation in physics, in fact if we restrict ourselves to the values of

$$\pi \langle Z_1\ Z_2\ Z_3\ Z_4 \rangle, \text{ where } \pi = \pi^3,$$

then $\Delta\pi(L_3)$, $\Delta\pi(L_9)$, $\Delta\pi(L_{16})$ are constrained by

$$\Delta\pi \langle Z_1\ Z_2\ Z_3\ Z_4 \rangle = 0$$

This gives a *relation of constraint* as

$$\Delta\pi(L_3) + \Delta\pi(L_9) + \Delta\pi(L_{16}) = 0$$

This also illustrates how we intend to construct a pattern on the simplices of $K_Y(X)$ from a mapping defined on the Y_i of Y. Provided there is no fear of ambiguity we can use the same word 'pattern' to describe both of these but in considering $\Delta\pi$, as above, we must be careful to specify π on the actual simplices of $K_Y(X)$. The population pattern above gives us an overall view which is the following, taking account of the various simplicial identities between the L_i.

$$\pi : K_L(A3) \to J$$

simplex σ_t	identical L_i	value of $\pi = \pi^t$
$\langle Z_3 \rangle$	L_1, L_{18}	$\pi^0 = 107$
$\langle Z_1\ Z_2 \rangle$	L_2	$\pi^1 = 75$
$\langle Z_1\ Z_2\ Z_3\ Z_4 \rangle$	L_3, L_9, L_{16}	$\pi^3 = 250$
$\langle Z_1\ Z_3 \rangle$	L_4	$\pi^1 = 66$
$\langle Z_1 \rangle$	L_5, L_{17}	$\pi^0 = 114$
$\langle Z_1\ Z_2\ Z_4 \rangle$	L_6	$\pi^2 = 54$
$\langle Z_1\ Z_3\ Z_4 \rangle$	L_7	$\pi^2 = 58$
$\langle Z_2\ Z_3\ Z_5 \rangle$	L_8	$\pi^2 = 160$
$\langle Z_2\ Z_4 \rangle$	L_{10}, L_{11}	$\pi^1 = 27$
$\langle Z_2\ Z_3\ Z_4 \rangle$	L_{12}, L_{14}	$\pi^2 = 92$
$\langle$all others$\rangle$	nil	$\pi^t = 0$

and so we obtain the grading

$$\pi = \pi^0 \oplus \pi^1 \oplus \pi^2 \oplus \pi^3$$

The problem of forming $\Delta\pi$ can be represented as a (graded) operator in the scheme

$$\Delta\pi: \pi^0 \xrightarrow{\Delta} \pi^1 \xrightarrow{\Delta} \pi^2 \xrightarrow{\Delta} \pi^3 \xrightarrow{\Delta} 0$$

by which we mean (e.g.) $\Delta\pi^1$ is free in the domain of π^2, etc., and $\Delta\pi^3$ is not free.

As another illustration of a graded pattern let us consider a hypothetical set of numbers which represent consumer-spending in a specific monthly period on the listed trades of A1. This will give rise to a pattern on the conjugate $K_{A1}(L)$, built up from values attributed to the seven elements — the units being the shilling and the values being based on zero data, but bearing in mind that the records show the annual rent for a piece of pasture land to be three shillings and fourpence (with twelve pence to the shilling) and the annual rent for a market stall could range from three pence to seven pence. Since the simplices representing the X_i are distinct in $K_{A1}(L)$ we can identify the pattern directly via:

$$\pi: K_{A1}(L) \to J$$

simplex σ_t		value of $\pi = \pi^t$
$\langle L_5\ L_6\ L_8\ L_{11}\ L_{13}\ L_{14}\ L_{16} \rangle$	X_1	$\pi^6 = 240$
$\langle L_3\ L_5\ L_7\ L_{16} \rangle$	X_2	$\pi^3 = 180$
$\langle L_{10} \rangle$	X_3	$\pi^0 = 40$
$\langle L_{11}\ L_{12} \rangle$	X_4	$\pi^1 = 80$
$\langle L_9\ L_{10}\ L_{13} \rangle$	X_5	$\pi^2 = 75$
$\langle L_{10}\ L_{12} \rangle$	X_6	$\pi^1 = 200$
$\langle L_{12}\ L_{14}\ L_{15} \rangle$	X_7	$\pi^2 = 60$
$\langle$all others$\rangle$	nil	$\pi^t = 0$

with the grading $\pi = \pi^0 \oplus \pi^1 \oplus \pi^2 \oplus \pi^3 \oplus \pi^6$

It follows that $\Delta\pi^6 = 0$, there can be no *free* change in the 6-level pattern, since there are no 7-simplices in the complex. This means that changes in π^6 must be induced by 'forces' of some kind, of a social nature, which are the manifestation of pressures from the inside, or the outside, of the urban community. For example, an increase of outside financial interests in the economy of Saffron Walden (over a period of many months) can result in the building of a new malthouse or the destruction of one of the inns. This must alter X_1 or X_2 and produce a new complex $K_{A1}(L)$ with new connectivity patterns, thereby affecting π^6 or π^3. Another outside force might be the isolation of the town due to an attack of plague, another inside might be a destructive fire which guts all the buildings in L_{10}, L_{12}, and L_{13}. The latter will drastically alter the connectivities of X_3, X_4, X_5, and X_6 — forming a change in the patterns π^0, π^1, and π^2, both in their values and in their orders. Thus if π^1 becomes a π^0 then the possibility of a free change $\Delta\pi$ has increased. In this way we can begin to *describe the effect of the pressures in terms of the changes in the patterns.* We consider therefore two situations: the first is one in which there is a non-trivial change in the population pattern, and the second is one in which the consumer-spending pattern changes.

In the first case we suppose that, over some specified period of time, say, between 1600 and 1605, the population pattern changes as follows.

$$\Delta\pi^0 = -30, \Delta\pi^1 = +20, \Delta\pi^2 = -15, \Delta\pi^3 = +42$$

The fact that $\Delta\pi^3 \neq 0$ can be interpreted by saying that there is an effective extra vertex which, if it were actually present, would allow a free change π^3 of the value of $+42$. Thus this change of $+42$ in π^3 is in some sense a measure of the lack of freedom to change, of the extraneous pressure or force which results in the change. Since the other components π^0, π^1, π^2 are all defined on simplices which are faces of the one 3-simplex the corresponding changes can be viewed as free changes which can take place without any appeal to these extraneous pressures or forces. We shall consequently describe this situation of

$$\pi \to \pi + \Delta\pi, \text{ over a specified time interval,}$$

as one which *exhibits an attractive force at the 3-level,* described by the value of $\pi^3 = +42$. We call it attractive because it results in an increase in π^3. Such a social force is extraneous to the 3-simplex on which π^3 is defined, it need not be associated with the 'outside' of the complex $K_L(A3)$ in the ordinary sense. Nor is it unreasonable to warn against too glib an identification between this use of the word 'force' and that found in physics. But the parallel, vis-à-vis our complexes, should not be misleading since, in physics a force is measured by an acceleration (or change of velocity per unit of time) — and it is a philosophical convention to say that the force causes the motion. What it 'causes', and this is exactly the same as in our new use of the word 'force', is for a new vertex (or set of vertices) to be effectively added to the complex so that changes in π^t are possible. The fact that we allow various values of t corresponds to the physicist's use of general tensors as an extension of the order (2-simplex order) of force.

But this analogy with the idea of force in physical science would suggest that we only need appeal to the idea of a social force when π^t patterns change on $(t + 1)$-disconnected components of the complex. Since this can happen at more than one value of t, we *need to describe a force as a t-force* (a 1-force, a 4-force, etc.). And, for a particular t-value, how are we to distinguish the 'strength' of this t-force — assuming this is possible? Because of the great diversity of vertices and simplices involved in the complexes of $S(N)$ it would appear to be futile to think in terms of specific qualitative units for our t-force. Rather it seems more sensible to regard the rational number $\Delta\pi^t/\pi^t$ ($\pi^t \neq 0$) as a measure of this strength, for comparison purposes, and to call the t-force *attractive* when *this ratio is positive,* and *repulsive* when the ratio is *negative.*

The result of using this vocabulary to describe the hypothetical population pattern change $\Delta\pi$ is to say that *it is expressive of an attractive 3-force of strength 42/250 acting in the complex K_L (A3)*.

A similar hypothetical change of pattern $\Delta\pi$, defined on K_{A1} (L), *viz.*, $\pi^0 = +5$, $\pi^1 = -30$, $\pi^6 = +40$, would be described as consisting of an attractive 6-force, of strength 40/240, together with a repulsive 1-force, of strength 30/280, acting in the complex.

When there is zero t-force, for any value of t, in the complex then all changes which take place in patterns π are free changes, without constraints. Since, under these conditions, $\Delta\pi^t$ is a π^{t+1}, so every π^{t+1} can be regarded as a possible (source of) $\Delta\pi^t$. Hence this kind of *force-free pattern change* is characterised by a *flow of pattern* values *down* the sequence of q-values (from a σ^2 to a σ^1, etc.), not up that sequence. Characteristically a force-full pattern change will be able to exhibit a flow of pattern values up the sequence of q-values, and this includes the creation of an effective σ_{t+1} where one did not exist before.

Is it thereby too fanciful to regard the t-forces present in a community as descriptive of the drives to expand, to build, and to widen the horizons, and which lift the human condition out of the frozen patterns of physics?

6.5 Algebraic patterns for town planning

If we refer to Appendix D we see there an outline of the algebraic possibilities of discussing the structure of complexes and the dynamics of patterns on them. The static backcloth of any particular urban community thereby becomes expressible by a polynomial

$$\pi_s = \sum_{i,\,p} \sigma_p^i$$

where σ_p^i is the ith p-simplex in some K contained in $S(N)$, and which is the algebraic monomial term (say) $x_{\alpha_0} x_{\alpha_1} \ldots x_{\alpha_p}$ in the appropriate algebra (ΛV or $\mathbb{C}(V)$), the x's being in a (1–1) correspondence with the vertex set V. Thus π_s is a special pattern such that,

if $\sigma_p \in K$, then $(\sigma_p, \pi_s) = 1$

and if $\sigma_q \notin K$, $(\sigma_q, \pi_s) = 0$

When we refer to the backcloth $S(N)$ as *static* we have in mind only that, with respect to some agreed time interval T_0 (say), the complex K (or that union of complexes K_i which go to make up $S(N)$) remains unaltered. In contradistinction to this time scale T_0 we naturally allow for other time intervals $T_1, T_2, \ldots$, which are such that

(1) $T_i < T_0$, for all $i \neq 0$ and
(2) there exist patterns $\pi : K \to J$ which are such that each π is constant in some T_i but variable in T_0.

These latter patterns define the *dynamics* of the urban community, and their variations describe what we have called the t-forces in the structure.

An obvious example of this idea is provided by the dynamic pattern π of a modern vehicular traffic on the streets (lozenge-areas) of a town. If, say, the values of π represent the numbers of parked vehicles at any instant, then we might be able to agree that there exists a time interval (T_1) such that π is constant in this interval — whilst it is patently variable over the much longer period T_0. Precisely, we might well take T_0 as the period of 1 month whilst T_1 is the period of 30 minutes. During T_0 we regard the backcloth as static, and described by π_s, and during any intermediate time T (where $T_1 < T < T_0$) there will be a variation in the values of π. These changes in π (values of $\Delta\pi$) are a reflection of the vehicle-parking t-forces which exist in the urban structure: naturally, these t-forces are functions of the activities A_i (the vertex set) which define the simplices in $K_L(A; \lambda)$ on which π is defined.

In a similar way, we obtain a dynamical view of the leisure-pursuits of the urban population by studying the pattern π' — which tells us how many people are enjoying the separate activities A_j (which happen to describe those particular leisure vertices). Thus π' is most naturally taken as a pattern on the simplices of $K_A(L; \lambda^{-1})$; changes in π' are a reflection of the social-cultural-sporting t-forces which are acting in the urban structure.

Such patterns as π, π' above have the algebraic representations

$$\pi = \sum_{i,p} n_i \sigma_p^i \quad n_i \in J, \ \sigma_p^i \in K_L(A; \lambda)$$

$$\pi' = \sum_{j,q} n_j' \sigma_q^j \quad n_j' \in J, \ \sigma_q^j \in K_A(L; \lambda^{-1})$$

and where, for example, the vertices in $K_L(A)$ correspond to the variables x_i, whilst those of $K_A(L)$ correspond to the variables y_j.

We can now see the immediate effect of changes in the static backcloth $S(N)$ vis-à-vis the dynamical patterns $\pi, \pi', \ldots$, which might interest us. If, for example, one vertex A_1 in $K_L(A; \lambda)$ is removed completely from the scene then every term in π_s which contains the variable x_1 is reduced in degree by 1. For example,

$$x_1 x_2 x_4 x_5 \text{ becomes the term } x_2 x_4 x_5$$

and this corresponds, in the geometry in E^h, to the tetrahedron $A_1 A_2 A_4 A_5$ being reduced to the single face $A_2 A_4 A_5$. It follows that any dynamical pattern, say, π which contains the term

$$n \ x_1 x_2 x_4 x_5$$

is *forcibly altered* by *this change in the geometry of the backcloth*. Since the term must become $n \ x_2 x_4 x_5$ the change is effectively as if π had undergone the change

$$\Delta\pi = -n \ x_1 x_2 x_4 x_5 + n \ x_2 x_4 x_5$$

This means that there is effectively introduced into the structure

(1) a 3-force (of repulsion) which evacuates the simplex $A_1 A_2 A_4 A_5$,
(2) a 2-force (of attraction) which attracts towards the simplex $A_2 A_4 A_5$.

An individual motorist (assuming our π refers to the parking-pattern) will therefore experience these t-forces as a part of his intuitive sense of the dynamics of the community. Before the change in π_s he parks his car in some lozenge-area L_i which corresponds (via λ) to the activities A_1, A_2, A_4, A_5 — because he is contributing to the π^3-component of π (if he were only interested in activity A_1 then he would not be contributing to this term of the polynomial π, but to the coefficient of the monomial x_1). After the change in π_s he finds that his L_i now corresponds to the activities A_2, A_4, A_5 only. This situation increases the flexibility for parking (for the individual's choice) since, changing his mind about parking requires only the existence of a 2-connection in the geometry as opposed to the previous 3-connection. But the price paid by the individual person is the reduction of his effective community simplex from a σ_3 to a σ_2. This latter corresponds to the repulsive 3-force, whilst the greater flexibility corresponds to the attractive 2-force.

In a similar way, suppose that in $K_A(L; \lambda^{-1})$ the static backcloth polynomial π_s contains the monomial term

$$y_1 y_2 y_4 y_5 y_7$$

and that we consider the removal of y_1 (this might correspond to the demolition of a street, or part of a street, due to some new development). Then every π' which contains the variable y_1 is altered appropriately, as before. The forcible alteration in the geometry of the backcloth automatically introduces a repulsive 4-force (away from the activities which correspond to the areas L_1, L_2, L_4, L_5, L_7) together with an attractive 3-force (towards the activities which correspond to the areas L_2, L_4, L_5, L_7). An individual person experiences these t-forces as social pressures in the urban structure; pressures which deprive him of physical space (the L_1) and yet which increase his flexibility among the remaining leisure-pursuits which remain.

In either of the cases considered the individual in the community obtains an overall feeling about the structure which reflects the importance which he personally attributes to either his own simplex dimension in $S(N)$ or to the connectivity pattern of the conjugate complexes $K_L(A)$, $K_A(L)$. In other words, he must eventually strike a balance between his reaction to the various t-forces of repulsion and those of attraction which embody the changes in π_s.

When proposals for new Town Plans or specific Town Developments are being considered by the community then it is clear that they can be completely described by a collection of polynomials — which include the appropriate π_s and dynamical π's. This, of course, requires that there shall be an adequate amount of data available for the definitions of the pattern polynomials as well as appropriate Q-analyses for their interpretation.

This would suggest that Planning Policies for urban structures could be represented in terms of the dynamics and the statics of the community patterns. For example, a knowledge of the q-connectivities of the static backcloth clearly sets limits to the pattern changes which the geometry allows and, against this backcloth, a knowledge of the pattern changes gives a dynamic view of the community which represents the 'norm' at some particular time. Then a community might allow the existence of t-forces in the structure provided they are well-defined and constrained within specific limits. For example, the inhabitants of our Suffolk village, Lavenham, might be so enamoured of the Tudor appearance of their houses that they might well demand that the connectivity values of the simplices in $K_L(A; \lambda)$ — where A is a set of specific Tudor properties of buildings in streets L_i — must not be allowed to fall below certain values; in other words, that the bottom-q value of every L_i must not be less than (say) $\check{q} = 4$. This places a *Planning Policy in the context of the algebra of pattern polynomials;* it would result in constraints on any Development Plan to alter the backcloth $S(N)$; it naturally imposes limits on the values of 't', when reckoning with the t-forces which result from any change in a dynamic π. If π is a density of tourist sightseers in the village, then $\pi^{\check{q}}$ is the lowest order component in the graded pattern π. Lowering the value of $\check{q}$ is likely to decrease the obstruction vector which, as we have seen in a previous section, is a measure of how diverse is the visual attraction of the village. In a similar manner might the inhabitants (assuming that they are in command of their destinies) place upper limits on the *intensities* of the t-forces which the structure is to be allowed to carry. If the backcloth $S(N)$ is to be altered in some hypothetical way so that some specific lozenge-areas (L_1, L_2, ...) increase their simplex dimensions vis-à-vis a set of commercial (retail) activities, then it is likely that a dynamic pattern π defining consumer spending will suffer a definite change — due to a redistribution over L. This will result in the existence of attractive as well as repulsive t-forces (which will accurately describe the gain and loss of trade in different parts of the town). These forces will have intensities (described in the previous section) which may be expressed as simple percentages. Should there be limits (upper and lower?) placed on these forces so as to limit the affect on the whole community? When there are no such limits imposed then towns, or parts of towns, die, whilst others grow.

It is therefore being suggested that Urban Development and Urban Planning can be precisely expressed in the algebraic language of pattern polynomials, and detailed under the following broad headings:

(1) Policy constraints on the connectivities of the backcloth $S(N)$,
(2) Policy constraints on the intensities of the t-forces which the structure should be permitted to carry, consequent upon any change in $S(N)$.

Such a development would allow every interested party, every age group, every cultural society, to have a foot in the door when decisions are to be taken. With a common language in which to express the problems there is a greater possibility of understanding just what a community is and how it functions. If we may make use of the fact that this language of connectivities is its own metalanguage, then we can say that it acts as an extra vertex in all sets A and complexes $K_P(A; \lambda)$, P being a set of people. It therefore makes a contribution to the connectivity of any such complex, and this contribution helps to reduce the obstruction vector; hence, for example, patterns of ranking (priorities needed before decisions can be arrived at) can consequently flow in the complex more easily; agreement is more likely, not less.

Even so we must not underestimate the human ability to find new reasons for doubt and suspicion when dealing in human affairs.

7 Politics and the University Bar

7.1 Shall we move the bar?

We take up the highly political question which we introduced in section 1.8, of whether we should move the university bar from its present position A to a proposed position B. We begin from the position we left in Chapter 1, with two relatively simplified relations

$$\Gamma_1 \subset Y \times X \quad \text{and} \quad \Gamma_2 \subset P \times X$$

where Y = a set of university activities,   card Y = 13
       X = a set of university committees, card X = 12
and   P = a set of individual people,   card P = 25.

The incidence matrices of Γ_1 and Γ_2 are given in section 1.8 and the structural analyses for both are given below.

For $K_Y(X; \Gamma_1)$:

Y1	Y2	Y3	Y4	Y5	Y6	Y7	Y8	Y9	Y10	Y11	Y12	Y13	
1	–	–	–	–	–	–	0	–	–	–	–	–	Y1
	0	–	–	–	–	–	–	–	–	0	–	–	Y2
		2	1	0	0	0	0	0	0	0	0	2	Y3
			1	0	–	–	–	–	–	–	–	1	Y4
				1	0	0	0	0	0	0	0	1	Y5
					2	1	1	1	1	1	1	0	Y6
						2	0	2	1	0	2	0	Y7
							4	0	1	2	1	1	Y8
								2	1	0	2	0	Y9
									3	2	2	1	Y10
										3	1	1	Y11
											4	1	Y12
												3	Y13

with components

at $q = 4$ {Y8}, {Y12}
at $q = 3$ {Y8}, {Y10}, {Y11}, {Y12}, {Y13}
at $q = 2$ {Y3, Y13}, {Y6}, {Y7, Y8, Y9, Y10, Y11, Y12}
at $q = 1$ {Y1}, {Y3, Y4, Y5, Y6, Y7, Y8, Y9, Y10, Y11, Y12, Y13}
at $q = 0$ {all}

For $K_X(Y; \Gamma_1^{-1})$:

X1	X2	X3	X4	X5	X6	X7	X8	X9	X10	X11	X12	
0	–	–	–	–	–	–	–	–	–	0	–	X1
	3	–	–	–	–	0	0	2	3	–	1	X2
		1	–	–	–	0	–	–	0	–	0	X3
			0	–	–	0	–	–	0	0	0	X4
				2	2	–	–	–	1	–	0	X5
					3	–	–	–	2	–	0	X6
						3	–	0	3	0	2	X7
							0	0	0	–	0	X8
								3	3	–	0	X9
									9	0	4	X10
										1	0	X11
											4	X12

with components

at $q = 9$ {X10},   at $q = 8$ {X10}
at $q = 7$ {X10},   at $q = 6$ {X10}
at $q = 5$ {X10},   at $q = 4$ {X10, X12}
at $q = 3$ {X2, X7, X9, X10, X12}, {X6}
at $q = 2$ {X2, X5, X6, X7, X9, X10, X12}
at $q = 1$ {X3}, {X11}, {X2, X5, X6, X7, X9, X10, X12}
at $q = 0$ {all}

The two structure vectors for Γ_1 are consequently,

$K_Y(X; \Gamma_1)$: $Q = \{\overset{4}{2} \ 5 \ 3 \ 2 \ \overset{0}{1}\}$

$K_X(Y; \Gamma_1^{-1})$: $Q = \{\overset{9}{1} \ 1 \ 1 \ 1 \ 1 \ 1 \ \overset{3}{2} \ 1 \ 3 \ \overset{0}{1}\}$

And for the relation Γ_2 we obtain,

For $K_P(X;\Gamma_2)$:

	P1	P2	P3	P4	P5	P6	P7	P8	P9	P10	P11	P12	P13	P14	P15	P16	P17	P18	P19	P20	P21	P22	P23	P24	P25
P1	5	2	3	3	0	2	0	0	1	0	1	1	1	0	1	1	0	0	0	0	0	0	1	1	1
P2		3	2	1	0	0	0	0	0	1	1	1	1	0	1	1	1	0	0	1	1	0	1	1	0
P3			4	4	0	0	0	1	0	1	1	0	0	0	0	1	0	0	0	0	1	1	0	1	0
P4				5	0	0	1	1	1	0	0	1	1	0	0	0	0	0	1	0	1	0	2	0	1
P5					—	1	1	0	1	0	0	1	1	1	1	1	1	1	1	1	0	0	0	0	0
P6						3	1	1	1	0	0	0	0	0	0	0	0	0	0	0	1	0	0	0	1
P7							1	0	0	0	0	0	0	0	0	0	0	0	0	0	0	0	0	0	0
P8								1	0	0	0	0	0	0	0	0	0	0	0	0	1	1	0	0	0
P9									2	0	0	0	0	0	0	0	0	0	0	0	0	0	0	0	1
P10										2	0	0	0	0	0	0	0	0	1	0	0	0	0	0	—
P11											2	0	0	0	0	1	0	1	1	0	0	0	2	1	—
P12												3	1	0	0	0	0	0	0	0	0	0	0	0	—
P13													3	0	0	1	0	0	0	0	0	0	0	0	—
P14														0	0	0	0	0	0	0	0	0	0	0	—
P15															0	0	0	0	0	0	0	0	0	0	—
P16																1	0	0	0	0	0	0	0	0	—
P17																	0	0	0	0	0	0	0	0	—
P18																		0	0	0	0	0	0	0	—
P19																			0	0	0	0	0	0	—
P20																				0	0	0	0	0	—
P21																					2	1	0	0	0
P22																						1	0	0	0
P23																							3	2	0
P24																								2	0
P25																									1

with components

at $q = 5$ {P4}, {P1},
at $q = 4$ {P1}, {P3}, {P4}
at $q = 3$ {P1, P3, P4, P5}, {P2}, {P6}, {P12}, {P13}, {P23}
at $q = 2$ {P1, P2, P3, P4, P6, P23}, {P5}, {P9}, {P10}, {P11}, {P12}, {P13}, {P21}, {P24}
at $q = 1$ {P1, P2, P3, P4, P5, P6, P7, P8 P9, P10, P11, P12, P13, P16, P21, P23, P24, P25}, {P22}
at $q = 0$ {all}

For $K_X(P; \Gamma_2^{-1})$:

X1	X2	X3	X4	X5	X6	X7	X8	X9	X10	X11	X12	
5	0	0	1	1	1	–	–	0	1	0	2	X1
	5	0	–	1	1	1	0	0	2	2	1	X2
		3	–	1	0	0	–	0	1	–	–	X3
			4	–	0	0	0	1	0	–	1	X4
				5	0	0	–	–	2	0	1	X5
					6	–	0	–	4	1	2	X6
						5	0	2	1	0	1	X7
							2	0	–	1	0	X8
								3	0	0	0	X9
									9	1	3	X10
										5	3	X11
											8	X12

with components

at $q = 9$ {X10},
at $q = 8$ {X10}, {X12}
at $q = 7$ {X10}, {X12}
at $q = 6$ {X6}, {X10}, {X12}
at $q = 5$ {X1}, {X2}, {X5}, {X6}, {X7}, {X10}, {X11}, {X12}
at $q = 4$ {X1}, {X2}, {X4}, {X5}, {X6, X10}, {X7}, {X11}, {X12}
at $q = 3$ {X1}, {X2}, {X3}, {X4}, {X5}, {X6, X10, X11, X12}, {X7}, {X9}
at $q = 2$ {X1, X2, X5, X6, X10, X11, X12}, {X3}, {X4}, {X7, X9}
at $q = 1$ {all}
at $q = 0$ {all}

The structure vectors for Γ_2 are consequently,

$K_P(X; \Gamma_2)$: $Q = \{\overset{5}{2} \ 3 \ 6 \ \overset{2}{9} \ 2 \ \overset{0}{1}\}$

$K_X(P; \Gamma_2^{-1})$: $Q = \{\overset{9}{1} \ 2 \ 2 \ 3 \ \overset{5}{8} \ 8 \ 8 \ \overset{2}{4} \ 1 \ 1\}$

For convenience we repeat the lists which describe the sets X and Y, *viz.*,

X1	minor-works finance committee	X7	social amenities committee
X2	student welfare committee	X8	housing committee
X3	landscape committee	X9	student affairs committee
X4	catering committee	X10	senate
X5	academic department committee	X11	finance committee
X6	faculty board	X12	council

and

Y1	capital expenditure	Y8	catering provision
Y2	external decor	Y9	student recreation
Y3	room allocation	Y10	general amenities
Y4	departmental rooms	Y11	public relations
Y5	faculty room	Y12	student residences
Y6	cleaning detail	Y13	staff amenities
Y7	security		

We must also now take into account the network of committees (which is what most writers on politics would consider the 'structure' of the political situation), that is to say, the tree which represents which committees may send resolutions to which other committees. We shall not be too unrealistic if we adopt the following as the relation, Γ_3, which describes the open statement 'committee —— sends its recommendations forward to committee ——'. The usual network representation is shown in Figure 7.1.

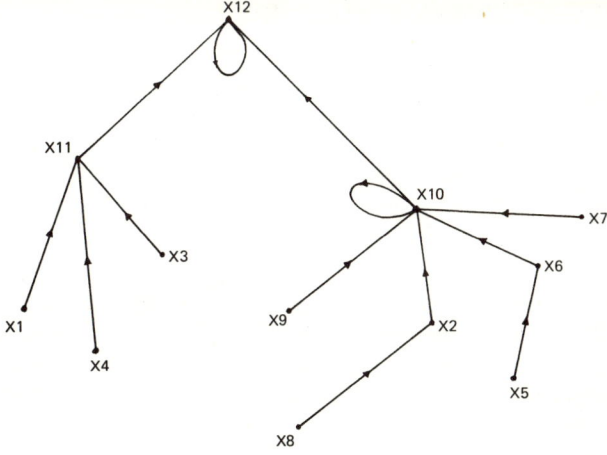

Figure 7.1 Conventional tree of committees; relation Γ_3

146 *Mathematical Structure in Human Affairs*

In Γ_3, if a committee XJ may take a decision itself we interpret it as Γ_3-related to itself. It will therefore appear that only X10 (the senate) and X12 (the council) may take decisions, and this is indicated in Figure 7.1 by the presence of a loop on X10 or on X12.

Γ_3	X1	X2	X3	X4	X5	X6	X7	X8	X9	X10	X11	X12
X1	0	0	0	0	0	0	0	0	0	0	1	0
X2	0	0	0	0	0	0	0	0	0	1	0	0
X3	0	0	0	0	0	0	0	0	0	0	1	0
X4	0	0	0	0	0	0	0	0	0	0	1	0
X5	0	0	0	0	0	1	0	0	0	0	0	0
X6	0	0	0	0	0	0	0	0	0	1	0	0
X7	0	0	0	0	0	0	0	0	0	1	0	0
X8	0	1	0	0	0	0	0	0	0	0	0	0
X9	0	0	0	0	0	0	0	0	0	1	0	0
X10	0	0	0	0	0	0	0	0	0	1	0	1
X11	0	0	0	0	0	0	0	0	0	0	0	1
X12	0	0	0	0	0	0	0	0	0	0	0	1

This relation Γ_3 is a subset of $X \times X$, and the simplicial complexes which describe it are $K_X(X; \Gamma_3)$ and $K_X(X; \Gamma_3^{-1})$. The first of these is $K_X(X; \Gamma_3) = \{\sigma_1, \sigma_0^i; i = 1, \ldots . 5\}$

where

$\sigma_1 = \langle X10, X12 \rangle$ with the name X10

$\sigma_0^1 = \langle X11 \rangle$ with the names X1, X3, X4

$\sigma_0^2 = \langle X10 \rangle$ with the names X2, X6, X7, X9

$\sigma_0^3 = \langle X6 \rangle$ with the name X5

$\sigma_0^4 = \langle X2 \rangle$ with the name X8

$\sigma_0^5 = \langle X12 \rangle$ with the names X11, X12

These simplices describe the connected pattern between the *committees which send forward recommendations;* we might therefore speak of $K_X(X; \Gamma_3)$ as the *outgoing-complex*. By comparison the structure $K_X(X; \Gamma_3^{-1})$ describes the connections between the *committees which receive recommendations;* we might therefore speak of $K_X(X; \Gamma_3^{-1})$ as the *incoming-complex*. This possesses the following simplices,

$$K_X(X; \Gamma_3^{-1}) = \{\sigma_4, \sigma_2^1, \sigma_2^2, \sigma_0^1, \sigma_0^2\}$$

where

$\sigma_4 = \langle X2, X6, X7, X9, X10 \rangle$ with the name X10
$\sigma_2^1 = \langle X1, X3, X4 \rangle$ with the name X11
$\sigma_2^2 = \langle X10, X11, X12 \rangle$ with the name X12
$\sigma_0^1 = \langle X5 \rangle$ with the name X6
$\sigma_0^2 = \langle X8 \rangle$ with the name X2

We notice that the domain of Γ_3^{-1} is a proper subset of X, which is the domain of Γ_3. We notice too that Figure 7.1 (which *conventionally* represents the 'committee structure') is an attempt to represent both complexes at the same time, and to do so by using nothing more than 1-simplices; we do not recommend it as an adequate tool for a full discussion of the relations between the committees. The geometry of the incoming-complex $K_X(X; \Gamma_3^{-1})$ gives rise to the structure vector

$$Q = \{\overset{4}{1} \quad 1 \quad 3 \quad 3 \quad \overset{0}{4}\}$$

showing that $Q_0 = 4$; there are four distinct entry points (better, *entry zones*) for committee recommendations. These entry zones are the separate sub-complexes which make up the whole, and they are constituted as follows:

$$\{\sigma_4, \sigma_2^2\}_1, \{\sigma_2^1\}_2, \{\sigma_0^1\}_3, \{\sigma_0^2\}_4$$

Their structure vectors are separately,

$$Q_1 = \{\overset{4}{1} \quad 1 \quad 2 \quad 2 \quad \overset{0}{1}\}$$
$$Q_2 = \qquad \{1 \quad 1 \quad \overset{0}{1}\}$$
$$Q_3 = \qquad\qquad \{\overset{0}{1}\}$$
$$Q_4 = \qquad\qquad \{\overset{0}{1}\}$$

with the sum $\quad Q = Q_1 + Q_2 + Q_3 + Q_4$

The vector Q_1 refers to the complex which contains the senate and the council; this is the only complex with a non-zero obstruction vector

$$\hat{Q}_1 = \{\overset{2}{1} \quad 1 \quad 0\}$$

7.2 The political backcloth

The structures which are associated with the relations $\Gamma_1, \Gamma_2, \Gamma_3$ form the backcloth, $S(N)$, against which all the political action must be played out. It is therefore important for us to examine those structures and to appreciate the implications of the various connectivity patterns, before we can hope to fully understand any specific political scenario.

Beginning with Γ_1 and the complex $K_Y(X; \Gamma_1)$ we see that there are two 4-simplices, Y8 and Y12; each of these have top-q value of 4 and bottom-q

value of 2. They stand out from the rest with their relativity high eccentricities; even at $\check{q} = 2$ they are not directly connected to each other, this only occurs at $q = 1$. It is probably not surprising that Y8 (= catering provision) should be eccentric in this context, but the equal role played by Y12 (= student residences) is certainly more of a surprise. At the next top-q value of 3 the elements Y10 (= general amenities), Y11 (= public relations), and Y13 (= staff amenities) come into the picture; each of these possesses the same bottom-q value of 2. At the value of $\hat{q} = 2$ the element Y6 (= cleaning detail) comes in as a disconnected component and Y3 (= room allocation) comes in as a face of Y13. At the level of $\hat{q} = 1$ a distinct component occurs with Y1 (=capital expenditure), and the only 0-simplex is Y2 (= external decor). This 0-simplex, Y2, is only connected to one other element, namely, the 3-simplex Y11 (= public relations), and this connection is of zero order. Finally, the complex is in one piece, with $Q_0 = 1$, and it possesses an obstruction vector of

$$\hat{Q} = \{\overset{4}{1} \quad 4 \quad 2 \quad 1 \quad 0\}$$

containing a relatively high component at $q = 3$.

The conjugate complex $K_X(Y; \Gamma_1^{-1})$ gives us a picture of the dynamic functioning of the committees vis-à-vis the set Y. The simplex of highest dimension is X10 (= the senate) at $\hat{q} = 9$, and with $\check{q} = 4$ this committee possesses eccentricity of 5. Indeed we can see that the senate exists in splendid isolation for all the $\hat{q}$-values of 9, 8, 7, 6, 5 until it is joined at $\hat{q} = 4$ by X12 (= the council). This structure therefore confirms the fact that it is the senate (and to a lesser degree the council) which discusses most of the problems, both in theory and in practice. Since the senate consists of members of the academic staff (wearing various hats) then these are the people who are running the university (an assertion which might come as something of a surprise to a few colleagues). After the dominating position of X10 and X22, we find that X2 (= student welfare), X7 (= social amenities), and X9 (= student affairs committee) enter the picture at $\hat{q} = 3$ and as faces of X10 or X12. Also at $\hat{q} = 3$, but disconnected, we find X6 (= faculty board); each of these new simplices becomes connected at this next level with $\check{q} = 2$. Then at $\hat{q} = 1$ we find X3 (= landscape) and X11 (= finance) as separate components, but each committee possesses a bottom-q value of $\check{q} = 0$, so that $Q_0 = 1$. Although the structure vector **Q** possesses a component at $q = 9$ (due to X10) the obstruction vector is only

$$\hat{Q} = \{\overset{3}{1} \quad 0 \quad 2 \quad 0\}$$

and this is due to the fact that, at the high q-values between 4 and 9, the complex behaves like one simplex (X10 = the senate) which offers zero obstruction between its faces. This latter fact is an important characteristic of any organization in which complicated decisions must be made. If there is one committee (or its equivalent) which may discuss *all* issues then that committee becomes a single n-simplex, σ_n, for a suitably large value of n. Furthermore this σ_n is identical with the appropriate complex K, which contains this σ_n. Hence the obstruction vector is $\hat{Q} = 0$ — because, at the practical level, all matters may not only be discussed but (consequently) can be traded off against each other, may be juggled with in the sense of priorities, and so decisions can always be arrived at. When $\hat{Q} \neq 0$ this process is naturally obstructed (by the multi-dimensional geometry which obtains), and decision-making is much harder. The classical difference between totalitarian and democratic systems is this difference — the first possesses a zero obstruction vector $\hat{Q} = 0$, the second does not. The first case is unlikely to be a genuine illustration unless the top committee (the σ_n) contains only one man, and he must be free of schizophrenia. To be precise, the vector $\hat{Q}$ is a measure of the obstruction to a free change $\Delta\pi$ in any pattern π defined on the complex (cf. section 6.4). In this case, where we are contemplating a decision-making process, such a pattern π could well be a set of priority rankings (values in J) on the simplices. If then the complex consists of one simplex σ_n and π contains a component π^n we must have the case of

$$\Delta\pi^n = 0$$

This can then give rise to a 'conservation-law' situation where, for example,

$$\sum_i \Delta\pi^n(Y_i) = 0$$

the Y_i being the names of the σ_n. This situation is no more nor less than that contained in the proverb, 'what you lose on the swings you gain on the roundabouts'.

Returning to the details of our backcloth $S(N)$ we look at the relation Γ_2 and the complex $K_P(X; \Gamma_2)$. The highest order simplex occurs with the individual P4, with $\hat{q} = 5$ and $\check{q} = 3$, and P1 and P3 enter the lists at $\hat{q} = 4$ and with $\check{q} = 2$. It follows that P4 sits on six committees and P1 and P3 sit on five committees, which are not the same five in each case because P1 and P3 are only 3-connected (so they share four committees). If we are giving equal weight to each individual and to each committee then P4 must be the most influential person in the structure, closely followed by P1 and P3. Such equal weights are of course unrealistic and fortunately our language of complexes need not make such crude concessions to abstraction. In fact, the way to allow for unequal weighting, either of people or of committees, is by defining a ranking pattern π on the relevant complex. But, failing that, at this stage we can see that P4, P1, P3 are *potentially* the most influential people in the complex. The rest of the structure shows a high degree of disconnection, with $Q_3 = 6$ and $Q_2 = 9$. The consequent obstruction vector is

$$\hat{Q} = \{\overset{4}{2} \quad 5 \quad 8 \quad 1 \quad 0\}$$

and the *experience* of this pattern is, reminiscent of our Tudor village example in Chapter 6, one which cannot be gained from any one vantage point (any one committee). The observer can only get the feel of what all these individuals are like (in this political backcloth $S(N)$) by seeing them in action in many committees. And although our hypothetical list of people only contains twenty-five names P1, ..., P25 — and thus might give the impression of an oligarchical rule — the high values in the vector $\hat{Q}$ show that there is a premium

150 *Mathematical Structure in Human Affairs*

on disagreement, assuming, that is, that these people meet and interact only in these twelve committees. It is not unreasonable, in the light of this discussion, to therefore say that if *oligarchy is bad because card P is too small then democracy (card P large) is only good if the obstruction vector $\hat{Q}$ is small.*

The conjugate complex $K_X(P; \Gamma_2^{-1})$ now describes the committee structure as a connectivity pattern dependent on the sharing of people. As in the case of Γ_1 we find that X10 (= the senate) is the largest simplex, at $\hat{q} = 9$, and that the council follows closely on this at $\hat{q} = 8$. The eccentricities of these committees are remarkably high with $\hat{q} = 4$, for X10, and $\hat{q} = 3$ for X12. The faculty board, X6, is the third high order simplex with non-trivial eccentricity via $\hat{q} = 4$ and $\hat{q} = 6$. This means that the academic staff are spread over senate, council, and the faculty board to quite a wide extent, because of the high $\hat{q}$ values, and the $\check{q}$-values describe the level of sharing between the committees. The overall picture is again one with high Q_q values, the resulting obstruction vector being

$$\hat{Q} = \{\overset{8}{1}\ 1\ 2\ \overset{5}{7}\ \overset{4}{7}\ \overset{3}{7}\ 3\ 0\ 0\}$$

This 'bulge' of high values at $q = 5, 4, 3$ suggests a considerable obstacle to any $\Delta \pi^t$, for $t \geq 3$; it can mean that the ranking of any issue, as between different committees, which requires the agreement of at least four individuals is relatively rigid — $\Delta \pi^t$ is not free. This must mean also that any decision which is the result of a compromise position will be extremely difficult to obtain, given the voting significance of $t \geq 3$ in these committees where $\hat{q} \leq 9$. From this point of view the most promising alliance can be forged *via* the 4-connection which exists between X6 (= the faculty board) and X10 (= the senate). This is stronger than that between X10 and X12 (= the council).

We have already discussed the detailed structures of the relation Γ_3; it seems to the writer that these structures are very much the bare bones of the political backcloth, the necessary but far from sufficient geometry for any political action. Also, it is probably true that these Γ_3-structures are the easiest to alter if by so doing decisions for action can be expedited. This illustrates very simply the idea that when *political will* is present all practical committee-structures (meaning the crude Γ_3-structures) need not be an obstacle. This is because the Γ_3-structures are not really important as political entities, except in that they can be used (*via* the manipulation of $\hat{Q}$) to aid and abet the *real* political actions which occur in the *significant* Γ-structures.

7.3 Round-1

Against the backcloth $S(N)$ which we have described, let us now come to the actual-situation which arises as soon as one individual out of the set P feeds into the system the startling proposal 'to move the bar from A to B'. We need to consider (1) a plausible choice of individual and (2) a plausible point of entry into $S(N)$.

It is a poor state of affairs if *any* choice of individual is not a plausible choice; we shall begin by supposing that P21 is the culprit who begins to cause trouble by introducing his proposal. But where does he introduce it? He is the 2-simplex P21 = ⟨X3, X7, X9⟩, where X3 = landscape committee, X7 = social amenities committee, and X9 = student affairs committee; he therefore has a choice of three as a point of entry. The idea came to him at the vertex X3, when he and his three colleagues (X3 is a 3-simplex in $K_X(P; \Gamma_2^{-1})$) were discussing the central justification for the committee's existence, *via.*, the facades and aesthetic appeal of the university buildings. It had emerged that there was some concern, vis-à-vis public relations, that the bar was generating a waste-paper-and-empty-beer-bottles eyesore on certain occasions. Surely one solution for this indelicacy would be to move the bar, preferably indoors and out of sight. Our man, P21, therefore introduced his proposal into the entry point X3 — where better? His associates on X3 = P5, P11, P12, P21 were plainly sympathetic, all sensitive un-vulgar men, and X3 was able to send recommendations straight to X11 and thence to the very top at X12. The chairman of X3, P12, was politically astute — as far as P21 could see — and pointed out that an alternative position must accompany the proposal and that, in order to be successful, all that was needed was for the overall financial cost of the move to be safely brought down to a few hundred pounds. The complete proposal was therefore argued out on X3, including details of the final position B and a suitably optimistic guess at the cost of the operation. Since P5 was on X1 (= minor-works finance committee) and he felt sure that there was enough money in the kitty for this kind of adjustment, then X3 accepted the proposal from P21 and dutifully sent forward its recommendation to X11. At this stage we might suppose that P21 regarded the possible argument around his proposal to be centred on the issues A2, A3, A4, and A7 (listed on page 18 in section 1.8) and his own favourites B2, B3, B5, and B6 (listed on page 19). At the same time his sense of the political structure of the university amounted to a more or less clear picture of the diagram in Figure 7.1, (without the sophisticated loops).

When the proposal reaches X11 it has no practical support (because X3 and X11 are disconnected); it is therefore 'aired' rather than proposed, and the chairman of X11, spotting some wider implications, stresses the roles of X4 and X1 in such a radical proposal, and so X11 invites comment from these two sub-committees before proceeding further. Hence the proposal is delayed by the first hand-off at X11, and it now trickles through to X1 and X4 — X1 is 0-connected to X11 and X4 is not connected to X11. The message comes back to P21 that 'it is being considered by X1 and X4' and, since he knows that P5 is on X1, he blithely thinks that things are moving and that his proposal is safely bedded into the system. What perhaps he does not see is that it is destined for a long sleep this way.

The state of play at this stage, although somewhat thin, is nevertheless interesting. The proposal has been injected (if that is not too strong a word) into the σ_2^1 of $K_X(X; \Gamma_3^{-1})$, which is one of the *completely disconnected* entry zones discussed in section 7.1. Thus, although it offers a zero obstruction vector, as a subcomplex of $K_X(X; \Gamma_3^{-1})$, this entry zone leads nowhere in the sense that it cannot immediately be recommended to a decision-making committee (X10 or X12). It could perhaps have been worse, by being introduced into X5 or X8, but enough is enough. Thus the relation Γ_3 has not been properly understood; more precisely it is a knowledge of Γ_3^{-1} which is lacking, illustrating again the inadequacy of the conventional tree of Figure 7.1. Furthermore, no allowance has been made for the relation Γ_1, which effectively identifies the nature of the proposal and allocates it (if allowed to do so) to suitable points in the committee pattern. As far as P21 is concerned, he has effectively introduced the proposal into the simplex

$$X3 = \langle Y2, Y11 \rangle$$

which is of order $\hat{q} = 1$ and restricts the issue to 'external decor' and 'public relations'. The only hope for the issue to exist on a wide stage (on a bigger dimensional subcomplex) is *via* the 0-connection between X3 and X7, X10 and X12. But this 0-connection is *via* the single vertex Y11, a matter of policy – not of votes by people. Finally P21 has the support of, say, P5 and P11, both being 2-simplices in $K_P(X; \Gamma_2)$, and of these only P11 being a vertex in the senate committee X10. So far, too, we are supposing that all men are equal, in P, but we know that P21 should know, and act on, the Orwellian improvement of this, *viz.*, that some are more equal than others. Thus, P21 has misunderstood the significance of $K_X(X; \Gamma_3^{-1})$, the connectivity of $K_X(P; \Gamma_2^{-1})$, or the existence of $K_X(Y; \Gamma_1^{-1})$.

The consequence of this is that X1, X4 consider the proposal, notice the new points A5, A6, A9, A10 and B1, B4, B10, B11 and B13, and recommend to X11 that no action be taken at the present time. The finance committee send the proposal back to X3 with a promise to reconsider it at a more propitious moment; P21 gets that brick wall feeling. 'Where', he cries in frustration, 'does the power lie in this place?'. We leave him with the complaint, that his question is too simple and its answer is too complicated, for further discussion at this time.

7.4 Round-2

Fortunately for P21 his colleague P11, who is a vertex in X10, was sufficiently keen on the proposal to mention it to P3, who is a 4-simplex in $K_P(X; \Gamma_2)$. Since P3 possesses a top-q value of 4 and a bottom-q value of 3, he is not particularly eccentric in this complex. But the top-q value of 4 makes him influential; his simplex is in fact

$$P3 = \langle X1, X4, X6, X10, X12 \rangle$$

and, being on X4 the proposal is not entirely new to him – its original route to him had merely induced a certain amount of indifference. Now it seemed to P3 that there was merit in the proposal, chiefly because he had campaigned for some time for a new and more luxurious bar in the university, something to rival the spitoon-and-sawdust affair which posed as a bar at the moment. Hence P3 saw a way of getting a better bar by moving the present one; he was struck by the B9 aspect as an additional possibility. By incorporating B9 into the proposal P3 saw a way of interesting more of his sophisticated colleagues; he decided therefore to adopt the proposal and to make it his own. Where, then, was he to inject it into the system? No mistakes this time; into the component $\{\sigma_4, \sigma_2^2\}_1$ of $K_X(X; \Gamma_3^{-1})$, preferably into X10 itself. The possibilities were in fact any of X2, X6, X7, X9, X10, X11, X12, but knowing from experience that X10 is the place where the effective decision could be taken, he decided against X11, X12. He also rejected X9 and X7 because each had a bottom-q value of $\check{q} = 2$ in $K_X(P; \Gamma_2^{-1})$, and then they were only connected to each other; as far as connection with X10 was concerned they only came into the same component at $q = 1$. A better entry point would have been X2 (= student welfare committee), as far as connectivity with X10 was concerned ($q = 2$), but he did not wish to make it primarily a student welfare issue – having in mind the welfare of some of the more mature members of the university. It remained therefore a straight choice between X6 (= faculty board) and X10 itself. He settled finally on X6, because an immediate rush at X10 might precipitate attitudes which once hardened could not be altered, noting that X6 and X10 were 4-connected in $K_X(P; \Gamma_2^{-1})$.

The proposal was therefore introduced into X6 by P3, at the end of a particularly thirsty agenda, under A.O.B. with a mock flippancy which easily carried the day. Why not vote ourselves a well-earned perk after so many hours devoted to heady faculty business? It would be proposed at the next senate meeting (X10) and, coming from such a sober source, would be seriously discussed (the 4-connectivity would also ensure this). Since it was now injected at X6 the relation Γ_1 shows that it was now associated with entirely different issues than hitherto. Indeed in $K_X(Y; \Gamma_1^{-1})$ we see that

$$X6 = \langle Y3, Y4, Y5, Y13 \rangle$$

being essentially a matter of staff amenities and room allocation, of the proper use of university facilities; no more of this stuff about whether it looks pretty; real meaty sober matters; an intellectual challenge.

A price which has to be paid for introducing the proposal into the subcomplex $\{\sigma_4, \sigma_2^2\}$ of $K_X(X; \Gamma_3^{-1})$ is the presence of a non-zero obstruction vector

$$\hat{Q}_1 = \{\overset{2}{1} \quad 1 \quad 0\}$$

but this is not insuperable. The value of 1 at $q = 2$ in $\hat{Q}$ indicates a single unbridgeable gap between the two components, at $q = 2$, in the structure vector Q_1. This gap is between $\sigma_2^1 = \langle X1, X3, X4 \rangle$ and $\sigma_2^2 = \langle X10, X11, X12 \rangle$ and means that they do not share any committees. But there is an adequate link between these committees *via* $K_X(P; \Gamma_2^{-1})$ – among the people P1, P3, P11, P12, P24. Thus P3 found that P11, P12, and P24 were amenable to being sympathetic to the proposal; in particular P24 (*via* X1 and X12) would be a valuable ally when the final financial nod had to be given.

Of course P3 realized that the issues in X6, in $K_X(Y; \Gamma_1^{-1})$, were too restrictive in the matter and that, at X10, the chairman would be obliged to refer it to committees which would widen the vertex set to take in almost the whole of Y. The best way therefore to anticipate the next stage would be to cover $K_X(Y; \Gamma_1^{-1})$ as economically as possible. Once more, this could be achieved by concentrating on X6 and X10; with X6 characterized by $\hat{q} = 3$ and $\check{q} = 2$, whilst X10 is characterized by $\check{q} = 3$ and $\hat{q} = 9$. As we have seen in section 7.2 the significance of X10 in this context is to provide practically a zero obstruction vector between $q = 9$ and $q = 4$. Thus P3's tactics would be to assume the proposal would be referred to, say X1, X2, X4, and X7 but then to wait until its return to X10 where, at a high q-level in $K_X(P; \Gamma_2^{-1})$, the zero obstruction would make it easier to argue away the conflicting rankings which would return with it. Once it could be approved by X10 the financial arrangements through X1 and X11 would be a matter of a report (only) to X12.

So in round-2 of this saga the proposal from P3 came to X10 *via* X6; a sober discussion ensued and X10 approved the 'idea in principle' but, wanting some concrete advice, invited their respective comments from the committees X2, X4, and X7. Although these committees are only 1-connected in $K_X(P; \Gamma_2^{-1})$, P3 felt that it was safe to allow them to function without any campaigning among their members. Indeed he felt that if conflicting recommendations came back to X10 it would make the task easier; compromise at X10 is *unobstructed* and senators grasp at it eagerly.

But P3 had only grasped the *static nature* of the political structure; the *dynamic forces* which play on the backcloth S(N) had eluded him; this was borne out by the subsequent course of events.

At the report-back stage, X2 opposed the proposal on the grounds of B2, B3, and B7, but supported the proposal on the basis of B1, B6, and B9; X4 opposed the proposal outright because of the loss, under A10, of business to the coffee bar and also because of their fears, under B9 and B10, that the new bar would lose its present profit-making potential; X7 supported the proposal, chiefly on the grounds of B1, B3, B9, but drew attention to the difficulties inherent under B11 and B13. The result was therefore an evenly balanced dilemma for X10, with B3 and B9 being bases for both support and opposition. Nor was it known to P3 that some fears about the cost of the proposal had begun to influence P1 and P2, so much so that P2 and P4 were becoming anxious about the prejudicial allocation of funds under the minor-works programme — to the detriment of certain departmental proposals. The chairman of X10, *viz.*, P1, responded to this situation by proposing that, in order to resolve the dilemma, a *Working Party on the siting of licensed-bar facilities* be set up and that P3 should be the chairman. Furthermore he proposed that, in order that no stone be left unturned, the Working Party should be free to discuss the matter with any interested party and that it should also send a preliminary report to X11, X12, and X10.

P3, unable to understand the significance of this piece of dynamism, was obliged to accept the situation and to try to make the best of things. His colleagues on the Working Party would be chosen for him, to be representative of general interests in the university. For himself, he had not been able to execute his tactics at senate — they had suddenly appeared to be irrelevant —

and now he felt himself peculiarly marked out as a zealous advocate of a narrow and controversial proposal which, three months earlier he had thought to be just a good idea 'worth a try'. In some sense, which was somewhat confused in his mind, P3 felt isolated (disconnected), and *eccentric*.

In fact the situation was now structurally altered, the backcloth $S(N)$ had responded to the political dynamics which was being played; it was comparable in physical science, to someone altering the law of gravity when an astronaut was in flight. But how had this dynamics occurred, and what were the structural consequences?

What P3 had missed was the significance of patterns on the various complexes of $S(N)$, patterns π which provided rankings (e.g.) of people (elements of the set P), of areas of interest (elements of the set Y). Add to this a static view of the backcloth $S(N)$, a lack of awareness of the structural changes which can easily be generated from within the system, rather like a chess player who underestimates a trivial little pawn move, and we can begin to appreciate that P3 was extremely vulnerable.

In the first place, the responsibilities of the individuals in the set P naturally induce a pattern of ranking which reflects these. Since P1 is chairman of X10, which is the most decisive committee in the whole structure, then quite apart from any other considerations, this must require a ranking value for P1 which is higher than that of any other individual. After this the dimensions of the simplices which other individuals represent are an indication of their potential influence and ranking — with a suitable weighting for membership of X10 and X12, the two decision-making committees. The result of all these considerations (and excluding any attempt at a deeper analysis based on popular ideas of personality) is that P3 could well have anticipated a ranking pattern on $K_P(X; \Gamma'_2)$ of something like the following.

$$\pi : P \to J$$

where

$\pi(P1) = 10$

$\pi(P2) = 5, \quad \pi(P3) = 6, \quad \pi(P4) = 7$

$\pi(P7) = 2, \quad \pi(P8) = 2, \quad \pi(P9) = 3$

$\pi(P11) = 3, \quad \pi(P12) = 4, \quad \pi(P14) = 2$

$\pi(P16) = 2, \quad \pi(P18) = 2, \quad \pi(P23) = 4$

$\pi(P24) = 3, \quad \pi(P25) = 2, \quad \pi(\text{rest}) = 1$

If now P2 and P4 are in opposition to P3 on an issue of this kind (that is to say, not an issue over which P3 is likely to resign and thereby so upset the community as to cause a widespread *structural* disruption) and if P1 has some sympathy with the reasons for this opposition, then the decisive action of X10 is likely to be set against a backcloth $S'(N)$ in which $K_X(P; \Gamma_2^{-1})$ is based on an effectively modified relation Γ_2 which, to be reasonably generous to the members of the set P, includes only those PJ for which $\pi(PJ) \geq 4$. This gives a (dynamic) structure as follows.

$K_P^t(X; \Gamma_2)$:

P1	P2	P3	P4	P12	P23	
5	2	3	3	1	1	P1
	3	2	1	1	1	P2
		4	1	0	0	P3
			5	1	2	P4
				3	2	P12
					3	P23

with components

at $q = 5$ {P1}, {P4}
at $q = 4$ {P1}, {P3}, {P4}
at $q = 3$ {P1, P3, P4}, {P2}, {P12}, {P23}
at $q = 2, 1, 0$ {all}

and structure vector

$$Q' = \{\overset{5}{2} \ 3 \ 4 \ 1 \ 1 \ \overset{0}{1}\}$$

which was previously

$$Q = \{\overset{5}{2} \ 3 \ 6 \ 9 \ 2 \ \overset{0}{1}\}$$

$K_X'(P; \Gamma_2^{-1})$:

X1	X2	X3	X4	X5	X6	X7	X9	X10	X11	X12	
1	0	–	0	–	1	–	–	1	0	1	X1
	3	0	–	1	0	1	0	3	1	1	X2
		0	–	0	–	0	–	0	–	–	X3
			0	–	0	–	–	0	–	0	X4
				2	0	0	–	2	–	0	X5
					2	–	–	2	0	2	X6
						1	0	1	0	0	X7
							0	0	0	0	X9
								5	1	3	X10
									1	1	X11
										3	X12

with components,

at $q = 5$ {X10}
at $q = 4$ {X10}
at $q = 3$ {X2, X10, X12}
at $q = 2$ {X2, X5, X6, X10, X12}
at $q = 1$ {X1, X2, X5, X6, X7, X10, X11, X13}
at $q = 0$ {all}

and structure vector

$$Q' = \{\overset{5}{1} \ 1 \ 1 \ 1 \ 1 \ \overset{0}{1}\}$$

which was previously

$$Q = \{\overset{9}{1} \ 2 \ 2 \ 3 \ \overset{5}{8} \ 8 \ 8 \ 4 \ 1 \ \overset{0}{1}\}$$

We see at once that there has been a drastic reduction in the obstruction vector on $K_P(X; \Gamma_2)$; agreement among P1, P2, P3, P4, P12, P23 is relatively easy, particularly at $q = 2$. At this level the obstruction vector now has a zero component whereas it was previously 8. Thus this hidden party of influence can, without the person of P3, manipulate the political structure to achieve some desired end — and this structure (viewed from the dynamics of this ranking pattern) is stable at the $q = 2$ level, that is to say, more than three committees would have to step out of line to upset the agreed end, and if P3 is the only person who might want to oppose, it is practically (dynamically) impossible. What emerges from this is the proposal that a Working Party be set up, with P3 in the chair; the membership will be effectively chosen by P1, P2, P4 and probably P12, P23. We notice too, at this stage, that the dynamic complex $K_X(P; \Gamma_2^{-1})$ has possessed a zero obstruction vector $\hat{Q}' = 0$, showing that (with respect to this ranking pattern) all the committees allow free pattern changes without constraint. The Q-analysis also shows that each simplex is a face of X10, and this includes X12, and so all decisions will be effectively (dynamically) settled in senate.

But if this is the real politics of the situation why did not senate, influenced by P1, P2, P4, P12, and P23, simply outvote P3's proposal and put an end to it there and then? The answer to this is equally simple, if a trifle long. Because the issues involved were not so desperate as to call for such do-or-die tactics; because P3's standing required that his advocacy should be treated with sympathy and tact; because it might just be a good idea after all and it should therefore be given the chance to prove it, in a medieval sort of way, by overcoming a few more innocent hurdles; because university business must be conducted with donnish elegance and sensivity, if the young scholars are to acquire some of the delicacies of civilization.

The structural consequence of creating the Working Party is manifest *via* an alteration in the relation Γ_3, the set X now contains thirteen committees; X13 is the new Working Party. We now suppose that each of the committees

158 Mathematical Structure in Human Affairs

X1, X2, X3, X4, X6, X7, and X9 can send recommendations to X13, whilst X13 is required to send its recommendations to X10, X11, and X12. The resulting structures are summarized in the following.

For $K_X(X; \Gamma_3)$:

$$Q = \{\overset{2}{1} \quad 4 \quad \overset{0}{3}\}$$

with components,

at $q = 2$ {X13}
at $q = 1$ {X13}, {X1, X3, X4}, {X2, X6, X7, X9}, {X10}
at $q = 0$ {X1, X2, X3, X9, X6, X7, X9, X10, X11, X12, X13}, {X5}, {X8}

For $K_X(X; \Gamma_3^{-1})$:

$$Q = \{\overset{7}{1} \quad 1 \quad 2 \quad 2 \quad 2 \quad 2 \quad 2 \quad \overset{0}{3}\}$$

with components,

at $q = 7, 6$ {X13}
at $q = 5, 4$ {X10}, {X13}
at $q = 3$ {X10, X13}, {X11}
at $q = 2, 1$ {X10, X11, X13}, {X12}
at $q = 0$ {X9, X10, X11, X12, X13}, {X2}, {X6}

These structure vectors should be compared with the previous ones, when X13 did not exist, viz.,

for $K_X(X; \Gamma_3)$ $\quad\quad Q = \{1 \quad \overset{0}{4}\}$

for $K_X(X; \Gamma_3^{-1})$ $\quad\quad Q = \{\overset{4}{1} \quad 1 \quad 3 \quad 3 \quad \overset{0}{4}\}$

The outgoing-complex, $K_X(X; \Gamma_3)$, has suffered a reduction in Q_0, from 4 to 3, and now none of the subcomplexes in it offers any obstruction vector. This is a manifestation of the senate suggestion that X13 should act as a general receiver of views on P3's proposal (notice that this gives a long column of 1's under X13 in Γ_3's incidence matrix and this helps to connect the outgoing-complex). This feature of the senate suggestion therefore supports the idea that it is a liberal move, a democratic move, but the conjugate complex is adversely affected by it. In $K_X(X; \Gamma_3^{-1})$ we see a big extension of the obstruction vector with non-zero components at $q = 5$ and 4; previously the non-zero components only occurred at $q = 2$. For this conjugate complex to be 'improved' (in the sense that $\hat{Q}$ is to decrease, and thus encourage political decisions) it would have been necessary for senate to suggest that X13 should be allowed to *send its recommendations to all committees*, as it was invited to *receive all recommendations*. The latter increases the connectivity of $K_X(X; \Gamma_3)$ and the former increases the connectivity of the incoming-complex $K_X(X; \Gamma_3^{-1})$; increasing the connectivity tends to lower $\hat{Q}$. In this case the incoming-complex shows a *marked increase* in its *obstruction vector*, and X13 is the largest simplex in the complex, replacing senate itself, X10. The eccentricities of X10 and X13 show up the new situation, with

$$X10 = (3, 5), \qquad \hat{q} - \check{q} = 2$$
$$X13 = (3, 7), \qquad \hat{q} - \check{q} = 4$$

Is it surprising that the new chairman P3 began to feel eccentric too?

In general terms the meaning of the *difference* between the two eccentricities of X13, $\hat{q} - \check{q} = 4$ in the incoming-complex and $\hat{q} - \check{q} = 2$ in the outgoing-complex, is that this committee possesses responsibility without power (if by 'power' we mean political, decisive influence). The responsibility is reflected in the 7-simplex which X13 represents in the incoming-complex, while the political influence is reflected in its 2-simplex in the outgoing-complex.

We can now see that the setting up of the Working Party X13 has radically altered the backcloth $S(N)$ in such a way that a static view of $S(N)$ makes it more difficult to arrive at a political decision. This does not necessarily mean that such a decision is ruled out altogether, or that we should view the move which set up X13 as a particularly sinister manifestation of political cynicism on senate. The reason for this lies in the paramount importance of the political dynamics which are available on any particular backcloth. If P3 is now despondent, as the eccentric chairman of an eccentric committee, it is a reflection of his persistently static view of the backcloth, even though his grasp of that backcloth is far superior to that shown by P21. In fact P3 feels the pressure of intangible *political forces;* we can show him that these are in fact t-forces of the kind discussed in Chapter 6 and Appendix D.

Thus, P3 was trying to ignore the dynamics induced by the existence of the mapping pattern $\pi : P \rightarrow J$; in effect this means that he was interpreting the static situation as if it were the real dynamic one. Thus we might say that P3 assumed a ranking pattern on the set P defined by

$$\pi_s = \pi_s^0 \oplus \pi_s^1 \oplus \pi_s^2 \oplus \pi_s^3 \oplus \pi_s^4 \oplus \pi_s^5$$

in which, for $P_i \in P$,

$$\pi_s(P_i) = \hat{q}(P_i) + 1$$

and when P_i is a t-simplex in $K_P(X; \Gamma_2)$ then $\pi_s(P_i) \equiv \pi_s^t$. This gives a ranking pattern (*cf.* the list on page 143) with

$$\pi_s^5(P1) = 6, \quad \pi_s^3(P2) = 4, \quad \pi_s^4(P3) = 5$$
$$\pi_s^5(P4) = 6, \quad \pi_s^3(P12) = 4, \quad \pi_s^3(P23) = 4, \qquad \text{etc.}$$

Hence P3's experience of the political situation is equivalent to a change in this π_s to π_d (that given on page 155, which is,

$$\Delta \pi^5 = 17 - 12 = +5 \qquad \Delta \pi^2 = 12 - 18 = -6$$
$$\Delta \pi^4 = 6 - 5 = +1 \qquad \Delta \pi^1 = 8 - 10 = -2$$
$$\Delta \pi^3 = 15 - 20 = -5 \qquad \Delta \pi^0 = 8 - 6 = +2$$

This means that the *dynamical political forces* in the complex $K_P(X; \Gamma_2)$

160 *Mathematical Structure in Human Affairs*

may be described as
(1) an attractive 5-force of strength 5/12,
(2) an attractive 4-force of strength 1/5,
(3) a repulsive 3-force of strength 5/20,
(4) a repulsive 2-force of strength 6/18,
(5) a repulsive 1-force of strength 2/10,
(6) an attractive 0-force of strength 2/6.

These forces are an expression of *political pressures in the complex,* and identify *centres* (subcomplexes) *of attraction* and *repulsion;* if the pattern π_d is realistic then the greatest political forces in the structure are manifest in P1 and P4. These forces are as 'real' as the forces which are manifest in the acceleration of a rocket which is propelled under chemical action, and which moves through a simplicial complex point-mesh called space.

But these dynamical forces are not the only ones acting in the backcloth $S(N)$. By themselves they do not explain why, on this particular issue, they should act to upset the static structure. The complexes defined by the relation Γ_1 possess a dynamic pattern of forces which are specifically involved with any political decision on the proposal. Such forces will be the result of a ranking pattern defined in the areas of policy Y and, having seen the actual situation on X10 which produced the Working Party X13, it would seem that at that stage a pattern like the following would have been sufficient to account for the action

$$\pi_d : Y \to J$$

$\pi_d(Y1) = 4,\quad \pi_d(Y2) = 0,\quad \pi_d(Y3) = 1,\quad \pi_d(Y4) = 3,$

$\pi_d(Y5) = 3,\quad \pi_d(Y6) = 0,\quad \pi_d(Y7) = 0,\quad \pi_d(Y8) = 0,$

$\pi_d(Y9) = 0,\quad \pi_d(Y10) = 2,\quad \pi_d(Y11) = 0,\quad \pi_d(Y12) = 0$

Taking the same pattern π_s for the static picture, *viz.,* $\pi_s(Y_i) = \hat{q}(Y_i) + 1$ we obtain the pattern of t-forces on the complex $K_Y(X; \Gamma_1)$ as,

$\Delta\pi^0 = -1$; repulsive 0-force of strength 1

$\Delta\pi^1 = +4$; repulsive 1-force of strength 4/6

$\Delta\pi^2 = -11$; repulsive 2-force of strength 11/12

$\Delta\pi^3 = -10$; repulsive 3-force of strength 10/12

$\Delta\pi^4 = -8$; repulsive 4-force of strength 8/10

This force pattern, based on a high ranking of capital expenditure, faculty and departmental requirements, catering and staff amenities, results in the dynamical picture with a large attractive force on the 1-simplices with vertices chosen from X1, X11, X10, and X12. This force is now simultaneously manifest on these simplices in $K_X(P; \Gamma_2^{-1})$, which is why P1, P2, P4 are sensitive to them. Thus the simultaneous play of the dynamic patterns π_d on $K_P(X; \Gamma_2)$ and π_d on $K_Y(X; \Gamma_1)$ produces the political movement (the actual dynamics) on X10. The *effect of the repulsive forces* is to *evacuate those* remaining committees and people from the centres of political decision-making. The overall effect, on X10, was consequently an expression of a kind of resonance between the attractive 1-force on $K_Y(X; \Gamma_2)$ and the attractive 5-force on $K_P(X; \Gamma_2)$.

The resultant *dynamics* against the backcloth was quite sufficient to explain the inevitable outcome of P3's Working Party. The membership of the Working Party was naturally (and fairly) adjusted so that all interests were taken into account. Hence X13 worked at its task with the *wrong* π_d on $K_Y(X; \Gamma_1)$, one which reflected the original π_s. So long as the *actual* π_d was effective on X10, in $K_X(P; \Gamma_2^{-1})$ most of the recommendations from X13 would amount to pouring liquid into a bottomless pit — because of the repulsive t-forces existing in $K_Y(X; \Gamma_1)$. Hence the work of X13 would appear to be forever 'missing the point' about the whole proposal — even if that 'point' were also elusive to everyone else. The inevitable result was a long rambling discursive document from X13 containing lukewarm proposals and vague financial reassurances; even P3 would be glad to see the back of it and to get out of this eccentric role. Naturally X10 and X12 were ready to oblige by noting the report, making sympathetic clucking noises, and leaving it in the air for future use when further developments might make it a clearer and less controversial issue.

7.5 The referee stops the fight

The discussion of the previous sections illustrates the dynamic nature of even the most innocent of political actions. As far as the original proposal is concerned its fate hinged on a dynamic pattern (of rankings) defined on the complex $K_Y(X; \Gamma_1)$ and the reaction to the effective t-forces by the (dynamic) influential subcomplex $K_P(X; \Gamma_2)$. Both of these complexes are part of the overall backcloth $S(N)$ and can be interpreted as either (1) an effective distortion of the backcloth (cf. the $K'_P(X; \Gamma_2)$ of section 7.4, or (2) a field of t-forces on the static backcloth. It is not fanciful to compare this situation with that in physics, where the gravitational force-field is either seen as a distortion of the geometry of space-time (the Einstein view) or as a force which acts at a distance in a static (rigid) space-time structure (the Newtonian view)[22]. The difference does not seem to be one of truth so much as a matter of taste, although it might transpire in the future to be influenced by the successes or failures of specific mathematical techniques.

If we restrict ourselves to a backcloth $S(N)$ defined by the static relations Γ_1, Γ_2, and Γ_3 then we have seen that the dynamic forces which exist in Γ_1 and Γ_2 were able to produce changes in the complexes induced by Γ_3. It was very easy for these forces to alter card X, by creating at least one extra committee and adjusting the relation Γ_3 accordingly. It would have been equally easy for these forces to have reduced the value of card X or to have otherwise altered the relation Γ_3. Since Γ_3 is responsible for the bare-bones of the structure, the crude physical channels for the flow of recommendations and decisions, its function in the backcloth $S(N)$ — under the action of the dynamical forces arising in Γ_1 and Γ_2 — is comparable to the physical engineering which is to act as the stage-for-action when the particles and fluids and electric sparks interact in a predictive fashion in a physical experiment. It is likely, therefore, that most practising scientists would prefer the *Newtonian view of politics* (as here outlined) to the Einsteinian view; it is more likely to lead to successful engineering.

If we insist on trying to settle the matter of the university bar against the backcloth $S(N)$ herein outlined, if we wish to take either one of the silly sides, then we must turn our attention to the dynamical forces which either exist or can be made to exist. For it seems to the writer that the essence of political campaigning is the effort to induce a favourable t-force-yield on a given static backcloth. Thus the mapping pattern π can be both created and destroyed by active people in the complexes of their interactions. The forces which are thereby generated in $S(N)$ — forces which might involve more important people than a handful of dons and which might act on a backcloth which sweeps across the whole of a society — can produce radical changes in the static backcloth, or act as defensive conservatism against such changes. In all, the picture is one of a constantly changing 'actual-space', suffering and inducing a vast collection of patterns and t-forces as political (or merely 'social') fortunes sway back and forth.

The simplest way to get our university bar moved to position B, being the most direct, would be to campaign for a new dynamic pattern π_d on $K_Y(X; \Gamma_1)$ and to link this with a simultaneous acknowledgement of the π_d on $K_P(X; \Gamma_2)$. If the financial facts of the affair are too tough to crack then the proposer must bend, either by having an extra position C up his sleeve (which must be cheaper and, possibly, must reduce the value of card Y drastically). If the attractive 1-force on $K_Y(X; \Gamma_1)$ can be made into a repulsive 1-force whilst at the same time the higher order t-forces can be made less repulsive (even attractive) then the effect on the people in $K_P(X; \Gamma_2)$ would be profound. But to achieve this it would be essential to work backwards from the t-force centres in $K_P(X; \Gamma_2)$ — due to the π_d on P. This is old-fashioned campaigning.

A more drastic, and desperate way, is to try and destroy the pattern π_d on $K_P(X; \Gamma_2)$ — even, at times, going so far as to destroy the static pattern on Γ_2 altogether. This is a frontal attack on 'the establishment'; it might even be described as revolution. If successful this must be replaced by a new establishment at once, dedicated to the party line 'we must move the bar'. Clearly this will not be achieved without a considerable struggle since a big change in the π_d on $K_P(X; \Gamma_2)$ is too serious to be viewed as merely a device for achieving one rather innocuous political end. But the ability to dent that pattern π_d (perhaps the 5-force can be reduced in strength from 5/12 to 3/12?) by argument and persuasion can be sufficient to produce the political end — the deterrent effect.

But we must leave P21 and P3 licking their wounds; it would not be politic to lay out a detailed computer program for political success in this specialized field of 'bar moving'. It is difficult enough at the moment to find any university bar without the added handicap induced by enthusiastic dons getting them all moved. But perhaps we have discussed the details sufficiently for the boxing fans to tolerate that most frustrating finish when the referee stops the fight?

Appendix A
Sets and Relations

1   We denote sets by capital letters A, B, X, S etc., and elements of a set by small letters x, p, q, t, etc. The property of *set-membership* is indicated by the Greek letter ϵ, so that for example, the statement 'P is a member of the set S' is commonly written as P ϵ S; and this may equally well be read as 'p belongs to S'; the negation of ϵ is simply written as $\notin$.

A set may be defined by predicating a specific property of its members (but there are some dangers of ambiguities in this, as indicated in the text) or by listing its members; this latter implies that there is a finite number of elements in the set. Thus we might have

$$X = \{p : p \text{ is an odd number}\}$$

or $$F = \{\text{Tom, Dick, Harry}\}$$

The first is read as 'X is the set of elements p for which p is an odd number', whilst the second reads as 'F is the set whose three elements have the names Tom, Dick, Harry'.

It is convenient to take the set of positive integers as a reference set in matters of counting and so we adopt a fixed notation for this set, *viz.*, J_+, and indicate its elements by writing

$$J_+ = \{1, 2, 3, \ldots\}$$

Similarly we shall denote by J the set of all integers, and write

$$J = \{0, -1, +1, -2, +2, -3, +3, \ldots\}$$

If we can place the elements of two sets A and B into a mutual correspondence so that

(1) to every a ϵ A there corresponds one and only one element b ϵ B and
(2) to every b ϵ B there corresponds one and only one element a ϵ A, then we say that

$$\text{A and B are in a (1-1) correspondence.}$$

For example, if A = {Tom, Dick, Harry} and B = {Mary, Jane, Susan} we can set up a (1-1) correspondence between them in many ways. One such correspondence is specified by assigning

$$\text{Tom} \longleftrightarrow \text{Jane}$$
$$\text{Dick} \longleftrightarrow \text{Susan}$$
$$\text{Harry} \longleftrightarrow \text{Mary}$$

This idea of a (1-1) correspondence is not restricted to sets with a finite number of elements. Thus in projective geometry in the plane the points on two lines A and B can be *in perspective from a vertex* O. This perspectivity, as it is called, is actually a (1-1) correspondence between the infinite sets of points on A and on B, as shown in Figure A.1.

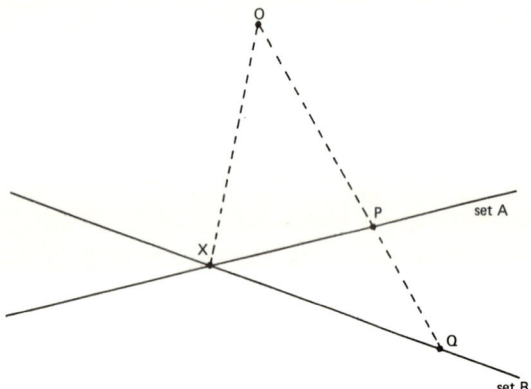

Figure A.1 A geometrical (1-1) correspondence

To find that unique point on B which corresponds to the point P on A we join O to P and let Q be the point of incidence between OP and B. The point X, lying on both A and B, is an example of a *self-corresponding* point in the (1-1) correspondence.

When there is a (1-1) correspondence between any two sets A and B we say also that

A *and* B *have the same cardinality*

The correspondence is a mathematical way of saying that A and B have the same number of elements, but the idea precedes the idea of counting — because counting is really the expression of setting up a (1-1) correspondence between the set which 'is being counted' and another set which contains some of the members of J_+. Thus the idea of cardinality (which, incidentally, does not involve the notion of ordering) is an idea associated with all the set which can be put pairwise into (1-1) correspondence with each other. When a set X can be put into a (1-1) correspondence with the positive integers J_+ we say that it possesses the cardinality $\aleph_0$ (aleph zero) which symbol (following Cantor) we reserve for the cardinality of J_+.

We shall write the cardinality of a set S as card S. In this book we are mostly concerned with the case when card S is a finite number, and this is sometimes indicated by writing card $S < \infty$.

2   A subset of a set S is any set T such that whenever $x \in T$ then $x \in S$. Thus the set T = {x : x is an even number} is a subset of J. Also, of course, any set S must be a subset of itself, but in that case it would not be called a proper subset of S. It is reputed that Galileo first pointed out that a proper subset of

an infinite set can have the same cardinality as the whole set. This can be seen by considering J_+ and the set

$$X = \{x : x \text{ is the square of an integer}\}$$

whence we get the correspondence

X	1^2	2^2	3^2	4^2	...	n^2	...
J_+	1	2	3	4	...	n	...

so that card X = card J_+. This situation cannot arise with finite sets.

The notation for 'A is a subset of B' is simply $A \subset B$; this can also be read as 'the set A is included in the set B'.

3   The *intersection* (or *meet*) of two sets A and B is written as $A \cap B$ and defined by

$$A \cap B = \{x : x \in A \text{ and } x \in B\} = B \cap A$$

(It is usually read as 'A cap B'.)

The *union* (or *join*) of two sets A and B is written as $A \cup B$ and defined by

$$A \cup B = \{x : x \in A \text{ or } x \in B\} = B \cup A$$

(It is usually read as 'A cup B'.) The 'or' in the definition is not exclusive. We see from these definitions that, for example,

$$\text{if } A \subset B \text{ then } A \cap B = A \text{ and } A \cup B = B$$

The *complement* of a set A is written as A^c (sometimes as A') and defined by

$$A^c = \{x : x \notin A\}$$

so that, for example, $(A^c)^c = A$.

If we consider a predicate property π and the set

$$B = \{x : x \text{ possesses } \pi\}$$

then if

$$A = \{x : x \in B \text{ and } x \notin B\}$$

the elements of A must be both 'members' and 'not-members' of B. We call such a set A the *empty set* and denote it always by the Greek letter ϕ.

Thus we have $\phi \cap S = \phi$ for every set S

and $\phi \cup S = S$ for every set S.

It is therefore consistent of us to treat ϕ as a subset of every set S; $\phi \subset S$. An example of ϕ from pure mathematics is the following

$$\phi = \{x : x < 0 \text{ and } x \in J_+\}$$

and in a non-mathematical vein

$$\phi = \{x : x \text{ is a man and } x \text{ is immortal}\}$$

The *difference* of two sets A−B (and distinct from B−A) may be defined as those elements of A which are not members of B. This is the same as

$$A-B = \{x : x \in A \text{ and } x \notin B\}$$

or as
$$A-B = A \cap B^c$$

Notice that
$$B-A = A^c \cap B.$$

The *symmetric difference* of A and B is often written as A △ B and is defined by

$$A \triangle B = (A \cap B^c) \cup (A^c \cap B) = B \triangle A$$

or by
$$A \triangle B = (A-B) \cup (B-A)$$

We notice that
$$A \triangle A = \phi$$

and that
$$A \triangle \phi = A = \phi \triangle A \text{ for all sets } A.$$

The complement of ϕ is often called the *universal set* U (it must contain 'everything'), $\phi^c = U$ and then, as an alternative to some of the above,

$$A^c = U-A$$
$$U^c = U-U = \phi = (\phi^c)^c$$

The set of all subsets of a set A is called the *power set* P(A) of A. If card $A = n$ then card $P(A) = 2^n$. If (for example) $A = \{a, b, c\}$ then

$$P(A) = \{\phi, \{a\}, \{b\}, \{c\}, \{ab\}, \{bc\}, \{ac\}, A\}$$

4 The symbols for sets can be manipulated according to basic rules which arise directly from the definitions. This means that we can regard such symbols as forming an *algebra* of sets — an example of what is called a *Boolean Algebra*. The basic rules for this algebra are listed below.

B1:	$A \cup (B \cup C) = (A \cup B) \cup C$ $A \cap (B \cap C) = (A \cap B) \cap C$		The associative laws
B2:	$A \cup B \quad = B \cup A$ $A \cap B \quad = B \cap A$		The commutative laws
B3:	$A \cup (B \cap C) = (A \cup B) \cap (A \cup C)$ $A \cap (B \cup C) = (A \cap B) \cup (A \cap C)$		The distributive laws
B4:	$A \cup \phi \quad = A \, ; A \cup U = U$ $A \cap U \quad = A \, ; A \cap \phi = \phi$		The identities ϕ and U
B5:	$A \cup A \quad = A$ $A \cap A \quad = A$		The idempotent laws
B6:	$(A \cup B)^c \quad = A^c \cap B^c$ $(A \cap B)^c \quad = A^c \cup B^c$		De Morgan's laws

In each of the above pairs of rules, one example of the law is obtained from the other by interchanging $\cup$ with $\cap$ and ϕ with U, where relevant. One such form of the law is called the *dual* of the other. Boolean Algebra is *self-dual*.

Any theorem in the algebra therefore possesses a dual form of itself and this will be proved by rewriting the first proof with $\cup$, $\cap$, and ϕ, U interchanged. Thus the dual theorem can be stated without further proof once the original theorem is established.

5   The *Cartesian product* of two sets A and B is a new set, denoted by A $\times$ B, which consists of all elements of the form (a, b) where a ϵ A and b ϵ B. For example, if A = {a, a', a''} and B = {1, 5} then A $\times$ B consists of six elements, *viz.*,

$$A \times B = \{(a, 1), (a, 5), (a', 1), (a', 5), (a'', 1), (a'', 5)\}$$

The elements of A $\times$ B are also referred to as *ordered pairs* (a, b), with a ϵ A and b ϵ B; ordered because we distinguish the first symbol in (a, b) from the second. Thus we regard (a, 1) as distinct from (1, a) and consequently we expect, in general, that A $\times$ B $\neq$ B $\times$ A. An exception occurs when A = B for then A $\times$ A = A $\times$ A – not because (a, a') = (a', a) but because the elements of A $\times$ A exhaust every combination of pairs of elements selected from A; if (a, a') occurs in A $\times$ A then every such pair occurs in A $\times$ A, where a ϵ A and a' ϵ A.

A *relation* λ from the set A to the set B is a rule which associates some of the elements of B with some of the elements of A. Looked at in another way, suppose we are given a statement Σ which has two vacancies in it where names (of elements of sets) can be inserted; for example,

Σ_1 —— is greater than ——

Σ_2 —— and —— are members of the same club

Σ_3 —— is located in ——

Such a statement can be denoted by Σ (–, –) and referred to as an *open proposition*. It can be applied to an ordered pair of the Cartesian product A $\times$ B to give a specific proposition Σ (a, b) about any particular ordered pair (a, b) in that product set. Thus, symbolically,

$$\Sigma (-, -) (a, b) = \Sigma (a, b)$$

Now Σ (a, b) has a truth value, *true* or *false,* although Σ (–, –) does not.

A *relation* λ can now be viewed as *the result of the application of such an open proposition* Σ (–, –) *to the product set* A $\times$ B. Of every pair (a, b) ϵ A $\times$ B we must be able to answer Yes or No to the question, is Σ (a, b) true?

It is therefore sufficient, in identifying λ, to know which collection of the pairs (a, b) satisfy the open statement – which make Σ (a, b) a true statement. Since this collection of *pairs related via* λ is a subset of A $\times$ B we commonly say that 'a relation λ between sets A and B is a subset of the set A $\times$ B'. We therefore denote λ as if it were a subset of A $\times$ B and write $\lambda \subset$ A $\times$ B; this is a relation from A to B; the associated relation from B to A is called the inverse relation and denoted by λ^{-1}; we write the latter as $\lambda^{-1} \subset$ B $\times$ A.

If the pair (a, b) is such that Σ (a, b) is true, that is to say, if (a, b) is in the subset λ of A × B, we also write

$$a \lambda b$$

which reads as 'a stands in the relation λ to b', and this is equivalent to

$$b \lambda^{-1} a$$

which reads as 'b stands in the relation λ^{-1} to a'.

If λ denotes the relation '—— is the child of ——' then λ^{-1} denotes the relation '—— is the parent of ——'.

When we represent the relation λ between A and B as that subset λ ⊂ A × B identified by saying

$$\Sigma (a, b) \text{ is true}$$

then we naturally obtain a simple mathematical array which contains the relation. This array is an example of a *matrix array* of numbers λ_{ij}, with each λ_{ij} either 0 or 1. The resulting matrix is also called the incidence matrix of the relation λ ⊂ A × B.

We illustrate the incidence matrix $\Lambda = (\lambda_{ij})$ with two simple examples.

Example 1

λ	B → 4	12	15	24
A ↓ 3	0	1	1	1
5	0	0	1	0
6	0	1	0	1
15	0	0	1	0
17	0	0	0	0

Here the relation λ ⊂ A × B is derived from the open statement:

' —— divides —— exactly'

Thus 3 divides 12 but not 4, etc. The subset of A × B which effectively is the relation λ corresponds to the positions of the 1's in the array, viz.,

$$\lambda = \{(3, 12), (3, 15), (3, 24), (5, 15), (6, 12), (6, 24), (15, 15)\}$$

Example 2

λ	B1	B2	B3	B4	B5
P1	1	0	0	0	1
P2	0	1	1	0	0
P3	1	0	1	1	0
P4	0	0	0	1	1
P5	1	0	1	0	0

Here the relation λ is derived from the open statement:

'the person named —— sits on the committee called ——'

where the names of the committees are B1, B2, B3, B4, B5. Hence A is a set of people called P1, ... P5 and precisely the relation $\lambda \subset A \times B$ is the set with members

$$\lambda = \{(P1, B1), (P1, B5), (P2, B2), (P2, B3), (P3, B1), (P3, B3), (P3, B4),$$
$$(P4, B4), (P4, B5), (P5, B1), (P5, B3)\}$$

When we wish to indicate that we are taking the incidence-matrix view of a relation λ between A and B we shall use the shorthand description of λ as follows:

λ	B
A	(λ_{ij})

with

λ^{-1}	A
B	(λ_{ij}^{-1})

with $\lambda_{ij}^{-1} = \lambda_{ji}$.

The *domain* D of a relation λ is the subset of A which occurs *via* the first members of all the ordered pairs $(a, b) \in \lambda$.

6 A function, or *mapping*, from a set A to a set B is a special kind of relation, *viz.*, one in which there is at most one 1 in any one row of the incidence matrix Λ. Thus if μ is a mapping from A to B and if we denote by μ(A) that element of Ḃ which is made to correspond to $a \in A$, then $\mu(a) \neq \mu(a')$ implies that $a \neq a'$. Only one element of B can correspond to a given element of A; this element is the one denoted by μ(A) and called the *image* of a under the mapping μ. We usually represent a mapping μ by

$$\mu : A \rightarrow B$$

and the set of all $b \in B$ which are examples of μ(a), for $a \in A$, is the *range* of μ. The *domain* of μ must always be (the whole of) A; that is to say we always restrict A to the set of elements {a} such that $\mu(a) \in B$ for every $a \in A$. Some writers reserve the word 'mapping' for this case (when the whole of A is the domain of μ) and use the word function for the more general relation when the domain of μ (or f) is possibly a proper subset of A.

Generally, we speak of a mapping being *into* the set B, in the sense that $\mu(A) \subset B$. Sometimes of course the mapping might be *onto* the set B, in which case every $b \in B$ can be identified with μ(a) for some $a \in A$, every b is the image under μ of some $a \in A$. When a mapping is both *one-to-one* and *into* we call it an *injection;* that is to say, when $\mu(a) = \mu(a')$ implies $a = a'$ (there cannot be more than one 1 in any row or column) although there might be some b's in B which are not images under μ. When μ is an onto map we call it a *surjection,* and when it is both onto and injective we call it a *bijection.*

Example 3

The set of prizes in a lottery number 5 in all, with values £1, £2, £3, £4, £5.

The set F = {Tom, Dick, Harry} are allotted (or win) various prizes in fictional situations which can be described in terms of different kinds of maps.

(1) An *into* map μ_1 distributes prizes as follows (sharing is allowed)
$$\mu_1(\text{Tom}) = £1; \quad \mu_1(\text{Dick}) = £1; \quad \mu_1(\text{Harry}) = £5$$
The range of μ_1, *viz.*, $\mu_1(F)$, is a proper subset of B = {prizes}.

(2) An *injective* map μ_2 distributes prizes as follows:
$$\mu_2(\text{Tom}) = £1; \quad \mu_2(\text{Dick}) = £2; \quad \mu_2(\text{Harry}) = £4$$

(3) An extension to the set F, which then becomes
$$F' = \{\text{Tom, Dick, Harry, Jane, Mary, Susan}\}$$
allows a *surjective* map μ_3 via $\mu_3 : F' \to B$ with
$$\mu_3(\text{Tom}) = \mu_3(\text{Jane}) = £1; \mu_3(\text{Dick}) = £2 \text{ and}$$
$$\mu_3(\text{Harry}) = £3; \mu_3(\text{Mary}) = £4; \mu_3(\text{Susan}) = £5$$
Now we see that $\mu_3(F') = B$; no prize escapes from μ_3.

(4) Supposing that Susan drops out of the competition so that F' becomes F' = {Tom, Dick, Harry, Jane, Mary} then a *bijective* map μ_4 can arise with the following prize distribution:
$$\mu_4(\text{Tom}) = £5; \mu_4(\text{Dick}) = £1; \mu_4(\text{Harry}) = £2 \text{ and}$$
$$\mu_4(\text{Jane}) = £3; \mu_4(\text{Mary}) = £4$$
In this case no prizes are shared, no prizes escape, and no one fails to receive a prize.

7   Apart from a relation becoming a mapping it can possess other properties of importance, and these arise when $\lambda \subset A \times A$ (the case of B = A, when we speak of λ being a relation 'on a (single) set A'); they are the following:

λ might be *reflexive*, that is to say, $(a, a) \in \lambda$ for all $a \in A$

λ might be *symmetric*, that is to say, $(a, a') \in \lambda$ implies $(a', a) \in \lambda$

λ might be *transitive*, that is to say, $(a, a') \in \lambda$ and $(a', a'') \in \lambda$ together imply that $(a, a'') \in \lambda$.

'—— has the same colour as ——' is a reflexive relation on a set of coloured objects; it means that, in the incidence matrix, the leading diagonal is a set of 1's, or $\lambda_{ii} = 1$ for all i. A symmetric relation on a set A corresponds to the incidence matrix being symmetric, that is to say, it is unaltered by transposing the rows and columns, or $\lambda^{-1} = \lambda$; thus '—— differs from —— by a multiple of 3' is a symmetric relation on the set J. Finally, '—— is blood-related to ——' is a transitive relation on the set of people, since if Tom is related to Henry and Henry is related to Jane, then Tom is related to Jane.

If a relation λ on A ($\lambda \subset A \times A$) is reflexive, symmetric, and transitive it is called an *equivalence relation*. Its effect on the set A is to create a *partition* of A, that is to say, λ identifies subsets $A_1, A_2, \ldots A_i$

of A such that   (1) $A_i \cap A_j = \phi$ whenever $i \neq j$

and   (2) $A = \underset{i}{U} A_i$

In other words, a partition of A is a collection of subsets whose union is the whole set A but which pairwise have no common elements.

We can argue this partition property of an equivalence relation in the following way. Let (e.g.) A_1 be the subset of A which is related (*via* λ) to a particular element a_1. Then because $(a_1, a_1) \in \lambda$ (reflexive) we know that $a_1 \in A_1$. Let a_2 be a distinct element of A which is $\notin A_1$ (if no such a_2 exists then $A_1 = A$ and the partition trivially exists) and let A_2 be the set which is λ-related to this a_2. If A_1 and A_2 have a common member (so that $A_1 \cap A_2 \neq \phi$), say a', then $(a_1, a') \in \lambda$ and $(a_2, a') \in \lambda$; hence, by symmetry, $(a', a_2) \in \lambda$ and so we deduce that $(a_1, a_2) \in \lambda$ (transitivity). It therefore follows that $a_2 \in A_1$, which is a contradiction; hence A_1 and A_2 must be disjoint. Now by finding an element $a_3 \in A$ which is not in A_1 nor in A_2 we can repeat the argument and deduce that $A_1 \cap A_3 = \phi$ and $A_2 \cap A_3 = \phi$. Proceeding in this way we eventually exhaust the set and so obtain a partition of A by the subsets $A_1, A_2, A_3, \ldots A_i, \ldots$.

The separate subsets A_i of the above argument are called the *equivalence classes* of the relation λ on A. The relation λ derived from the open statement

'—— is the same height as ——'

applied to the set {people} is an equivalence relation. The equivalence classes are sets of people of the same height; these are pairwise disjoint because no one person can be simultaneously two different heights (let us say).

The collection of equivalence classes forms a set of sets and this is denoted by A/λ (read 'A by λ') and called the *quotient set* of A by the equivalence relation λ. The reader will easily convince himself that 'being in a (1–1) correspondence with' is an equivalence relation on the set of all sets and that the sets which are contained in an equivalence class all possess the same cardinality. In exhibiting an example of a set X with a given cardinality, say card X = 100, it is clearly immaterial which set of the relevant equivalence class we choose since cardinality is a class-property. Having chosen a set X out of the 'card X = 100'-equivalence class we refer to it as a representative of that class, and then we denote the class itself by the symbol [X]. The commonest and most intuitive choice of X is a specific subset of J_+, what we call the first one hundred natural numbers. The following example is another arithmetic illustration.

Example 4

We define an equivalence relation λ on the set of integers J by stating that $(a, b) \in \lambda$ if and only if $a - b$ is a multiple of 5. This also means that b is the remainder after dividing a by 5. There are therefore 5 distinct equivalence classes in J/λ since there are only 5 possible remainders, *viz.*, 0, 1, 2, 3, 4. We might therefore write

$$J/\lambda = [0], [1], [2], [3], [4]$$

This is an example of a modular arithmetic, $(a, b) \in \lambda$ being also written as
$$a \equiv b \text{ (modulo 5)}$$

read as   'a is congruent to b modulo 5'.

In this case we would also write J/λ as J_5; it is a finite set derived from an infinite set. The actual members of the equivalence classes look like:

[0] = {0, −5, +5, −10, +10, −15, +15, ...}
[1] = {1, −4, +6, −9, +11, −14, +16, ...}
[2] = {2, −3, +7, −8, +12, −13, +17, ...}
[3] = {3, −2, +8, −7, +13, −12, +18, ...}
[4] = {4, −1, +9, −6, +14, −11, +19, ...}

Appendix B
The Structure of a Relation

1 We shall first define what is called a *simplicial complex,* and this will be the concept of structure which is the basic theme of this book. We shall then see how a relation λ exhibits this particular kind of structure; in a very natural way we can say that a relation *is* a simplicial complex. Our intuitive recognition of structure as a kind of geometrical fabrication is sustained in this discussion by the introduction of a geometrical representation of a relation, although it is based on algebraic foundations.

We first consider a finite set

$$V = \{v^i; i = 1, \ldots k\}$$

and a collection K of its subsets. We denote any one of these subsets by the symbol σ_p when it contains $(p + 1)$ distinct elements of V, and we call such a subset a *p-simplex* (or a simplex of *order p*). If σ_q is a q-simplex defined by a $(q + 1)$ subset of the $(p + 1)$ elements which define the first we say that σ_q is a *face* of σ_p, and we write

$$\sigma_q < \sigma_p$$

This relation $<$ is a partial ordering on the collection K.

This collection K is called a *simplicial complex* if and only if

(1) each singleton set $\{v^i\}$ is a member of K, each being a σ_0
(2) whenever $\sigma_p \in K$ and $\sigma_q < \sigma_p$ then $\sigma_q \in K$.

The set V is called the *vertex set* of the complex K. Each p-simplex is said to be of dimension p; the largest integer n for which $\sigma_n \in K$ is called the *dimension* of K, and written dim K.

As a matter of notation, if the p-simplex σ_p is defined by the vertices $v^1, v^2, \ldots v^{p+1}$ we write

$$\sigma_p = \langle v^1\ v^2\ \ldots v^{p+1} \rangle$$

When the order in which the vertices are so written is irrelevant, as our definition implies, then we describe the complex K as unoriented. But it is always possible to define an *orientation* on a complex K. This is done by deciding on a positive sequence for the vertices in any one simplex σ_p, then any even permutation of that sequence defines the same σ_p (that is to say, $+\sigma_p$) and any odd permutation defines the corresponding $-\sigma_p$. This process is not necessarily a systematic process as we proceed from one simplex to another. By comparison a natural and systematic procedure is to settle on a positive sequence for the vertex set V and let this provide an *induced orientation* (by acting as a kind of template) for each σ_p. This induced (positive) orientation is identified with any even permutation of that $(p + 1)$ subset of V which defines that σ_p. In any event most of the global properties of a complex K, such as the homological structure studied in Appendix C, are invariant under a change of orientation, although an orientation is required to define some of them. We shall indicate the presence of an orientation only when it is relevant to do so.

Another set-theoretic idea can be taken into account by noticing that the empty set ϕ is a subset of every set; may we not therefore include it in the collection K? We certainly may but when we do so it is important to indicate its presence, both because of its formal effect and because of the consequences which can arise in a specific application of the idea of a complex. Since ϕ, as a subset of V, contains no vertices it must be denoted by the formal simplex σ_{-1}, and it is a face of every simplex of K. When this σ_{-1} is attached to K we say that the latter is an *augmented complex* and usually denote it by K^+.

The value of including σ_{-1} is potentially more than one of tidying up the notation vis-à-vis set theory since it allows us the concept of 'not-V' in the context of identifying the vertex set — so that V = U and $\phi = V^c$.

2   We can obtain a *geometrical representation* of a complex K in terms of *connected convex polyhedra*, in the following manner. If we take two points P_1, P_2 in the Euclidean plane E^2 then the set of points which lie between them, that is to say, points P with co-ordinates symbolically represented by

$$P = \theta_1 P_1 + \theta_2 P_2 \quad \text{where} \quad 0 \leq \theta_1, \theta_2 \leq 1$$

and with $\theta_1 + \theta_2 = 1$, is the *closed convex set* defined by P_1 and P_2. Furthermore the points P_1 and P_2 are well-defined by the convex set, being the only points of the set which do not lie between two other points of the set. This mutual defining relation is exactly that between the vertices of a simplex and the simplex itself. It follows that if v^1 and v^2 are two vertices of a simplicial complex K and if we associate the Euclidean points P_1 and P_2 with them (more precisely, if we introduce a mapping $\sigma: \{v^1, v^2\} \to E^2$, where $\sigma(v^1) = P_1$ and $\sigma(v^2) = P_2$) then there is an unambiguous association of the 1-simplex $\langle v^1 v^2 \rangle$ with the convex set defined by P_1 and P_2. Indeed it seems natural to denote this convex set by the same sort of symbol $\langle P_1 P_2 \rangle$. In other words the map σ induces a map, which we can agree to denote by the same symbol σ, viz. $\sigma: \langle v^1 v^2 \rangle \to E^2$, where the image of the 1-simplex is the convex set $\langle \sigma(v^1), \sigma(v^2) \rangle$.

In a similar way we can represent a 2-simplex $\langle v^1 v^2 v^3 \rangle$ by the convex set

$$P = \theta_1 P_1 + \theta_2 P_2 + \theta_3 P_3$$

where $\theta_i \geq 0$ and $\theta_1 + \theta_2 + \theta_3 = 1$, that is to say, by the triangle $P_1 P_2 P_3$ — including the 'inside' and the edges.

Generally we can represent a p-simplex σ_p by a *convex polyhedron* with $(p + 1)$ vertices in the Euclidean space E^p and a complex K by a collection of such polyhedra in some suitable space E^h. Although it would be safe to say that the dimension h of this representation space can be the sum of all the simplex dimensions plus card V, the fact that many of the simplices share common faces suggests that a smaller value for h might suffice. In fact it can be shown that if dim $K = n$ an economical but sufficient value for h is $2n + 1$. For example, if dim $K = 1$ the highest order simplex is of dimension 1 and we expect to need a space of 3 dimensions (E^3) for a geometric representation of K. This necessity is illustrated by the party-game problem of trying to draw in a plane (in E^2) the lines which join three houses, H1, H2, and H3, with the three utilities gas, water, and electricity, and to do this without the lines crossing. There are six vertices in the complex and if two lines cross, other than at a vertex, then such a point of crossing would be another vertex — if the drawing is to be a true geometric representation of the complex. The fact that this particular problem cannot be represented without such a crossing illustrates the theorem: Figure B.1 illustrates the dilemma in E^2, whilst Figure B.2 shows its solution in E^3.

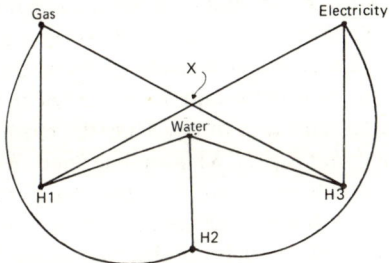

Figure B.1 Gas, water, and electricity connections in E^2 to houses H1, H2, and H3. A point like X is unavoidable

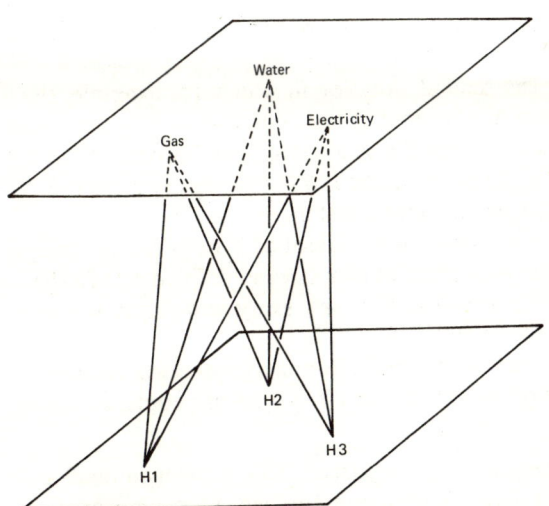

Figure B.2 Gas, water, and electricity connections in E^3 to houses H1, H2, and H3. No two lines meet except at a vertex

3   A *relation* λ from the finite set Y to the finite set X ($\lambda \subset Y \times X$) *defines a simplicial complex* — which we shall denote by $K_Y(X; \lambda)$. The inverse relation $\lambda^{-1} \subset X \times Y$ defines a complex $K_X(Y; \lambda^{-1})$. We shall speak of these complexes as *conjugates;* they arise in the following manner.

$K_Y(X; \lambda)$ refers to the pattern denoted by

$$
\begin{array}{c|c}
\lambda & X \\
\hline
Y & (\lambda_{ij})
\end{array}
$$

where we suppose the incidence matrix $\Lambda = (\lambda_{ij})$ contains m rows and n columns, that is to say, card Y = m and card X = n. *The set X is the vertex set and a subset of (p + 1) elements of X form a p-simplex if there exists at least one element Y which is λ-related to each of them.* Such an element of Y, say Y_1, acts as a connection between the vertices of such a σ_p and therefore serves the same purpose for any face of σ_p. Thus the closure under the 'face of' relation, $<$, is satisfied and $K_Y(X; \lambda)$ is well-defined. We notice too that the simplices are not uniquely represented by the elements of Y although there is one simplex represented by each element of Y which is of greater dimension than that of any other such simplex (assuming, for the moment that the domain of λ is the whole set Y). When there is no danger of confusion we shall speak loosely of the Y_i as the simplices of $K_Y(X; \lambda)$ — bearing the above ambiguities in mind.

In the same way, by regarding the set Y as the vertex set we obtain a complex $K_X(Y; \lambda^{-1})$; each X_i in the domain of λ^{-1} represents a closed simplex σ_p and all its faces.

To allow for the general situation in which, for example, the domain of λ is a proper subset of Y — so that at least one row in Λ is composed entirely of zeros, we can assume that K is augmented and becomes K^+. This then allows the 'offending' Y_i to be regarded as σ^{-1} (the empty subset of X) and the idea that each Y_i is a simplex can be sustained.

In $K_Y(X; \lambda)$ every non-empty subset of Y defines a *subcomplex L of K*, in the sense that the collection of simplices so defined satisfy the conditions in the definition of a complex. Similarly every non-empty subset of X defines a subcomplex of the complex $K_X(Y; \lambda^{-1})$.

Let us take a simplex example from a hypothetical relation $\lambda \subset Y \times X$, where X is a set of social roles and Y is a set of people, as shown.

X: X1 = a teacher, X2 = a parent, X3 = a town-councillor,
    X4 = a student, X5 = a householder, X6 = a motorist

Y: Y1 = Fotheringay, Y2 = Deveraux, Y3 = Blenkinsop
    Y4 = Beauchamp, Y5 = Carter-Smith

Let the matrix be:

λ .	X1	X2	X3	X4	X5	X6
Y1	1	1	0	0	1	1
Y2	0	1	1	0	0	0
Y3	0	0	0	1	0	1
Y4	0	0	1	0	1	0
Y5	0	1	0	0	0	1

In $K_Y(X; \lambda)$ we have dim $K = 3$ and

Y1 = ⟨X1, X2, X5, X6⟩   a 3-simplex
Y2 = ⟨X2, X3⟩   a 1-simplex
Y3 = ⟨X4, X6⟩   a 1-simplex
Y4 = ⟨X3, X5⟩   a 1-simplex
Y5 = ⟨X2, X6⟩   a 1-simplex

with a geometric representation shown in Figure B.3.

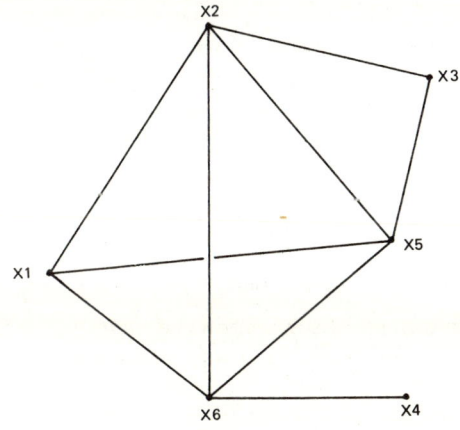

Figure B.3

We notice that Fotheringay (Y1) is a 3-simplex since he combines the roles of teacher, parent, householder, and motorist. The others are separate 1-simplices with Carter-Smith (Y5) being a face of Fotheringay — *via* the edge X2, X6 of the tetrahedron.

In $K_X(Y; \lambda^{-1})$ we have dim $K = 2$ and

X1 = ⟨Y1⟩   a 0-simplex   X4 = ⟨Y3⟩   a 0-simplex
X2 = ⟨Y1, Y2, Y5⟩   a 2-simplex   X5 = ⟨Y1, Y4⟩   a 1-simplex
X3 = ⟨Y2, Y4⟩   a 1-simplex   X6 = ⟨Y1, Y3, Y5⟩   a 2-simplex

with a geometric representation shown in Figure B.4.

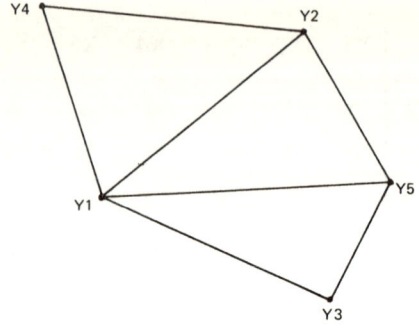

Figure B.4

We notice that the role of parent is a 2-simplex, as is that of the motorist. These correspond to the filled-in triangles Y1, Y2, Y5 and Y1, Y5, Y3 in the figure. The triangle Y1, Y2, Y4 is hollow however since only the edges are in K, *via* parent, householder, and town-councillor.

4 We now look more deeply into the structure of a simplicial complex in order to express, in a precise manner, the way its simplices are connected together. To this end we give a *definition of q-connectivity* and associated ideas.

Given two simplices σ_p, σ_r in a complex K, we shall say that they are joined by a *chain of connection* if there exists a finite sequence of simplices

$$\sigma_{\alpha_1}, \sigma_{\alpha_2}, \ldots \sigma_{\alpha_h}$$

such that

(1) σ_{α_1} is a face of σ_p
(2) σ_{α_h} is a face of σ_r
(3) σ_{α_i} and $\sigma_{\alpha_{i+1}}$ have a common face, say σ_{ρ_i}, for $i = 1, \ldots (h-1)$

We shall say that such a chain of connection is of *length* $(h-1)$, and we shall say that the chain is a *q-connectivity* if q is the least of the integers

$$\alpha_1, \beta_1, \beta_2, \ldots \beta_{h-1}, \alpha_h$$

As a special case we notice that a simplex σ_p must be regarded as *p*-connected to itself by a chain of length zero, the chain consisting of σ_p itself ($\beta_1 = p$). If we refer to Figure B.3 in the previous section we notice that

Fotheringay is 1-connected to Carter-Smith, *via* $\langle X2, X6 \rangle$;

Fotheringay is 0-connected to Deveraux, *via* $\langle X2 \rangle$;

each of the chains of connection being of zero length. On the other hand Blenkinsop is 0-connected to Beauchamp, *via* the chain $\langle X6, X5 \rangle$, a connection of length 1. Fotheringay is the only person who is 3-connected, the others are 1-connected, but not to each other.

It is not difficult to see that if σ_p and σ_r are *q*-connected then they are also $(q-1)$-, $(q-2)$-, ..., 1-, 0-connected in K. Furthermore we can set up a relation γ_q between the simplices of K by the open statement:

'——— is q-connected to ———'.

It then follows that

(1) $\sigma_p \in K$ implies that $(\sigma_p, \sigma_p) \in \gamma_q$
(2) $(\sigma_p, \sigma_r) \in \gamma_q$ implies that $(\sigma_r, \sigma_p) \in \gamma_q$
(3) $(\sigma_p, \sigma_r) \in \gamma_q$ and $(\sigma_r, \sigma_s) \in \gamma_q$ imply that $(\sigma_p, \sigma_s) \in \gamma_q$.

Hence γ_q is an *equivalence relation on the complex K* (which is a set of simplices) and the *equivalence classes* are the elements of the quotient set K/γ_q. We shall denote the cardinality of K/γ_q by Q_q,

$$Q_q = \text{card } K/\gamma_q$$

so that Q_q is the *number of q-connected components* of K, a component being all the members of an equivalence class under γ_q.

If we let q take all possible integral values from 0 to dim K and find K/γ_q in each case, we shall describe the whole procedure as a *Q-analysis* of K.

In the example of Figure B.3 of the previous section we obtain the following Q-analysis:

$q = 3$ (= dim K)	$Q_3 = 1$	Fotheringay
$q = 2$	$Q_2 = 1$	Fotheringay
$q = 1$	$Q_1 = 4$	Fotheringay, Carter-Smith; Blenkinsop; Beauchamp; Deveraux
$q = 0$	$Q_0 = 1$	Fotheringay, Carter-Smith, Deveraux, Blenkinsop, Beauchamp

In the conjugate complex of Figure B.4 we obtain the Q-analysis:

$q = 2$ (= dim K)	$Q_2 = 2$	parent; motorist
$q = 1$	$Q_1 = 3$	parent, motorist; town-councillor; householder
$q = 0$	$Q_0 = 1$	parent, motorist, student, teacher, town-councillor, householder

We notice that when $Q_0 = 1$ the whole complex K is in one piece, being joined at least *via* vertices. In performing the Q-analysis we notice too that the idea of the lengths of the chains of connection is not involved.

Looking for the q-connected components, for a fixed value of q, means that we are looking for all simplices σ_p with $p \geqslant q$ to see if they share any common faces of dimension greater than or equal to q. Of course, all the simplices in a particular component need not have q-simplex interfaces in a pairwise choice, but rather there will be *multi-dimensional tubes of simplices which join the members* of the component. These tubes embody the local structure of the simplicial complex, and therefore of the relation λ which defines K.

5   If we have a complex $K_Y(X; \lambda)$ in which dim $K = n$ a Q-analysis gives us the numbers of the q-connected components for values of q from 0 to dim K. If now we imagine a *vector space over the rationals $\mathscr{Q}$*, of dimension not less than n, denoted by $V(\mathscr{Q})$, we can regard the integers Q_q as defining a vector **Q** in this space. Indeed it is not necessary to use the field of rationals $\mathscr{Q}$ as the scalars in V but for the moment it will be convenient to do so.

Suppose dim $V = N$, with $N \geqslant n$, and let $\{e_1, e_2, \ldots e_N\}$ be a basis for V. Then every element (or vector) in V will be of the form

$$\mathbf{v} = x_1 e_1 + x_2 e_2 + \ldots + x_N e_N$$

with $x_i \in \mathscr{Q}$. Addition and multiplication by scalars (members of $\mathscr{Q}$) are defined in the usual manner *via*

$$\mathbf{v} + \mathbf{v'} = (x_1 + x'_1) e_1 + \ldots + (x_N + x'_N) e_N$$

and, if $y \in \mathscr{Q}$,

$$y\mathbf{v} = yx_1 e_1 + yx_2 e_2 + \ldots + yx_N e_N$$

together with the distributive property

$$y(\mathbf{v} + \mathbf{v'}) = y\mathbf{v} + y\mathbf{v'}$$

Also V contains the zero vector **0** in which each $x_i = 0$, and every vector **v** possesses an additive inverse $-\mathbf{v}$ obtained by replacing each x_i by $-x_i$.

Since this vector space V is to be used primarily for exhibiting the vectors **Q** we shall refer to it as a *Q-space associated with the complex K*. The vector **Q** will be called the *first structure vector* of K. If we contemplate a number of complexes K_i (which might arise from a number of relations $\lambda_i \subset Y \times X$) then each of them possesses a structure vector $\mathbf{Q}_i$ in the Q-space V. We must, of course, ensure that

$$\dim V \geqslant \max \{\dim K_i, \text{ for all } i\}$$

otherwise there will not be enough 'room' to fit in each $\mathbf{Q}_i$.

In the special case of a complex K for which $Q_0 = 1$ we introduce a slightly modified vector which we call an *obstruction vector*, the reasons for the name being discussed in the earlier chapters. This is defined in the following way.

If
$$\mathbf{Q} = \{Q_n, Q_{n-1}, \ldots Q_1, Q_0\} \quad \text{with } Q_0 = 1$$

define the *unit point* by the vector **U**, where

$$\mathbf{U} = \{1 \ 1 \ldots 1\}$$

in the n-dimensional subspace of V which contains **Q**. Then the obstruction vector, denoted by $\hat{\mathbf{Q}}$, is defined as

$$\hat{\mathbf{Q}} = \mathbf{Q} - \mathbf{U}$$

the geometrical relation in Q-space being shown in Figure B.5.

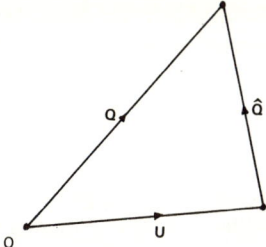

Figure B.5 Obstruction vector $\hat{Q}$ in Q-space

In the general case when $Q_0 = k\ (>1)$ the complex K is the union of k disjoint complexes

$$K = K_1 \cup K_2 \cup \ldots \cup K_k$$

and so there is a structure vector for each K_i and an obstruction vector $\hat{Q}_i$ for each K_i. It might then be valuable (but this depends on the specific application) to consider the overall vector of obstruction as

$$\hat{Q}_1 + \hat{Q}_2 + \ldots + \hat{Q}_k$$

6 In many applications of vector spaces the *concept of a metric* turns out to be significant. We shall introduce this idea by supposing that, for whatever reason, the Q-space, V, is an example of an *inner-product space*, that is to say, to every pair of vectors in V there corresponds a scalar (an element of $\mathscr{Q}$, the rational numbers) denoted by (Q_1, Q_2) and called the *inner-product,* satisfying the conditions:

(1) $(Q_1, Q_2) = (Q_2, Q_1)$
(2) $(aQ_1 + a'Q'_1, Q_2) = a(Q_1, Q_2) + a'(Q'_1, Q_2)$ for a, a' $\in \mathscr{Q}$
(3) $(Q, Q) \geq 0$ and $(Q, Q) = 0$ if and only if $Q = 0$.

The value of $\sqrt{(Q, Q)}$ is also introduced when the field of scalars is a *complete field,* for example, when $\mathscr{Q}$ is replaced by the reals $\mathscr{R}$. Thus when we take Q-space V to be $V(\mathscr{R})$ we can introduce $\sqrt{(Q, Q)}$ — called the *norm* of Q — and written $\|Q\|$. In this case we call the Q-space V a *metric space,* and define the *distance* (or *metric)* between two points of V with position vectors Q, Q' as d(Q, Q') where

$$d(Q, Q') = \|Q - Q'\|$$

This distance function may also be expressed in terms of a mapping from V × V into the field of scalars (say) $\mathscr{R}$. It is then expressed as

$$d : V \times V \to \mathscr{R}$$

with

(1) $d(Q, Q') = d(Q', Q)$
(2) $d(Q, Q') \geq 0$, $d(Q, Q') = 0$ if and only if $Q = Q'$
(3) $d(Q, Q') \leq d(Q, Q'') + d(Q'', Q')$

The last condition (3) is commonly referred to as the *triangle inequality;* it can be deduced by appealing to the Schwarz inequality for an inner product space, viz.,

$$(Q, Q')^2 \leq (Q, Q).(Q', Q')$$

The conditions (1), (2), (3) above may be used as defining conditions for any metric, viewed as a map d : V × V → F, provided F is a suitable field of scalars. The idea that F should be a complete field is needed in order to handle the notion of length (or norm) of a single vector. It is therefore needed to encompass the following idea, relevant to some applications of our Q-space.

The *first structure coefficient* of a relation $\lambda \subset Y \times X$, denoted by h, is defined by the equation,

$$\|Q\| . \|Q'\| . h = (Q, Q')$$

where Q, Q' are the structure vectors, in V($\Re$), of the complexes $K_Y(X; \lambda)$ and $K_X(Y; \lambda^{-1})$ respectively.

The most familiar example of an inner-product (and metric) space is Euclidean space in $(n + 1)$-dimensions, E^{n+1}. In this case V($\Re$) is of dimension $(n + 1)$ and if

$$Q = Q_0 e_0 + Q_1 e_1 + \ldots + Q_n e_n$$

then
$$(Q, Q') = Q_0 Q_0' + Q_1 Q_1' + \ldots + Q_n Q_n'$$

so that
$$\|Q\| = +\sqrt{(Q_0^2 + Q_1^2 + \ldots + Q_n^2)}$$

This is a straightforward generalization of the common Euclidean 3-space, E^3, and so it is plausible to interpret h as $\cos \theta$, where θ is the 'angle' between the vectors Q and Q'.

In the numerical example of section 3 of this Appendix we see that the Q-space must be at least 4-dimensional and that, if we make it Euclidean E^4, we get

$$\|Q\| = \sqrt{19}, \|Q'\| = \sqrt{14}, \text{ and } (Q, Q') = 15$$

with a structure coefficient $h = 0.92$.

7   The above ideas about the structure of a relation may clearly be applied to any data which can be displayed in a two-dimensional array. It is therefore possible to compare the ideas with those which are relevant to a statistical view of the data, in particular to the method of *regression analysis* and the evaluation of the (linear) *correlation coefficient*.

The idea behind regression analysis is to find a best-fit curve (usually a straight line) between the points with co-ordinates (X_i, Y_j), where the data is (really) a relation between the sets X and Y — with X = $\{X_i\}$ and Y = $\{Y_j\}$. As an illustration suppose that card X = 5 and that card Y = 4, and that the data is represented by the crosses in Figure B.6.

For computational purposes we shall suppose that the axes of co-ordinates are so arranged that the pair (X_i, Y_j) possess the co-ordinates (i, j). Then the standard statistical theory defines the *regression lines* for the points in this relation λ, in the following way:

$$Y = a_0 + a_1 X \tag{B7.1}$$

is a regression line (of Y on X) if it is a *least square line;* that is to say that, if there are N points in λ, then

$$\sum_{i=1}^{N} (a_0 + a_1 X_i - Y_i)^2$$

is a *minimum*. This condition defines values for the scalars a_0, a_1; these scalars must be such that

$$\sum_i Y_i = a_0 N + a_1 \sum_i X_i$$
$$\sum_i X_i Y_i = a_0 \sum_i X_i + a_1 \sum_i X_i^2 \tag{B7.2}$$

Similarly the regression line of X on Y is the line

$$X = b_0 + b_1 Y \tag{B7.3}$$

where

$$\sum X = b_0 N + b_1 \sum Y$$
$$\sum XY = b_0 \sum Y + b_1 \sum Y^2 \tag{B7.4}$$

(where we have dropped the suffixes for ease of writing).

In the numerical example above these two regression lines have the equations

$$Y = 1.9 + 0.29 X \tag{A}$$

and $\qquad X = 0.43 + 0.05 Y \tag{A'}$

and are illustrated in Figure B.7.

The point of intersection of (A) and (A') is the centre of gravity, or mean, $(\bar{X}, \bar{Y})$ of the data (relation) λ; the value of $\cos \theta$ is the *linear correlation coefficient*

$$r = \cos \theta$$

Now when the two regression lines are coincident we say that there is perfect linear correlation, and express this by the condition $\theta = 0$ or $\theta = \pi$, which is the same as $r = \pm 1$.

In our specific example of Figure B.6 we can compute the value of r and find it to be $r = 0.24$. We take this as a measure of the extent to which the set of points in the data (the members of λ) can be replaced by a new set of points lying on a single straight line. This idea is approximately illustrated by the dotted line in Figure B.6, which is supposed to be one of the angle-bisectors of the two regression lines (A) and (A').

But it is fair to say that this process throws away most of the points in the original data insofar as those points illustrate the essential structure of the relation λ. The two (possibly coincident) regression lines of Figure B.7 are intended to replace the two conjugate complexes $K_Y(X; \lambda)$ and $K_X(Y; \lambda^{-1})$ –

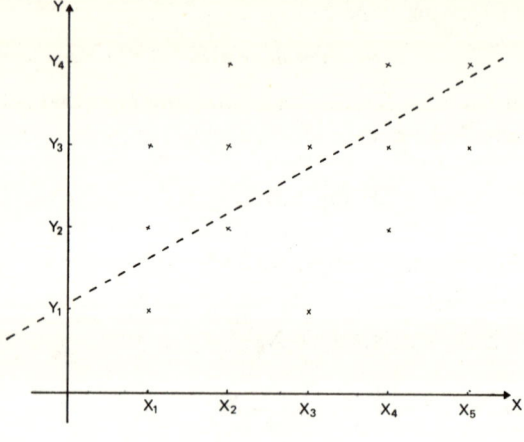

Figure B.6

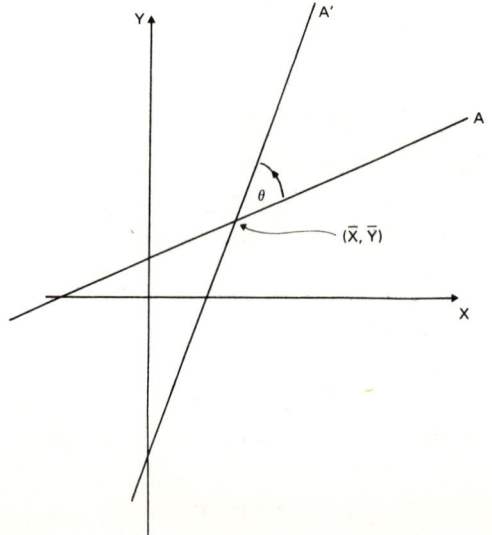

Figure B.7

which actually contain the structure of the data. When we accept any one of these regression lines as a substitute for (say) $K_Y(X; \lambda)$ then we are regarding the structure of the relation λ as being equivalent to a collection of disconnected (at the $q = 0$ level) 0-simplices. With card $X = n$ the complex $K_Y(X; \lambda)$ is replaced by a regression-line complex (via equation (A)) whose structure vector is given by $Q_0 = n$ and $Q_q = 0$ for all $q > 0$. Similarly, with card $Y = m$ the complex $K_X(Y; \lambda^{-1})$ is replaced by a regression-line complex whose structure vector is given by $Q_0 = m$ and $Q_q = 0$ for all $q > 0$.

It is clear that, in mathematical terms, replacing a relation λ (which is not a mapping) by a mapping must always reduce the structure vector of the simplicial complexes to this kind of thing.

Appendix B The Structure of a Relation 185

By comparison with this regression analysis we can perform a Q-analysis on the relation λ embodied in Figure B.7. The relation is the following:

λ	X_1	X_2	X_3	X_4	X_5
Y_1	1	0	1	0	0
Y_2	1	1	0	1	0
Y_3	1	1	1	1	1
Y_4	0	1	0	1	1

and this gives the following structure vectors.

For $K_Y(X; \lambda)$:

$$Q = \{\overset{4}{1}\ 1\ 1\ 1\ \overset{0}{1}\}$$

For $K_X(Y; \lambda^{-1})$:

$$Q = \{\overset{2}{2}\ 1\ \overset{0}{1}\}$$

Calculation of our first structure coefficient now gives

$$h = 0.94$$

We can also see that h is defined in certain cases when r is not. Thus consider the relation (which is a perfect linear relation between X and Y) shown in Figure B.8, there being N points in all.

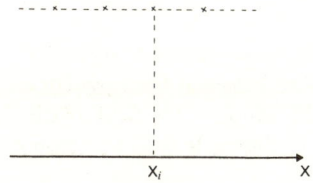

Figure B.8

Then the two complexes are as follows:

$K_Y(X; \lambda) = \{\sigma_{N-1}, \text{only}\}, \quad Q_{N-1} = 1 = Q_{N-2} = \ldots = Q_0$

$K_X(Y; \lambda^{-1}) = \{\sigma_0, \text{only}\}, \quad Q_0 = 1$ and all other $Q_i = 0$ for $i > 0$.

In this case the value of h is given by the equation

$$N^{1/2} \cdot 1 \cdot h = 1$$

so that

$$h = 1/N^{1/2}.$$

This illustrates that h is not a measure of 'linearity' but of structural dependence. Its value of $N^{-1/2}$ is a measure which corresponds closely to the intuitive idea that $K_X(Y)$ is only '$1/N$ th' as structured as is $K_Y(X)$.

On the other hand we would expect the structure coefficient h to give us a value of unity when the structures are identical. This will occur, for example, when the incidence matrix Λ is a square matrix and when $\lambda_{ij} = 1$ for all values of i and j. In such a case each of the two complexes consists of a single $(n - 1)$-simplex and each possesses the structure vector with $Q_i = 1$ for $i = 0, 1, \ldots, (n - 1)$. Hence we get $\|Q\| = \|Q'\| = n^{1/2}$, $(Q, Q') = n$ and so $h = 1$.

8 An *algorithm* for finding the connectivity pattern, and the consequent structure vector, for a relation $\lambda \subset Y \times X$ is constituted by the following discussion; it is suitable for pencil-and-paper work, although it is not the basis of the author's computer programs.

Starting with the incidence matrix $\Lambda = (\lambda_{ij})$ we notice that the scalar product of any two rows gives an integer which equals the number of coincident one's in these two rows. If the rows denote two particular Y's this product therefore gives the number of vertices (the X's) which they share. We can therefore obtain the complete pattern for all the Y's by considering the normal matrix product of Λ with Λ^T, the superscript T denoting the transpose matrix. If we form a matrix of suitable dimension containing all 1's, say Ω, the pattern of connectivities between the Y's (the rows of Λ) is given by the elements of the matrix

$$\Lambda \Lambda^T - \Omega$$

If Λ contains m rows and n columns then $\Lambda \Lambda^T$ contains m rows and m columns, and so we need Ω to be an $m \times m$ matrix of 1's.

In a similar way, we find the connectivity pattern between the columns (the X's) by forming the corresponding matrix

$$\Lambda^T \Lambda - \Omega$$

Since each of these matrices is symmetric it is only necessary to exhibit a triangular form of connectivities between the rows (or columns). The whole operation can be illustrated by the simple numerical relation discussed in the previous section, λ being illustrated in Figure B.6. In this case Λ is a 4×5 matrix, *viz.*,

$$\Lambda = \begin{pmatrix} 1 & 0 & 1 & 0 & 0 \\ 1 & 1 & 0 & 1 & 0 \\ 1 & 1 & 1 & 1 & 1 \\ 0 & 1 & 0 & 1 & 1 \end{pmatrix}$$

The case of $K_Y(X; \lambda)$ is given by the matrix $\Lambda \Lambda^T - \Omega$, where Ω is a 4×4 matrix of 1's. Evaluating this matrix gives the triangular array:

Y_1	Y_2	Y_3	Y_4	
1	0	1	—	Y_1
	2	2	1	Y_2
		4	2	Y_3
			2	Y_4

The minus sign '−' in the table stands for −1, and shows that Y_1 and Y_4 are disconnected.

In the same way, by evaluating the matrix $\Lambda^T \Lambda - \Omega$ we obtain the pattern for $K_X(Y; \lambda^{-1})$:

	X_1	X_2	X_3	X_4	X_5	
	2	1	1	1	0	X_1
		2	0	2	1	X_2
			1	0	0	X_3
				2	1	X_4
					1	X_5

By reading away from the leading diagonal (upwards and to the left, or to the right and downwards) we can easily obtain the Q_q values for either complex. Thus for $K_Y(X; \lambda)$ we can read off the following structure:

$q = 4$ $Q_4 = 1$ Y_3
$q = 3$ $Q_3 = 1$ Y_3
$q = 2$ $Q_2 = 1$ Y_3, Y_2, Y_4
$q = 1$ $Q_1 = 1$ Y_1, Y_2, Y_3, Y_4
$q = 0$ $Q_0 = 1$ all

and for $K_X(Y; \lambda^{-1})$ we obtain:

$q = 2$ $Q_2 = 2$ $X_1; X_2, X_4$
$q = 1$ $Q_1 = 1$ all
$q = 0$ $Q_0 = 1$ all

Appendix C
Homology and Relations

1   We restrict the discussion to the case of a relation λ between two finite sets X and Y; in particular $\lambda \subset Y \times X$ and $\lambda^{-1} \subset X \times Y$. Either of the two simplicial complexes $K_Y(X; \lambda)$, $K_X(Y; \lambda^{-1})$ possesses a finite dimension and a finite number of simplices σ_p.

We therefore take the case of such a complex, say $K_Y(X; \lambda)$, in which dim $K = n$; we assume that we have an orientation on K, induced by an ordering of the vertex set X and that this is displayed by labelling the vertices $X_1, X_2, \ldots X_k$, with $k \geqslant n + 1$. We select an integer p such that $0 \leqslant p \leqslant n$ and we label all the simplices of order p as $\sigma_p^i, i = 1, 2, \ldots h_p$, where we suppose that there are h_p p-simplices in K.

We now form the formal linear sum of these p-simplices and call any such combination a *p-chain* — allowing multiples of any one σ_p. We denote the totality of these p-chains by C_p and one member of C_p by c_p. Thus a typical p-chain is

$$c_p = m_1 \sigma_p^1 + m_2 \sigma_p^2 + \ldots + m_{h_p} \sigma_p^{h_p}$$

with each $m_i \in J$. We can then regard this set C_p as a *group* (an *additive abelian group*, under the operation +, by demanding

$$c_p + c_p' = (m_1 + m_1') \sigma_p^1 + \ldots + (m_{h_p} + m_{h_p}') \sigma_p^{h_p}$$

together with the identity (zero) 0_p for which each $m_i = 0$. Combining every group C_p, for $p = 0, 1, \ldots, n$, we obtain by the *direct sum* the chain group C., written

$$C. = C_0 \oplus C_1 \oplus \ldots \oplus C_n$$

Any element in C. is of the form

$$c. = c_0 + c_1 + \ldots + c_n$$

[We notice here that every *chain of connection* (*cf.* Appendix B) is a member of C., but the converse is not true.]

With every p-chain c_p we now associate a certain $(p-1)$-chain, called its boundary, and denoted by ∂c_p. We define ∂c_p precisely in terms of the boundary of a simplex $\partial \sigma_p$, and if $c_p = \sum_i m_i \sigma_p^i$ we take

$$\partial c_p = \sum_i m_i \partial \sigma_p^i$$

In other words we require that ∂ should be a *homomorphism* from C_p into C_{p-1}.

Appendix C Homology and Relations

If a typical σ_p is $\sigma_p = \langle X_1\ X_2\ \ldots\ X_{p+1}\rangle$ we define $\partial \sigma_p$ by

$$\partial \sigma_p = \partial \langle X_1\ X_2\ \ldots\ X_{p+1}\rangle = \sum_i (-1)^{i+1} \langle X_1\ X_2\ \ldots\ \hat{X}_i\ \ldots\ X_{p+1}\rangle$$

where $\hat{X}_i$ means that the vertex X_i is omitted.

Figure C.1 shows a geometric representation of a $\sigma_2 = \langle X_1\ X_2\ X_3\rangle$ together with the orientation and the induced orientations on the edges. In this case

$$\partial \sigma_2 = \partial \langle X_1\ X_2\ X_3\rangle$$
$$= (-1)^2 \langle X_2\ X_3\rangle + (-1)^3 \langle X_1\ X_3\rangle + (-1)^4 \langle X_1\ X_2\rangle$$

which is $\quad \partial \sigma_2 = \sigma_1^1 - \sigma_1^2 + \sigma_1^3$

which is a 1-chain, a member of C_1.

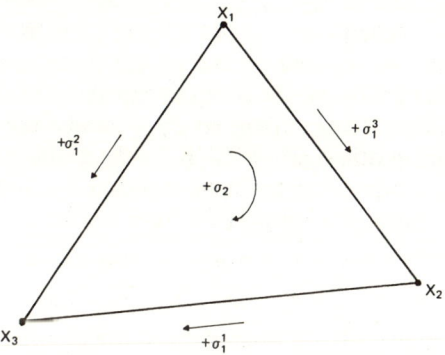

Figure C.1 A 2-simplex with its faces oriented

The boundary of a chain can be seen as its image under the operator ∂, which is a map

$$\partial : C_p \to C_{p-1} \text{ for } p = 1, \ldots n.$$

Not only is ∂ a homomorphism (it preserves the additive structure) but it is easily seen to be *nilpotent* — that is to say, $\partial (\partial c_p) = 0_{p-2}$,

or $\quad\quad\quad\quad\quad\quad \partial^2 = 0$ (the zero map).

In the case shown in Figure C.1 we have

$$\partial^2 \sigma_2 = \partial (\partial \sigma_2) = \partial (\sigma_1^1 - \sigma_1^2 + \sigma_1^3)$$
$$= \partial \langle X_2\ X_3\rangle - \partial \langle X_1\ X_3\rangle + \partial \langle X_1\ X_2\rangle$$
$$= \langle X_3\rangle - \langle X_2\rangle - (\langle X_3\rangle - \langle X_1\rangle) + \langle X_2\rangle - \langle X_1\rangle$$
$$= 0$$

Since $\partial : C_p \to C_{p-1}$ is a homomorphism the image of C_p, under ∂, must be a subgroup of C_{p-1}; we denote this image ∂C_p variously by im ∂ or by

B_{p-1}, and because ∂ is nilpotent we see that

$$\partial B_{p-1} = 0_{p-2} \text{ or } \partial (\text{im } \partial) = 0$$

Those p-chains $c_p \in C_p$ which are such that their boundaries vanish, that is $\partial c_p = 0$, are called *p-cycles*. They form a subgroup of C_p, being the kernel of the homomorphism ∂, and are usually denoted by the symbols z_p, the whole subgroup being Z_p. The members of B_p (which is ∂C_{p+1}) are clearly cycles too, by the above, and so $B_p \subset Z_p$. In fact B_p is a subgroup of Z_p.

The members of B_p are called *bounding cycles* (they are cycles in an identical or trivial sense), and those members of Z_p which are not members of B_p can be identified as representatives of the elements of the factor group (or quotient group) Z_p/B_p. The members of this factor group are of the form

$$z_p + B_p$$

and, if we select one member, say z_p, out of this equivalence class, we can also denote it by $[z_p]$. When two p-cycles z_p^1 and z_p^2 differ by a p-boundary, then $z_p^1 - z_p^2 \in B_p$ and we say that z_p^1 and z_p^2 are *homologous* (often written as $z_p^1 \sim z_p^2$). This is a relation on the set of cycles and it is easy to see that it is an equivalence relation. The quotient set $Z_p/\sim$, under the relation of 'being homologous to', is the quotient group Z_p/B_p — the group structure being determined by the operation + on the members $z_p + B_p$. In this group structure the set B_p acts as the additive identity (the 'zero'), since

$$(z_p + B_p) + B_p = z_p + B_p$$

for all z_p.

This pth factor group Z_p/B_p is what is called the *pth homology group* and denoted by H_p,

$$H_p = Z_p/B_p \quad p = 0, 1, \ldots, n$$

The group of cycles Z_p, being mapped to zero by the homomorphism ∂, is what is known as the kernel of ∂ (written ker ∂) and so we find the alternative form

$$H_p = \text{ker } \partial/\text{im } \partial$$

The operation of ∂ on the graded group C. can be indicated by the sequence:

$$C. = C_0 \oplus C_1 \oplus C_2 \oplus \ldots \oplus C_p \overset{\partial}{\underset{\leftarrow}{\oplus}} C_{p+1} \ldots \oplus C_n$$

together with the symbolic diagram of Figure C.2 below.

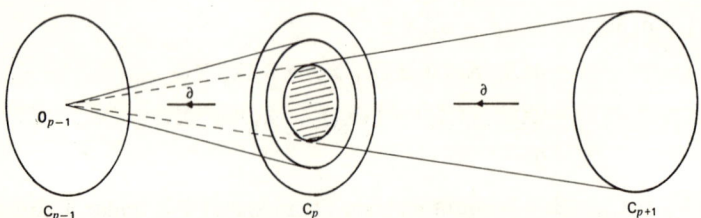

Figure C.2 A nilpotent ∂ operating on a graded group C.

In this diagram B_p is represented by the shaded bull's-eye in C_p; Z_p is the inner ring surrounding this shaded portion.

When $H_p = 0$ there is only one equivalence class in the factor group and this is B_p; every $z_p \in B_p$; every cycle is a bounding cycle. When $H_p \neq 0$ there is more than one element in the factor group and so there must be at least one cycle which is not a bounding cycle at this level. In Figure C.1 we have $H_1 = 0$ because the only 1-cycle is the combination $\sigma_1^1 - \sigma_1^2 + \sigma_1^3$ (and multiples thereof) and this is $\partial \sigma_2$. Because there is no C_3 there cannot be a B_2 (the σ_2 is not the boundary of anything) and since $\partial \sigma_2 \neq 0$, Z_2 is also empty. Under these conditions we also write $H_2 = 0$. When $H_p = 0$ we speak of the homology being *trivial* at the p-level; when we say that 'the homology is trivial', without specifying the values of p, we mean that $H_p = 0$ for all values of p other than $p = 0$. This latter group H_0 is never zero, except possibly when the complex K is augmented.

We can see, in Figure C.1 that the homology is trivial, and also that $H_0 \neq 0$. For any c_0 is of the form

$$c_0 = m_1 \langle X_1 \rangle + m_2 \langle X_2 \rangle + m_3 \langle X_3 \rangle$$

and taking the boundary of a point to be zero (this convention is hardly acceptable when K is the augmented complex K^+), it follows that c_0 must be a 0-cycle, $c_0 \in Z_0$. But the vertices X_1, X_2, X_3 form part of an arc-wise connected structure in the sense that 1-chains c_1, c_1' exist such that

$$\langle X_2 \rangle = \langle X_1 \rangle + \partial c_1$$

$$\langle X_3 \rangle = \langle X_1 \rangle + \partial c_1'$$

(in fact we need only take $c_1 = \sigma_1^3$ and $c_1' = \sigma_1^2$). Hence we have

$$c_0 = z_0 = (m_1 + m_2 + m_3) \langle X_1 \rangle + \partial \text{ (some 1-chain)}$$

Hence the vertex X_1 acts like a special chosen 0-cycle $\hat{z}_0$ and all the possible 0-cycles in the structure can be generated by writing

$$z_0 = m\hat{z}_0 + \partial \text{ (some 1-chain)}$$

and $\hat{z}_0$, referring to a single point, cannot be the boundary of any 1-chain. Hence $\hat{z}_0 \notin B_0$ and so $H_0 \neq 0$; in fact H_0 contains a single generator and, being an additive group, it is isomorphic therefore to the additive group of integers J (which is generated by a single symbol, *viz.*, 1). Thus we see that for the complex represented in Figure C.1

$$H_0 = J$$

or, preferably, we should use the symbol for *isomorphism* and write $H_0 \cong J$

The above argument shows that this structure is characteristic of the complex being arcwise connected and we can therefore generalize it to give the result:

if K possesses k connected components then

$$H_0(K) = J \oplus J \oplus \ldots \oplus J$$

with k summands.

This idea of arcwise connectedness is the same as our suggested 0-connectivity discussed in Appendix B. In those terms we would say that $H_0(K) = J \oplus J \oplus \ldots \oplus J$, with k summands, whenever $Q_0 = k$. This number k is also known as the *zero-order Betti number* of K and then it is written as β_0.

2 The groups C_p, Z_p, B_p already discussed are examples of finitely generated *free groups*, there being no linear dependencies between the generators of any of them. But this property of being 'free' is not necessarily true of the factor group H_p. Indeed, in general, we find that H_p can be written as the direct sum of two parts, one of which is a free group and the other is not. To explain this idea, and to illustrate it by a practical example, we write our general H_p in the form

$$H_p = G_p^0 \oplus \text{Tor } H_p$$

where G_p^0 is to be a free group and Tor H_p is to be called the *torsion subgroup* of H_p. Any element of Tor H_p, say h, is such that $n\text{h} = 0$ for some finite integer n (and 0 being the additive identity of the group H_p). In the context of boundaries and cycles this means that h can be written in the form $\text{h} = z_p + B_p$, because $\text{h} \in H_p$, and that there is an n such that

$$n\text{h} = nz_p + nB_p$$

and that this element must be in B_p (the zero of the factor group). But this means that, although $z_p \notin B_p$ it must be that $nz_p \in B_p$ for this particular value of n. This rather strange behaviour of certain torsion cycles is the property which the subgroup Tor H_p characterizes.

Members of the free group G_p^0 cannot behave in this way; if $z_p \in G_p^0$ and $z_p \notin B_p$ then $nz_p \notin B_p$ for any non-zero value of n. For this reason a free group is often called an *infinite cyclic group*, in contrast to the *finite cyclic groups* which go to make up Tor H_p. Thus G_p^0 will consist of summands J (the number of summands will equal the number of distinct generators of G_p^0) whilst Tor H_p will consist of summands like J_m (the additive integers, modulo m) for some choices of m. This must be so because a group like J_m is an additive abelian group with the property that if $\text{h} \in J_m$ then $m\text{h} = 0$. If Tor H_p contains a number of subgroups then each one will be isomorphic to some J_m, for a suitable m.

The number of generators of G_p^0 (the number of free generators of H_p) is called the *pth Betti number* of the complex K, sometimes written as β_p. We notice from our discussion in Appendix B that although

$$Q_0 = \beta_0$$

it is generally true that $Q_p \neq \beta_p$.

3 We have seen (*cf.* Figure C.1) the case of a complex K possessing a trivial homological structure; in that example $H_1 = 0$ because the triangle σ_2 is filled-in. If we cut out the inside of this σ_2, leaving only the edges, then we find that $H_1 = J$, because there is now a single generator in the shape of

$$\sigma_1^1 - \sigma_1^2 + \sigma_1^3$$

which is not the boundary of a σ_2, the σ_2 having been removed. Thus the single generator of H_1 represents the presence in K of a hole, bounded by 1-simplices (edges), what we shall call a *1-dimensional hole*. If the complex K contained two hollowed-out triangles then H_1 would be isomorphic to the direct sum of J and J, written $H_1 = J \oplus J$. In a similar vein, if a geometrical representation of the complex K possessed a spherical hole (bounded by the surface of a sphere) we would find that H_2 would contain a single generator $\hat{z}_2 \in B_2$; and if we found that $H_2 = J \oplus J$ we could interpret it as meaning that K possessed two 2-dimensional holes. Naturally too we can see that the 'hole' need not always be thought of as a neat Euclidean circle or sphere or hypersphere; a sort of squashed-up rubber sphere would still give us $H_2 = J$, provided the thing had not lost its essentially 'holey' nature. Pure mathematicians would describe such permissible malformations as *topological homeomorphisms*.

In general then we wish to stress the interpretation of the free group G_p^0 as an algebraic representation of the occurrence of *p-dimensional holes* in the complex K; the precise number of these holes is given by the pth Betti number β_p. A geometrical representation of the complex — as far as G_p^0 is concerned — therefore looks like a sort a multi-dimensional Gruyère cheese. The q-connectivity analysis discussed in Appendix B is more dedicated to showing us the structure of the cheese in between the holes. The possible interpretation of the torsion subgroup Tor H_p is more elusive in this cheese-like context, but the following example shows that it can have a very practical significance in another.

Example

Denote the faces of a gambler's die by the symbols $v^1, v^2, v^3, v^4, v^5, v^6$. Let these be the vertices of a 5-simplex and let K be this simplex together with all its faces; for example, a typical 1-simplex is the pair $\langle v^i v^j \rangle$ with $i \neq j$. Impose the induced orientation on K, induced by the natural ordering of the vertices. Now conduct a series of experiments in which the die is successively thrown until there is a repetition of a die-face; in this, interpret the sequence $\{v^i, v^j\}$ as the negative of the sequence $\{v^j, v^i\}$. The result of a series of successive throws is to observe an element in the graded chain group

$$C. = C_0 \oplus C_1 \oplus C_2 \oplus C_3 \oplus C_4 \oplus C_5$$

Notice that the boundary of the run $\langle 123 \rangle$ is the 1-chain $\langle 12 \rangle, \langle 23 \rangle, \langle 31 \rangle$.

In the first place we expect the experimenter to be able to observe every possible distinct run and series of runs. It would then follow that in the graded chain group every cycle is a boundary and so

$$H_p = 0 \text{ for } p = 1, 2, 3, 4$$

the homology is trivial.

But now let us alter the arrangement so that the experimenter suffers the handicap of working with a comic laboratory assistant who sees to it (by doctoring the records) that, let us say, the run $\langle 123 \rangle$ never occurs — either by itself or as a face of any other run. This results in a drastic alteration of the complex K and its associated chain group. For example, the sequence $\langle 123456 \rangle$ never occurs, since it contains $\langle 123 \rangle$. Furthermore, in the new complex K', there exists a cycle

$$z_1 = \langle 12 \rangle + \langle 23 \rangle + \langle 31 \rangle$$

which is not a boundary. Hence the intervention of the assistant is reflected in an increase in the 1st Betti number β_1 from the value 0 to the value 1. The assistant is responsible for punching a hole in the complex; the homology group H_1 is now isomorphic to J.

Let us go further than this however and admit that this is an artifical situation — since comic laboratory assistants do not exist. Let us instead alter the arrangements yet again and suppose that the experiment is conducted by two fair-minded gamblers. They begin by noticing that the probabilities of distinct runs corresponding to typical simplices $\sigma_1, \sigma_2, \sigma_3, \sigma_4, \sigma_5$ are 5/6, 5/9, 5/18, 5/54 and 5/324. Since they intend to bet on the experiment our two gamblers agree to weight the simplices so as to even up the chances. They do this by introducing new (weighted) simplices as generators for the new chain group $C'.$. These generators σ'_i are related to the old generators σ_i by the formulae

$$\sigma'_1 = 54\,\sigma_1;\ \sigma'_2 = 36\,\sigma_2;\ \sigma'_3 = 18\,\sigma_3;\ \sigma'_4 = 6\,\sigma_4;\ \sigma'_5 = \sigma_5$$

Now the homology has been altered yet again; for example,

$$54\,\{\langle 12 \rangle + \langle 23 \rangle + \langle 31 \rangle\}$$

is in Z'_1 but not in B'_1, because the latter consists of multiples of $108\,\sum_i \sigma_1^i$, 108 being the lowest common multiple of 36 and 54. Hence there exists a cycle z_1 such that $2z_1 \in B'_1$. This makes a contribution to H_1 of the summand J_2; H_1 now contains a *torsion subgroup* Tor H_1. In fact

$$H_1 = J_2 \oplus J_2 \oplus \ldots \oplus J_2$$

there being 10 summands in all. The other H_p are not affected and $H_p = 0$ for $p = 2, 3, 4$.

The gamblers' complex therefore possesses torsion which is expressed in H_1. It is thereby clear that the torsion can be introduced into $H.(K)$ in different ways, which give different summands J_m, by altering the odds on the outcome of the experiments. Thus $\sigma_1' = 48\,\sigma_1$ leads to 10 summands J_3, with

$$H_1 = J_3 \oplus J_3 \oplus \ldots \oplus J_3$$

4 We can associate with a chain group C. (with coefficients in J) a *dual concept,* namely that of mappings from C. into J (or into some other abelian group). In doing this we are said to introduce the *cochain,* dual to the chain; every such cochain being a mapping from C. into J. Precisely, we denote a *p-cochain* by c^p and whilst

$$c^p : C_p \to J$$

we also demand the additive structure

$$c^p(c_p + c'_p) = c^p(c_p) + c^p(c'_p)$$

We can build up any particular p-cochain c^p in terms of a set of mappings from the p-simplices σ_p into J. Hence, prior to the notion of a cochain we can have the notion of a *cosimplex* σ^p which is simply a mapping

$$\sigma^p : \{\sigma_p{}^i\} \to J$$

without any additive structure assumed. If there are h_p p-simplices in K we can define a *basis* for the cosimplices as the set of h_p mappings $\{\sigma_i{}^p, i = 1, 2, \ldots h_p\}$ where

$$\sigma_i{}^p(\sigma_p{}^j) = 0 \quad \text{if } i \neq j$$
$$= 1 \quad \text{if } i = j$$

Then every cosimplex σ^p is the sum of the $\sigma_i{}^p$

that is
$$\sigma^p = \sum_i \sigma_i{}^p$$

and every p-cochain is a linear combination

$$c^p = \sum_i m_i \sigma_i{}^p$$

together with the linearity condition. The zero cochain map (for any p) is the one defined by $m_i = 0$, for all values of i, and the whole set of p-cochains form an additive group C^p. Hence the *graded cochain group* is the direct sum

$$C^{\cdot} = C^0 \oplus C^1 \oplus \ldots \oplus C^n$$

where $n = \dim K$. To complete the duality we can define a *coboundary operator* δ which is the adjoint of ∂. Adopting the inner product notation (c_p, c^p) for the value (in J) of $c^p(c_p)$, we define δ by

$$(\partial c_{p+1}, c^p) = (c_{p+1}, \delta c^p)$$

which shows that $\delta : C^p \to C^{p+1}$

in the sequence:

$$C^0 \oplus C^1 \oplus \ldots \oplus C^p \stackrel{\delta}{\to} C^{p+1} \oplus \ldots \oplus C^n$$

It is also clear that δ is nilpotent, $\delta^2 = 0$, since

$$0 = (0, c^p) = (\partial^2 c_{p+2}, c^p)$$
$$= (\partial c_{p+2}, \delta c^p)$$
$$= (c_{p+2}, \delta^2 c^p) \qquad \text{for all choices of } c_{p+2},$$

and so $\delta^2 c^p$ must be the zero map.

We now have the dual cohomology groups, $H^p(K; J)$ defined by

$$H^p = Z^p/B^p = \ker \delta / \operatorname{im} \delta$$

5 An important illustration of homology and cohomology arises *via* the concept of an *exterior algebra* over a finite dimensional vector space V(F), F being the field of scalars and dim V = n. If $\{u_1, u_2, \ldots u_n\}$ is a basis for V we form the *exterior products* (or *wedge* products) $u_i \wedge u_j$ which satisfy the antisymmetric condition

$$u_i \wedge u_j = - u_j \wedge u_i$$

and we use the resulting $^nC_2$ products (notice that $u_i \wedge u_i = 0$) as the basis of a vector space which we denote by $\Lambda^2 V$. Similarly we form a vector space of dimension $^nC_3$, spanned by products like $u_i \wedge u_j \wedge u_k$, denoted by $\Lambda^3 V$. Finally we obtain a 1-dimensional vector space $\Lambda^n V$ with a basis vector $u_1 \wedge u_2 \wedge \ldots \wedge u_n$ and, denoting V itself by $\Lambda^1 V$ and the field of scalars F by $\Lambda^0 V$, we obtain the graded vector space ΛV (read 'wedge' $-V$)

$$\Lambda V = \Lambda^0 V \oplus \Lambda^1 V \oplus \ldots \oplus \Lambda^n V$$

This graded vector space can be extended to the *exterior algebra* ΛV by defining a product (the wedge product) $x \wedge y$ such that if $x \in \Lambda^p V$ and $y \in \Lambda^q V$ then $x \wedge y \in \Lambda^{p+q} V$ — and demanding that $\wedge$ be distributive over +.

If we restrict F to be an algebraic ring (for example, J) then V is called a *module*, rather than a vector space, but this does not invalidate the construction of the algebra ΛV.

If we denote the vectors in $\Lambda^p V$ by the symbols x_p then any such $x_{\hat{p}}$ is a linear combination (coefficients in F) of the basis vectors — of which a typical one is $u_1 \wedge u_2 \wedge \ldots \wedge u_p$. We can now make the formal identity, *viz*., let $\{u_1, u_2, \ldots u_n\}$ be the *vertex set* V of a *simplicial complex* K, let the p-simplices of K be the basis elements of $\Lambda^{p+1} V$, and let the p-chains of K be the members of $\Lambda^{p+1} V$. We can then define the boundary operator ∂ by

$$\partial \langle u_1 u_2 \ldots u_{p+1} \rangle = \Sigma (-1)^{i+1} \langle u_1 u_2 \ldots \hat{u}_i \ldots u_{p+1} \rangle$$

where $\hat{u}_1$ means that u_i is removed from the simplex. Imposing the usual linearity conditions on ∂ ensures that it is a homomorphism

$$\partial : C_p \to C_{p-1}$$

and nilpotent. We thereby obtain an associated homology group with this exterior product space, *viz*.,

$$H.(\Lambda V; F) = H_0 \oplus H_1 \oplus \ldots H_n$$

where $H_p = \ker \partial / \text{im } \partial$

Dual to these ideas, we can regard the differential du^i as a function defined on the basis set $\{u_j\}$ by setting its value on u_j equal to δ_j^i (that is, 0 if $i \neq j$, 1 if $i = j$). Writing this value as (u_j, du^i) we have

$$(u_j, du^i) = \delta_j^i$$

Thus $du^i : \{u_1, u_2, \ldots u_n\} \to J$ and so we can consider n such mappings, one for each u_j. We therefore obtain a basis $\{du^1, \ldots du^n\}$ for the space V*, the dual of V. Every element $\theta \in $ V* is a mapping of V into J (or some other suitable F). Making this a homomorphism by requiring suitable linearity conditions ensures, for example, that if $x = a_1 u_1 + a_2 u_2$ and $\theta = b_1 du^1 + b^2 du^2$ then

$$(x, \theta) = (a_1 u_1 + a_2 u_2, b_1 du^1 + b_2 du^2)$$
$$= a_1 b_1 + a_2 b_2$$

If we regard V* as a vector space (or a module) over F we can, as before, form the exterior product space

$$\Lambda V^* = \Lambda^0 V^* \oplus \Lambda^1 V^* \oplus \Lambda^2 V^* \oplus \ldots \oplus \Lambda^n V^*$$

with $\Lambda^0 V^* = F$ and $\Lambda^1 V^* = V^*$.

If we use θ^p to denote a member of $\Lambda^p V^*$ and allow the wedge product so that $\theta^p \wedge \theta^q \in \Lambda^{p+q} V^*$ we once more obtain an exterior algebra structure on ΛV^*. This structure is associated with the single point P of V whose co-ordinates are $(u_1, u_2, \ldots u_n)$ and it may be extended to all points of V by interpreting the differentials du^i in their more usual role as increments in the co-ordinates. If then we allow the space $\Lambda^0 V^*$ to represent all scalar functions of $(u_1, u_2, \ldots u_n)$ with values in the original F and regard coefficients (such as b_1, b_2 above) as functions in $\Lambda^0 V^*$, we thereby obtain what are called *differential forms* on (the whole of) V. For example, an element of $\Lambda^1 V^*$ will be

$$\theta^1 = b_1 du^1 + \ldots + b_n du^n$$

where $b_1, \ldots b_n$ are functions of $(u_1, u_2, \ldots u_n)$ with values in F; an element of $\Lambda^2 V^*$ will be

$$\theta^2 = b_{12} du^1 \wedge du^2 + b_{23} du^2 \wedge du^3 + \ldots + b_{n-1,n} du^{n-1} \wedge du^n$$

where b_{ij} are functions of $(u_1, u_2, \ldots u_n)$ with values in F. All these coefficients are normally required to be sufficiently differentiable in all variables, to serve some specific purpose.

These differential forms associated with points of V give rise to what is called a *De Rham cohomology theory* under a nilpotent coboundary operator δ known as the *exterior derivative*. This is defined as follows.

(1) $\delta \theta^0 = d\theta^0$, the differential of the function $\theta^0 (u_1, u_2, \ldots u_n)$
(2) $\delta (\theta^p \wedge \theta^q) = (\delta \theta^p) \wedge \theta^q + (-1)^p \theta^p \wedge (\delta \theta^q)$
(3) $\delta^2 \theta^0 = \delta d\theta^0 = 0$ for all functions $\theta^0 \in \Lambda^0 V^*$.

These ensure that, if $\theta^p \in \Lambda^p V^*$, then $\delta^2 \theta^p = 0$, the zero map which sends every θ^{p+2} to zero. For if a typical term in θ^p is θ_1^p where

$$\theta_1^p = A(u_1, u_2, \ldots u_n) du^1 \wedge du^2 \wedge \ldots \wedge du^{p+1}$$

we have $\delta \theta_1^p = dA \times du^1 \wedge \ldots \wedge du^{p+1} + A \sum_i du^1 \wedge \ldots \wedge d^2 u^i \wedge \ldots \wedge du^{p+1}$

$$= dA \times du^1 \wedge \ldots \wedge du^{p+1} \text{ by property (3) above,}$$

and so $\delta \theta_1^p = \sum_{i > p+1} \frac{\partial A}{\partial u^i} du^i \wedge du^1 \wedge \ldots \wedge du^{p+1}$

and then $\delta^2 \theta_1^p = \sum_{i>p+1} \sum_{j>i} \dfrac{\partial^2 A}{\partial u^j \partial u^i} du^j \wedge du^i \wedge du^1 \ldots \wedge du^{p+1}$

If we now allow that $\dfrac{\partial^2 A}{\partial u^j \partial u^i} = \dfrac{\partial^2 A}{\partial u^i \partial u^j}$ and notice also that $du^j \wedge du^i = - du^i \wedge du^j$ we obtain the identity $\delta^2 \theta_1^p \equiv 0$.

The *De Rham cohomology groups* are then given by

$$H^p(\Lambda V^*) = \ker \delta / \operatorname{im} \delta$$

The members of im δ are called *exact* differential forms, being such that if $\theta^p \in \operatorname{im} \delta$ then there exists a $(p-1)$-form θ^{p-1} such that

$$\delta \theta^{p-1} = \theta^p$$

Every exact form is also a *closed* form, that is, such that δ (closed) = 0; 'exact' corresponds to being a coboundary whilst 'closed' corresponds to being a cocyle. If the pth cohomology group is trivial, $H^p = 0$, then $\ker \delta = \operatorname{im} \delta$, and every closed p-form is an exact p-form.

Appendix D
An Algebra for Patterns

1 If we are chiefly interested in the homological (or cycle) structure of a complex, as we find in physics, then the role of the cocycles, or the cohomology is paramount. But if this is not the case, as for example in complexes which arise naturally in a social context and which express relations between people etc., then we would expect the cosimplices to be of greater significance.

In this book we have introduced the word *pattern* for a set of cosimplices (with values usually in J) defined on a complex K. Such a pattern, as our previous definitions imply, will be a graded set of cosimplices; having introduced the symbol π for any pattern, in the text, we can therefore expect to write it in the graded form

$$\pi = \pi^0 \oplus \pi^1 \oplus \pi^2 \oplus \ldots \pi^t \oplus \ldots \oplus \pi^n$$

where $n = \dim K$.

The complex K itself may be regarded as justifying the existence of a particularly simple pattern, namely the one which places a '1' on every simplex in K. Such a pattern is implied whenever we are given the existence of K; and in the text we have sometimes used this to provide a picture of a static backcloth. Changes from this basic pattern can then be interpreted either in terms of changes in the complex K (by emphasis or deletion of simplices, in varying degrees) or by introducing the concept of a *force on the complex*. In the latter case the static complex is regarded as rigid and not involved in the changing patterns; it acts as a *framework under stress*, but its basic static geometry is to remain unchanged. A formal way of describing these complex-forces is to measure them precisely in terms of the numerical changes in the pattern π. Indicating any such change by $\Delta\pi$ we can identify the graded change *via*

$$\Delta\pi = \Delta\pi^0 \oplus \Delta\pi^1 \oplus \ldots \oplus \Delta\pi^t \oplus \ldots \text{etc.}.$$

When $\Delta\pi^t \neq 0$ we speak of a *t-force acting in the* (static) *complex K;* its interpretation depends heavily upon the interpretation of the original complex K.

An alternative approach, illustrated in the text, is to regard the change in pattern as defining a new complex backcloth (often by replacing the original K by a number of new complexes, for example, when π is a set of weightings on the simplices and various 'slicing views' are taken of it.

These two approaches seem to the author to mirror exactly the historical differences between the classical physical theories of Newton and the relativistic approach of Einstein. The static backcloth complex K was a geometrical structure attributed to space (or space-time); with a rigid vew of this geometry the gravitational theory of Newton was expressed in terms of classical forces (forces at a distance) existing in this complex; the relativistic approach was to demand that the phenomena of gravitation should be interpreted as a modification of the space-time structure itself.

An interesting example of a graded pattern can be associated with a *probability distribution* on a set of events. The complex K discussed in section 3 of this Appendix affords such an example; an event being one of the allowed 'runs' in the throws of the die. The probabilistic idea that the events are based on 'equally likely' occurrences can be seen as the expression of a static backcloth given by the simple pattern π which assigns to each simplex σ_p in K the value of 1, thus

$$\pi^0 : \sigma_0^i \to 1 \qquad \text{for } i = 1 \ldots 6$$
$$\pi^1 : \sigma_1^i \to 1 \qquad \text{for } i = 1 \ldots 15$$
$$\pi^2 : \sigma_2^i \to 1 \qquad \text{for } i = 1 \ldots 20$$
$$\ldots \ldots \ldots$$
$$\pi^5 : \sigma_5^i \to 1 \qquad \text{for } i = 1$$

The total number of simplices in K is $2^6 - 1 = 63$, and this equals the arithmetic sum of the values of π on K. Then the probability $p(1)$ attributed to a 'run of 1', on this equally-likely hypothesis, is the rational number

$$\sum_i \pi^0(\sigma_0^i) / \sum_{i,t} \pi^t(\sigma_t^i)$$

which equals 6/63. Similarly we obtain $p(2) = 15/63$, $p(3) = 20/63$, etc., and the ratios of the various probabilities are

$$p(1) : p(2) : p(3) : p(4) : p(5) : p(6) = 6 : 15 : 20 : 15 : 6 : 1$$

Now suppose that the pattern changes because the die is loaded so that it always throws a 'six'. Then we obtain a new pattern which describes this situation, *viz.*,

$$\pi^0(\sigma_0^6) = 1 \text{ and all other } \pi^t(\sigma_t^i) = 0$$

This means that, relative to the static backcloth of 'equally likely events',

$$\Delta\pi^0(\sigma_0^6) = 0$$

and all other
$$\Delta\pi^t(\sigma_t^i) = -1$$

Taking the 'Newtonian' view of this situation, we interpret this as showing that there are now t-forces acting in the static backcloth (in the original complex K), for $t = 0, 1, \ldots, 5$. We describe the t-forces due to $-$ve values of $\Delta\pi$ as *forces of repulsion* (in K); these are *forces away from certain events* (away from certain simplices); in fact there are forces of repulsion which act away from every simplex in K except the single 0-simplex $\langle 6 \rangle$. In the complex K it follows that the event $\langle 6 \rangle$ is a *relative attractive centre* for those forces; the only such centre; the event $\langle 6 \rangle$ is the only event. Probability theory takes this into account by the new value $p(\langle 6 \rangle) = 1$ and all other probabilities having zero value.

Taking the 'Einsteinian' view of this situation, we take the new pattern π as the one which defines the (effective) complex K of events. In our previous terms, we can 'slice' the complex at $\theta = 1$ and so obtain a new complex K' consisting of one simplex $\langle 6 \rangle$ only. The events now number 1; all ambiguity has been removed.

In the Newtonian view we must also allow for the implication that $\Delta \pi^t$ is to be regarded as 'free' if, and only if, it exists in a $(t + 1)$-connected component of K. (This idea is parallel to the physics inherent in the 'triangle of velocities' structure, in which a change of velocity is only representable by the third side of a triangle if the whole triangle is present in the space-backcloth.) But in this case it means that, for example, $\Delta \pi^5 \ne 0$, and so the 5-force in K is only 'free' if K is 6-connected. The *presence of this 5-force therefore implies the presence of an effective 7th vertex*, foreign to the original complex, which can form a 6-simplex with all the original vertices. This *external vertex* corresponds to the intuitive idea that the new situation is the result of 'forces from outside' the complex K. The external 7th vertex is therefore representing the 'event' which results in the new pattern, and that 'event' is the one we call 'the die is loaded'.

5   We can introduce an *algebraic representation* of patterns π and their changes $\Delta \pi$ in the following way.

Suppose that the complex K, which is under consideration, possesses the vertex set X, with card X $= n$. Introduce the algebraic indeterminates $x_1, x_2, \ldots x_n$ corresponding to the vertices $X_1, X_2, \ldots X_n$, respectively. Regard the algebraic x_i as the basis set for an n-dimensional module V(J) over the integers J — or, when it is convenient, a vector space V(F) over a field F.

Now we form the *exterior product space* ΛV, as discussed in section 5 of this Appendix, and with the convention that $x_i x_j$ stands for the exterior product $x_i \wedge x_j$, we consider algebraic *polynomials* in ΛV. The highest power of any variable x_i will be 1, since $x_i^2 = 0$, and the presence of (say) $x_1 x_2 \ldots x_{p+1}$ in a typical polynomial will correspond to the presence of the simplex $\langle X_1 X_2 \ldots X_{p+1} \rangle$ in the complex K.

A pattern π which attributes integer-values to the simplices of K will now be represented by a polynomial $\pi(x)$ in ΛV. For example,

$$\pi(x) = x_1 + 3x_2 + 5x_1 x_2 + 14 x_2 x_3 x_4 + 27 x_3 x_5 x_8$$

represents a pattern which assigns the following integers to the following simplices of K, viz.,

$\pi^0 : \langle X_1 \rangle \to 1$ and $\langle X_2 \rangle \to 3$

$\pi^1 : \langle X_1 X_2 \rangle \to 5$

$\pi^2 : \langle X_2 X_3 X_4 \rangle \to 14$ and $\langle X_3 X_5 X_8 \rangle \to 27$.

The 'equally likely' static backcloth K of the previous section is defined by the *pattern polynomial*

$$\pi(x) = x_1 + x_2 + \ldots + x_2 x_3 x_4 + \ldots x_1 x_2 x_3 x_4 x_5 x_6$$

containing every distinct combination of the x's, with weight 1.

We now define an operation 'the face of' denoted by f; it is similar to the boundary operator ∂ but in effect ignores the orientation inherent in the wedge product. Precisely, we put

$$f(x_1 x_2 \ldots x_p) = \sum_i (x_1 \ldots \hat{x}_i \ldots x_p)$$

where $\hat{x}_i$ means that the variable x_i is omitted. In its formal structure this operator f behaves like the differential operator D applied to polynomials in elementary algebra.

With this definition of f we can now define an operator Δ which is to describe 'free' changes in patterns $\pi(x)$. It is given by the adjoint operator, via.

$$(f\sigma, \pi) = (\sigma, \Delta\pi)$$

showing that, when π is defined on a t-connection then $\Delta\pi$ is defined on a $(t+1)$-connection.

If P(X) denotes all the possible polynomials on ΛV it follows that it can be written as a graded additive group (a module over J):

$$P(X) = P_0 \oplus P_1 \oplus P_2 \oplus \ldots \oplus P_t \oplus \ldots \oplus P_n$$

where P_t denotes all polynomials consisting of terms containing precisely t of the variable x_i, and n = card X. The term P_0 may be denoted by the integer 1, and we can regard this as a representation of the simplex σ_1 (the empty set ϕ) — containing none of the x_i. Thus the set of polynomials P(X) contains a representation of all the complexes K^+ (the augmented complexes) which can be constructed out of the vertex set X; the antisymmetry of the exterior product also automatically allows for each of these complexes to be oriented by the ordering induced by the natural integers. The mappings f and Δ are such that

$$f : P_t \to P_{t-1} \text{ and } \Delta : P_t \to P_{t+1}$$

and by insisting that they possess the obvious linearity properties we can always regard these as *homomorphisms* on the graded module P(X).

We notice, appropos the remarks in the text (Chapters 6 and 7), that we can formally write

$$(f\sigma, \pi) = (\sigma, \Delta\pi) \text{ as } (\sigma, \pi) = (f^{-1}\sigma, \Delta\pi)$$

where $f^{-1}\sigma$ will represent all the simplices in $K(X)$ which possess σ as a face. This is the algebraic illustration of the fact that the structure K needs to contain simplices σ_{t+1} to 'freely' allow general changes $\Delta\pi^t$.

The relation γ_q, which identifies '—— is q-connected with ——' on the simplices of K will have a counterpart in a relation on P(X), and will induce on that set a filtration

$$P = P^0 \supset P^1 \supset P^2 \supset \ldots \supset P^k \supset \ldots \supset P^n$$

where P^k denotes all those polynomials which are k-connected. [The use of the operator f to define filtrations on a complex K has been anticipated by Zeeman [55] in his theory of Dihomology.]

By using the wedge product $\wedge$ we have a natural product on the module of polynomials P(X), thus forming an *algebraic ring structure* P(X). When this ring contains a unity (the integer 1 which generates P_0) we may use it to define the inverse polynomial π^{-1} (when it exists) where

$$\pi \pi^{-1} = \pi^{-1} \pi = 1$$

the product being that of the wedge $\wedge$.

The product also ensures that, whenever two terms (say) $x_\alpha x_\beta \ldots$ and $x_p x_q \ldots$ contain a common variable (say) x_μ, then the product of the terms must vanish. Otherwise, it is clear that the product of two terms representing (say) simplices σ_r and σ_s will be a term representing a simplex σ_{r+s+1} [this would be what students of topology would call the *Lefschetz prism* based on σ_r and σ_s].

Suppose now that we consider two simplices in K, σ_r and σ_s, which we know share a 0-face. Then the polynomial terms which represent them will be something like $x_1 x_h x_k \ldots x_t$, $(r+1)$ variables, and $x_1 x_f x_g \ldots x_j$, $(s+1)$ variables — with one vertex x_1 in common. It follows that the product of these two polynomials — which we might allow ourselves to represent for the moment as $\sigma_r \wedge \sigma_s$ — must vanish. We can write this symbolically as

$$(f^0 \sigma_r) \wedge \sigma_s) = 0$$

f^0 indicating the identity map.

We can now extend this idea and consider the case when σ_r and σ_s share a 1-face; their algebraic representative polynomials (monomials) will now have two variables in common, say, x_1 and x_2. It is then clear that the polynomial which represents (say) $f \sigma_r$ will consist of the sum of three kinds of terms, *viz.*,

1st kind of term will contain the variable x_1 (and not x_2)
2nd kind of term will contain the variable x_2 (and not x_1)
3rd kind of term will contain the variables $x_1 x_2$.

Since the representation of σ_s contains the variables $x_1 x_2$ it follows that the product (symbolically) represented by

$$(f^1 \sigma_r) \wedge \sigma_s = 0$$

Repeating this argument we see that if we know that σ_r and σ_s are two simplices which share a q-face, but not a $(q+1)$-face, then we can assert the following algebraic conditions on their representative monomials:

$$(f^i \sigma_r) \wedge \sigma_s = 0, \text{ for } i = 0, 1, \ldots q$$
$$\neq 0, \text{ for } i = (q+1), \ldots$$

The algebraic argument may be turned around to show that these must also be sufficient conditions for σ_r and σ_s to share a q-face (to be q-connected by a chain of length 1). We have therefore an algebraic theorem which relates the 'face of' operation to the ring product $\wedge$, *viz.*,

Theorem: Two simplices σ_r and σ_s in a complex K share a q-face (are q-connected by a chain of length 1) if and only if their monomial representatives in P(X) satisfy,

either $(f^i \sigma_r) \wedge \sigma_s = 0$, for $i = 0, 1, \ldots q$
$\neq 0$, otherwise

or $\sigma_r \wedge (f^i \sigma_s) = 0$, for $i = 0, 1, \ldots q$
$\neq 0$, otherwise

where $f^t = f(f^{t-1}), t = 1, \ldots$

If we multiply two pattern polynomials together, say, $\pi(x) \pi'(x)$, then we obtain the products of the values of π, π' on the Lefschetz prisms which are generated by the products of the underlying monomial terms — provided those terms contain no common variables. This process therefore automatically generates the value 0 for the product (say)

$$\pi(\sigma_r) \pi'(\sigma_s)$$

whenever the simplices σ_r and σ_s share any q-face ($q \geqslant 0$) in the original complex K. For example, with

$$\pi(x) = 2x_1 + 3x_2 x_3 \text{ and } \pi'(x) = 6x_4 + 3x_5 + 5x_1 x_2$$

we obtain the product

$$\pi\pi' = 12x_1 x_4 + 6x_1 x_5 + 18x_2 x_3 x_4 + 9x_2 x_3 x_5$$

This situation corresponds to the standard probability problem in which the probabilities of independent events (without common intersection in the sample space) are multiplied together to give the probability of a compound event.

If we extend the vertex set X so as to include all the vertices which are needed for a collection of distinct complexes, then the products of patterns π which are defined on the disjoint complexes always exhibit the property of such 'independent events'. These may then be regarded as patterns π on a new composite complex (formed from the Cartesian product of the vertex sets of the disjoint complexes). For a fuller discussion of the algebraic consequences of this and other features, the reader is referred to the author's paper [6].

3   The exterior algebra ΔV is itself a special case of a more general algebra, namely a *Clifford algebra* $\mathbb{C}(V)$ [33]. In this latter structure the antisymmetry of the product is maintained, except in the case when the two base vectors are identical; in that case the product is a constant (usually not zero). Thus, if $\{e_1, e_2, \ldots e_n\}$ is a basis for the vector space V(F), the Clifford algebra $\mathbb{C}(V)$ is defined by the following product rules:

(1) $e_i e_j = - e_j e_i$ when $i \neq j$
(2) $e_i^2 = 1$ for all values of i

Requiring the multiplicative associative property together with the distributivity of . over + results in the Clifford algebra $\mathbb{C}(V)$.

We now see that if we use this algebra to represent any simplicial complex K (with a finite vertex set, of course) then the introduction of the unity (the '1') seems more natural. It follows, as before, that any polynomial, with coefficients unity, represents a complex K^+ together with an orientation; the vertex which corresponds to the unity '1' is again the empty set, or σ_{-1}.

What we 'lose' in this representation of K is the theorem which describes the face-sharing properties of the simplices, since it is no longer true that (e.g.) $x_1 x_2 . x_2 x_3 = 0$. In $\mathbb{C}(V)$ we would have

$$x_1 x_2 . x_2 x_3 = x_1 . x_2^2 . x_3 = x_1 . 1 . x_3 = x_1 x_3$$

where the x's have replaced the e's of the first paragraph.

What we 'gain' is an algebraically more elegant way of describing the values of a pattern π on the simplices of K. For if we represent a typical simplex σ_p by the monomial $x_1 x_2 \ldots x_{p+1}$ we may express the value of π on this σ_p in a natural way *via* the Clifford algebra product. Thus, if π is to have the value θ on this σ_p then we can write the pattern polynomial π (as before) as

$$\pi = \theta \, x_1 x_2 \ldots x_{p+1}$$

and expect to find the value (the number θ) as the result of forming the product between π and the simplex σ_p. Thus we can write

$$(\sigma_p, \pi) = (x_1 \ldots x_{p+1}) . \theta . (x_1 \ldots x_{p+1})$$

and this
$$= \pm \theta$$

The $\pm$ sign is determined by the antisymmetry of the product, as follows.

$$(x_1 x_2 \ldots) . (x_1 x_2 \ldots) = x_1^2 (x_2 \ldots) . (x_2 \ldots) (-1)^p$$

because there have been p changes of sign as the x_1 moves through the first bracket expression to its new position. This is repeated as we move x_2 (through $(p-1)$ places) to its new position, etc., and finally we obtain

$$(x_1 \ldots x_{p+1}) . (x_1 \ldots x_{p+1}) = (-1)^H x_1^2 x_2^2 \ldots x_{p+1}^2$$
$$= (-1)^H$$

where

$$H = p + (p-1) + (p-2) + \ldots + 1$$
$$= p(p+1)/2$$

Thus if $\pi = \pi^2$ then $(\sigma_2, \pi^2) = -\theta$ whereas if θ is the numerical value of a π^3 then $(\sigma_3, \pi^3) = +\theta$.

This representation also gives the value of a pattern π^t on the faces of its σ_t as another pattern associated with what remains when that face is removed. For example, if we have the pattern

$$\pi^3 = \theta \, x_1 x_2 x_3 x_4$$

with the value $+\theta$ on the associated 3-simplex $x_1 x_2 x_3 x_4$, then, on a face (such as) $x_1 x_2$ of this simplex we obtain the 'value'

$$(x_1 x_2, \pi^3) = (x_1 x_2) . \theta . (x_1 x_2 x_3 x_4)$$
$$= \theta . (-1) . x_3 x_4$$
$$= -\theta \bar{x}_3 x_4$$

and this is the pattern π restricted to the face $x_1 x_2$ of the simplex σ_3. If we introduce the 'face of' operation denoted by f in the previous section, and allow additivity for the patterns π, we obtain the typical restriction of π to the whole face of a simplex as follows.

$$(f(x_1 x_2 x_3 x_4), \theta \ x_1 x_2 x_3 x_4) = (x_2 x_3 x_4, \theta \ x_1 x_2 x_3 x_4) +$$
$$(x_1 x_3 x_4, \theta \ x_1 x_2 x_3 x_4) +$$
$$(x_1 x_2 x_4, \theta \ x_1 x_2 x_3 x_4) +$$
$$(x_1 x_2 x_3, \theta \ x_1 x_2 x_3 x_4)$$

and this gives us the pattern

$$\pi^0 = \theta x_1 - \theta x_2 + \theta x_3 - \theta x_4$$

4 The *exterior algebra* may be extended to include terms like x_i^{-1} (the Clifford algebra already contains these in the formal sense that $x_i = x_i^{-1}$) and this can be arranged so that the algebra contains a representation of the *complementary complex* K^c of any given complex K (perhaps *anticomplex* would also be an effective same for K^c). To do this we extend the vertex set so as to include all those vertices $\bar{X}_i$ which are the *negations of the vertices* X_i. We then adopt the convention that the variable x_i^{-1} is to denote the vertex $\bar{X}_i$ when the variable x_i denotes the vertex X_i. Then, just as the algebraic product $x_i x_j$ means that there is a simplex $\langle X_i X_j \rangle$ in the complex under consideration, so must we interpret the algebraic term $x_i x_i^{-1}$ as meaning that the simplex $\langle X_i \bar{X}_i \rangle$ is in the complex. But this simplex must be the empty set σ_{-1} and so we must regard the algebraic product $x_i x_i^{-1}$ as equivalent to the unity symbol '1' — which represents σ_{-1} in every K. It follows that this now ensures that, even in the exterior algebra representation, *every simplex possesses an inverse* which is naturally related to the complementary complex K^c. Hence every monomial pattern π (with value θ) also possesses an inverse π^{-1}, excepting the case $\theta = 0$.

Also the algebra contains a representation of K^c which is dependent on the (1-1) correspondence between the variables x_i and x_i^{-1}. This fact must lead to the establishment of the following theorem.

Theorem: The structure of a complex K, in the sense of its q-connectivities, is identical with that of its complement K^c.

References and Bibliography

[1]   ABELL, P 'Structural Balance in Dynamic Systems', *Sociology,* 1968, **2**.
[2]   ATKIN, R.H. 'Abstract Physics', *Nuovo Cimento,* 1965, **38**.
[3]   ATKIN, R. H. 'Cohomology of Observations', in *Quantum Theory and Beyond,* (London: C.U.P., 1971).
[4]   ATKIN, R. H. 'From Cohomology in Physics to q-connectivity in Social Science', *Int. J. Man-Machine St.,* 1972.
[5]   ATKIN, R. H. 'Multi-dimensional Structure in the Game of Chess', *Int. J. Man-Machine St.,* 1972.
[6]   ATKIN, R. H. 'An Algebra for Patterns and Complexes', *Int. J. Man-Machine St.,* 1974.
[7]   ATKIN, R. H. *Research Reports I, II, III, IV,* Urban Structure Research Project (S.S.R.C.), University of Essex, 1972-74.
[8]   BARNES, J. A. 'Graph Theory and Social Networks', *Sociology,* 1969, **3**.
[9]   BOHR, N. *Phil. Mag.,* 1913, **26**, pp. 1, 476, 857.
[10] BOTVINNICK, M. M. *Computers, Chess, and Long-range Planning,* (Berlin: Springer-Verlag, 1970; Harlow: Longman, 1971).
[11] BUTTIMER, ANNE 'Social Space in Interdisciplinary Perspective', *Geog. Rev.,* 1969.
[12] CARTAN, E. *The Theory of Spinors,* (Massachusetts: M.I.T. Press, 1937).
[13] CHEVALLY, C. 'The Construction and Use of some Important Algebras', *Math. Soc. Japan,* 1965.
[14] CHOMBART de LAUWE, P. *Essais de Sociologie,* Paris, 1966.
[15] CLAGETT, M. *The Science of Mechanics in the Middle Ages,* (Chicago: Univ. of Wisconsin Press, 1961).
[16] CROMBIE, A. C. *Augustine to Galileo,* Vol. 2, (London: Heinemann, 1952).
[17] DE RHAM, G. *Variete Differentiables,* Paris, 1955.
[18] DIRAC, P. A. M. *Quantum Mechanics,* (Oxford: O.U.P., 1934).
[19] DOREIAN, P. *Mathematics and the Study of Social Relations,* (London: Weidenfeld and Nicolson, 1970).
[20] DOWKER, C. H. 'Homology Groups of Relations,' *Annals of Maths.,* 1952, **56**.

[21] EDDINGTON, A. *The Nature of the Physical World*, (London: C.U.P., 1928).

[22] EDDINGTON, A. *Space, Time, and Gravitation*, (London: C.U.P., 1921).

[23] ELGAR, F. *Mondrian*, (London: Thames and Hudson, 1968; Paris: Fernand Hazan, 1968).

[24] FISHER, R. A. *Phil. Trans. Roy. Soc. A*, 1922, **222**.

[25] FLAMENT, C. *Applications of Graph Theory to Group Structure*, (New York: Prentice-Hall, 1963).

[26] FLANDERS, H. *Differential Forms*, (New York: Academic Press, 1963).

[27] HAGGETT, P. *Locational Analysis in Human Geography*, (London: Arnold, 1965).

[28] HAGGETT, P., CHORLEY, R. J. *Network Analysis in Geography*, (London: Arnold, 1969).

[29] HALMOS, P. R. *Finite Dimensional Vector Spaces*, (New York: Van Nostrand, 1958).

[30] HALMOS, P. R. *Naive Set Theory*, (New York: Van Nostrand, 1960).

[31] HILTON, P. J., WYLIE, S. *Homology Theory*, (London: C.U.P., 1962).

[32] HODGES, J. L., LEHMANN, E. L. *Basic Concepts of Probability and Statistics*, (San Francisco: Holden-Day, 1970).

[33] HOGBEN, L. *Science in Authority*, (London: Allen and Unwin, 1963).

[34] HU, S. *Elements of General Topology*, (San Francisco: Holden-Day, 1965).

[35] KILMISTER, C. W. *Hamiltonian Dynamics*, (Oxford: O.U.P., 1967).

[36] KLEENE, S. C. *Introduction to Metamathematics*, (Amsterdam: North-Holland, 1964).

[37] LASKER, EMMANUEL *A Manual of Chess*, (London: Constable, 1932; New York: Dover, 1947).

[38] MACH, E. *The Science of Mechanics*, (Open Court, 1960).

[39] MACLANE, S., EILENBERG, S. 'Category Theory', *Trans. Amer. Math. Soc.*, 1945, **58**.

[40] MCGINNIS, R. 'A Stochastic Model of Social Mobility', *Amer. Soc. Rev.* 1968, **33**.

[41] MILLER, K. S. *Elements of Modern Abstract Algebra*, (New York: Harper and Row, 1964).

[42] O'HARA, C. W., WARD, D. R. *An Introduction to Projective Geometry*, (Oxford: O.U.P., 1949).

[43] RÉTI, R. *Masters of the Chess Board*, (London: Bell, 1953).

[44] ROBSON, B. T. *Urban Analysis*, (London: C.U.P., 1969).

[45] RUSSELL, B. *History of Western Philosophy*, (London: Allen and Unwin, 1946).

[46] SANTILLAN, G. DE *The Crime of Galileo*, (London: Heinemann, 1958).

[47] SCHILLING, O. 'The Theory of Valuations', *Amer. Math. Asscn.*, 1950.

[48] SORRE, M. *Les Fondements de la Geographie Humaine*, 3 vols., Paris, 1952.

[49] SORRE, M. *L'homme sur la Terre*, Paris, 1961.

[50] STOLL, R. R. *Sets, Logic, and Axiomatic Theories*, (New York: Freeman, 1961).

[51] WELDON, J. E. C. *The Politics of Aristotle*, (London: Macmillan, 1883).

[52] WHITTAKER, E. T. *Analytical Dynamics*, (New York: Dover, 1944).

[53] WHITTAKER, E. T. *From Euclid to Eddington*, (New York: Dover, 1958).

[54] ZEEMAN, E. C. 'The Topology of the Brain and Visual Perception', in *The Topology of 3-Manifolds*, (New York: Prentice-Hall, 1961).

[55] ZEEMAN, E. C. 'Dihomology I', *Proc. Lond. Math. Soc.*, 1962, (3), 12. 'Dihomology II', *ibid*

[56] ZNOSKO-BOROVSKY, E. *The Middle Game in Chess*, (London: Bell, 1953).

Index

ABRAHAMS, 46
Activities, 117
Anderssen, 56
Aristotle, 3

BACKCLOTH, 26, 105, 120, 138, 140, 147, 149, 154, 161
    static, 137, 199
Barber (paradox), 9, 22
Betti, 192
Bohr, 102
Boolean algebra, 166
Bottom-q, 33, 112, 148
Botvinnick, 50

CANTOR, 2, 8
Capablanca, 46
Cardinality (card), 10, 164
Cartesian product, 167
Chain (of connection), 28, 76, 178, 188
Checkmate, 54
Chess, 14, 46
Clifford, 100, 204, 206
Cocycle, 88, 90, 101, 102
Cohomology, 88, 93, 98, 101, 197
Complex, 86, 105, 146, 174, 179, 192, 206
Component, 31
Connectivity, 27, 30
Convex set, 174
Cosimplex, 45, 124, 195

DEMOCRACY, 150
Descartes, 83
Dirac, 100
Dowker, 88
Dynamics, 124, 137, 154, 160, 161

ECCENTRICITY, 34, 75, 148
Einstein, 91, 162, 199
Epimenides, 9
Equivalence relation, 170, 179
Euclid, 83
Exterior algebra, 89, 196, 206

FACE, 29, 203
Filtration, 122
Fisher, 10

GALILEO, 6, 13

HAMILTON, 93
Hierarchy, 117
Hole, 86, 103, 193
Homography, 91
Homological cycle, 87
Homology, 104, 190

KIESERITSKY, 56

LASKER, 46
Leibnitz, 82

MACH, 6
Mapping, 14, 169
Matrix, 168, 186
Maxwell, 95
Mesh, 86, 97
Metric, 181
Mode (game), 48
Mondrian, 65
Morphy, 53, 56

N-LEVEL, 117, 133
Newton, 82, 162, 199
Nimzowitsh, 50

OBSTRUCTION VECTOR, 41, 44, 72, 116, 125, 132, 147, 148, 150, 153, 158, 180
Oligarchy, 150

PARADOX, 8
Partition, 170
Pattern, 14, 44, 79, 120, 124, 133, 137, 140, 149, 155, 199, 201
Philidor, 50
Polyhedra, 174
Polynomial, 79
Probability, 10, 200
Pythagoras, 83

Q-ANALYSIS, 47, 75, 108
q-connectivity, 65, 106, 133, 178
Quantum, 103
Quantum theory, 98
Q-value, 31
q-value, 31

Index 212

RELATION, 7, 24, 27, 105, 167, 176
Relativity theory, 90
Reti, 50
Russell, 3, 9, 22

SAFFRON WALDEN, 126
Schrödinger, 99
Set, 2, 117, 163
Shakespeare, 25
Shannon, 14
Simplex, 27, 34, 109, 146, 173
Simplicial complex, 27, 173, 176, 196
Slicing parameter, 38, 67, 127
Spin, 104
Spinor, 101
Steinitz, 46, 50
Structure, 27, 65, 106, 145
Structure vector, 32, 58, 116, 130, 131, 142, 180

t-FORCE, 79, 126, 136, 138, 140, 159, 160, 162, 199, 200
Tempi, 55
Topology, 83
Top-q, 33, 112, 148

WEIGHTED RELATION, 37, 113

ZERMELO, 9
Znosko-Borovsky, 55